Radical Evil on Trial

CARLOS SANTIAGO NINO

Radical Evil on Trial

Yale University Press
New Haven and London

Set in Sabon type by Keystone Typesetting, Inc., Orwigsburg, Pennsylvania.
Printed in the United States of America.

Library of Congress Cataloging-in-Publication Data
Nino, Carlos Santiago.

  Radical evil on trial / Carlos Santiago Nino.
    p. cm.
  Includes bibliographical references and index.
  ISBN 0-300-06749-6 (c : alk. paper)
     0-300-07728-9 (pbk. : alk. paper)
  1. Civil rights — Argentina. 2. Human rights.
KHA3003.N56 1996   95-53689
323.4'9'0982 — dc20

A catalogue record for this book is available from the British Library.

The paper in this book meets the guidelines for permanence and durability of the
Committee on Production Guidelines for Book Longevity of the Council on
Library Resources.

10 9 8 7 6 5 4 3 2

Contents

Introduction

How shall we live with evil? How shall we respond to massive human rights violations committed either by state actors or by others with the consent and tolerance of their governments? In the wake of such atrocities, successor governments or occupying forces must decide whether to try or otherwise punish members of the defeated government or army accused of having committed atrocities. The most famous example, of course, is the Nuremberg war crimes trials after World War II. Sometimes new democratic governments must decide whether to use the newly enacted criminal law to prosecute members of the previous authoritarian regime for massive human rights violations. Such an undertaking is especially difficult during democratic transitions, such as those that occurred in southern Europe in the 1970s, in Latin America during the 1980s, and in Eastern Europe during the 1990s. Regardless of how successor governments deal with past human rights violations, and regardless of the difficulties, I believe and argue in what follows that some measure of retroactive justice for massive human rights violations helps protect democratic values.

Massive human rights violations involve what Kant deemed "radical evil" — offenses against human dignity so widespread, persistent, and organized that normal moral assessment seems inappropriate. If someone had confronted Adolf Hitler and told him that his acts were wrong, it would have sounded almost laughable. "Wrong" is too weak an adjective to describe actions that knowingly caused the deaths of more than twenty million people and the unimaginable suffering of millions more. Other words of moral condemnation, like "atrocious" or "abhorrent," express our emotional revulsion more strongly, but do not clarify the descriptive content. Thus, our moral discourse appears to reach its limit when dealing with deeds of this type.

Hannah Arendt wrote that we know very little about the nature of radical evil. She noted that we "are unable to forgive what [we] cannot punish and that [we] are unable to punish what has turned out to be unforgivable."[1] In her view, radical evil can be neither punished nor forgiven, and thus transcends the realm of human affairs and destroys the potentialities of human power. This image of powerlessness in the face of radical evil may at first appear as nothing more than a literary device, as a way of expressing the inadequacy of social evaluation, human justice, and our capacity to punish. But, more substantively, it points to the difficulty of responding to radical evil with the ordinary measures that are usually applied to common criminals.

Even the straightforward application of the criminal law seems too much to expect. In surveying the history of the criminal law when applied to massive human rights violations, we find blanket amnesties or pardons, widespread silence, and failure to prosecute anyone. At most, we see trials and punishment of the wrong people or punishment of the right people for the wrong acts. Low-ranking officials who committed some atrocities are used as scapegoats to quell public discomfort, while the political or military officials who gave the triggering orders remain untouched. In some instances, the leaders are prosecuted, but only for deeds that are much less important than those for which there is a demand of justice, as occurred when the former East German leader Erich Honecker was charged in 1992 with killings that had taken place more than forty years earlier.

One aim of this book is to examine the dynamics responsible for these failures of the law, focusing primarily on the case of Argentina. During Argentina's transition into democracy in the 1980s, the government tried and investigated some of those most responsible for the human rights violations committed by the military dictatorship from 1976 until its collapse in 1983. This was an extraordinarily difficult process, with different actors pressing for different courses of action; it ended when all the accused, even those convicted or sentenced, were granted presidential pardons. At several points, the democratic system as a whole seemed to be in imminent danger of collapsing as a result of the effort to deliver retroactive justice. Whether the experience as a whole has been worthwhile is a controversial issue that will be addressed in this book. Yet, no matter what the outcome of that discussion, Argentina's experience stands as a valuable source of information about the obstacles confronted when governments subject radical evil to moral evaluation and legal proceedings.

I will try to show that the problems of carrying out retroactive justice emerge on at least three different levels. The first is a moral one. As I have suggested, radical evil seems to surpass the boundaries of moral discourse; it embodies a form of life and a conceptual scheme that is alien to us. We seem unable to evaluate such acts from a moral vantage point because they are as incomprehensible to us as would be the behavior of people who did not share our concepts of time and space. The question then arises whether we can legitimately judge agents of such acts in terms of our own morality. Any possibility of grounding public moral evaluation in a consensus, however idealized, seems to be precluded in cases in which even moral agreement is foreclosed by extreme conceptual divergence.

Even if the problem of conceptual relativism is overcome, other moral problems emerge. For one thing, the kind of collective behavior that leads to radical evil would not have materialized unless carried out with a high degree of conviction on the part of those who participated in it. Sincere conviction, even when wrong, poses problems for moral evaluation, as evidenced by our tolerance of conscientious objection, regardless of whether we share its substantive content. Besides, the mistaken character of the conviction must be demonstrated. This raises problems concerning the foundations of human rights and their scope, as well as the priority among these rights when several of them conflict, and raises questions of self-defense, necessity, existence of a state of war, and the superior-orders defense.

Another moral problem arises from the diffusion of responsibility. Massive human rights violations could not be committed without the acquiescence of many people. There are those who planed the deeds and those who committed them. There are those who informed on neighbors or friends or who lent material resources to those who actually commit the atrocities. Some victims even helped to victimize others. There are also a host of people who may have cooperated by omission. Judges, for example, may have refrained from conducting proceedings that could have stopped the violations. Journalists may have failed to publicize the atrocities and helped contain reactions from within and without. Diplomats may have helped conceal what was occurring or even actively justified the actions of their governments. Even common people — like those who lived near concentration camps — often turned a blind eye to what was happening close to them. Some may have refrained from passing along knowledge to others and may even have mildly justified the deeds to themselves and each other. "It must be for something" was the common saying among Argentines when they learned that a neighbor or acquaintance had been kidnapped by security forces and made to "disappear." And if almost everybody is guilty, there is a feeling that nobody really is.

From a retributivist point of view, the diffusion of responsibility clearly presents acute problems. Retribution requires some measure of evenhandedness, which means either punishing everybody — which aggravates the strategic problems enormously — or letting everybody go free. Preventionist theories do not require such blanket judgments but nonetheless have their own problems. Using punishment as a means of preventing future violations as part of its moral justification allows the administration to make strategic judgments whether a greater evil, such as that of imperiling the stability of the democratic system, will likely result from punishing these deeds. On the other hand, it is questionable whether punishment of radical evil can effectively prevent such evil from recurring. Those deeds that collectively can be described as radical evil can only be performed under favorable political conditions, most commonly a totalitarian or authoritarian regime which constrains criticism and prevents the diffusion of knowledge. It is not clear whether punishing radical evil will prevent similar evil acts from taking place when these favorable conditions are present, nor is it clear whether punishment forestalls the emergence of these conditions. On the contrary, the risk of being punished for human rights violations tends to make the leaders of authoritarian regimes reluctant to surrender power in the first place.

These matters are not just of concern to the moralist but also are of special interest to political scientists. On this second level of intellectual concern — the political — the legacy of former human rights violations may be one of the greatest obstacles to the process of democratization. As some political scientists warn, excessive concern with the past may alienate entire social groups from the democratic system and cause dissension, hatred, and resentment, which in turn may interfere with the transition to democracy. To them, the energy of the transition process would be better employed in future-oriented endeavors, such as designing a constitutional structure capable of protecting democratic values. In contrast, another group of scholars, of which I am one, believe that some measure of retroactive justice for massive human rights violations helps protect democratic values. An aggressive use of the criminal laws will counteract a tendency toward unlawfulness, negate the impression that some groups are above the law, and consolidate the rule of law. In my view, some degree of investigation and prosecution of massive human rights violations is necessary for consolidating democratic regimes.

On a third level, the question of how to deal with massive human rights violations raises questions of legal theory. When deeds committed during one regime are investigated and tried under the rules of a successor regime, we must determine whether the rules in force at the time and place of the commission of the deeds, as opposed to those enacted afterward, should be binding upon the agency carrying out the investigation and trial. Human rights violations may have been lawful when committed, or, if not, after their commission an amnesty law may have effectively granted impunity for their commission. Should these amnesty laws be respected? A negative answer to this question may well clash with principles that prohibit retroactive criminal legislation.

Furthermore, the justifications and excuses available when the acts were committed may have been different from those provided by the law at the time and place of the trial. Alternatively, the statute of limitations in force when the acts were committed could be different than that in place at the time of the trial, especially when the statute has been purposely changed to facilitate the trial in question. Legal procedures may also have been modified to enable the investigation and trial, perhaps because the ordinary procedures are particularly inapt for dealing with crimes that are massive, have numerous agents, involve special problems for gathering evidence, and raise unique problems of national security. Another legal issue which frequently arises is that of jurisdiction. Often there are political and practical difficulties in having the alleged misdeeds investigated and tried by courts which were competent according to the laws in force at the time and place of their commission; new courts are needed, but they may not have jurisdiction over the crimes.

The ascription of legal responsibility may also be very problematic. In part this may be due to the problems of ascribing moral responsibility that I noted before, but in addition questions often arise as to agency and causality. It may be problematic to ascribe legal responsibility to agents when they are people who have not participated directly in the deeds but who instead planned and oversaw them — that is, the highest government officials under whom the abuses took place.

Some of these legal problems, mainly those having to do with retroactivity and jurisdiction, can be solved through resort to international law, but then we must confront another set of problems: What is the binding effect of international law? What is its relationship to municipal law? What are its contours when dealing with questions of crime and punishment? What is its capacity for empowering courts? Can an international tribunal legitimately resort to coercion? Some of these questions are related to oft-discussed issues such as whether foreign states or international agencies can intervene in the internal affairs of a state committing human rights abuses. These questions are particularly relevant today because the international court for trying the atrocities committed in the civil war of the former Yugoslavia has just begun its work.

A wide variety of responses may be possible to these moral, political, and legal problems. They include opening the gates to private revenge, remaining silent about the deeds, holding either full-fledged trials or trials only for the those most responsible, providing civil compensation to the victims or their families, dismissing perpetrators from civic or public organizations such as the armed forces, conducting an investigation that culminates in an official report, deploying symbols of repentance and forgiveness such as monuments to the victims, and enacting amnesties and pardons.

In the first chapter of this book, I shall offer a brief overview of the varied attempts to deal with radical evil during this century and note the wide variety of responses. I shall describe what was done following World War II; how radical evil was handled during the transition to democracy in southern Europe during the 1970s; what has happened in the wake of similar transitions in Latin America in the eighties; and, finally, the democratization of Eastern Europe following the collapse of the previous Communist regimes, focusing on the civil war in the former Yugoslavia. In the second chapter, I shall deal extensively with the case study closest to my heart — Argentina. After a brief discussion of the human rights abuses committed during the 1970s, I shall describe how the new democratic government dealt with these atrocities, as well as the political and legal difficulties it faced in implementing its policy. I will conclude that chapter with an evaluation of the successes and failures of the Argentine process.

The third chapter will address the political problems arising from retroactive justice, specifically those related to the consolidation of democracy. I will try to assess the dangers of going forward with retroactive justice, as well as the available alternatives. The fourth chapter will focus on the moral problems, mainly those of conceptual relativism and the justification of investigating and punishing the kinds of deeds embraced within the category of radical evil. The fifth chapter deals with legal questions: the continuity of the legal system to which these laws belong, the retroactivity of the definition of a crime, the statute of limitations, the jurisdiction, and the plausibility of some defenses. I close with a consideration of the role of international law as a means of coming to terms with radical evil.

PART **I**

The Historical Context

the ruthless invasion of Belgium, with the subsequent attack and destruction of the ancient city of Louvain; taking many civilians hostage and subsequently murdering many of them; raping women; killing adults and children during the occupation of France; launching zeppelins over London, killing more than two hundred civilians; sinking the *Lusitania,* with the loss of twelve hundred civilian lives; and executing the director of the nursing school in Brussels, Edith Cavell. As Telford Taylor writes, these atrocities reflected the German government's clumsiness, arrogance, and sheer brutality.[1]

Given such reprehensible conduct, popular sentiment, especially in France, pressed for punishment of the perpetrators, including the kaiser himself, who took refuge in Holland. In response, the victors established the Commission on the Responsibility of the Authors of the War and the Enforcement of Penalties at the 1919 Paris Peace Conference. The commission issued a report accusing Germany and its allies of violating the laws of war and recommended the formation of a twenty-two-member international tribunal to try those responsible for the atrocities, including the kaiser. National courts were charged with trying lower-level offenders. The commission found that waging an aggressive war was not a crime under international law, but advised that it should be morally condemned and made an international crime in the future.

Despite President Woodrow Wilson's reluctance to impose a type of "winner's justice," the American delegation to the Paris Peace Conference compromised with the other delegations. This compromise was reflected in articles 227–230 of the Versailles Treaty, determining that the kaiser should be tried before an international court, with judges from the United States, France, Britain, Italy, and Japan, for offenses against morality and the sanctity of treaties. Other individuals accused of violating the laws and customs of war were tried before the military courts of the victor countries. The Versailles Treaty also required Germany to extradite the alleged perpetrators. Similar clauses were included in peace treaties with Austria, Hungary, and Bulgaria.

All these arrangements amounted to little, however: Holland refused to hand over the kaiser, perceiving that the Allies were divided about the enforcement of this part of the treaty and that there were informal assurances that the Allies would not resort to coercion. When approached to hand over offenders to the aggrieved countries, Germany stalled on account of popular resistance. Fearing that such opposition would jeopardize the treaty, particularly the reparations provisions, the Allies accepted Germany's proposal to try the accused before the German Supreme Court in Leipzig. This trial began with the conviction of three German soldiers accused of beating some British prisoners; those convicted received six- to ten-month sentences. A U-boat commander accused of sinking a British hospital ship was acquitted on the grounds that he was following orders. Lt. Helmut Patzig, accused of sinking another British hospital ship, was unavailable for trial. Instead, two subordinates were convicted for manslaughter and sentenced to four years of imprisonment, but they escaped, apparently with the help of their jailers. Because German popular sentiment unduly influenced the outcome of these trials, the French and Belgians declared the Leipzig trials invalid under the Versailles Treaty.

Equally unsuccessful was the attempt to "vindicate" the Turks' genocide of the Armenians. Beginning in 1914, the "Young Turks" deported six hundred thousand Armenians—a third of the Armenian population in Turkey—to the Syrian desert, where they were massacred. Although the Turkish sultan wanted to placate the Allies, mainly the British, only two officials were convicted. While the 1923 Treaty of Lausanne included an amnesty for such crimes, individuals took retroactive justice into their own hands. For example, in 1921 an Armenian shot a primary architect of the massacre, Talaat Bey, in Berlin. The killer was tried and acquitted on the theory that he was motivated solely by a desire to avenge his people.

THE NUREMBERG TRIBUNALS

Never before World War II had humanity encountered an authoritarian power that combined a ruthless will to conquer the world with an explicit doctrine of racial superiority, leading to the enslavement and extermination of millions of Jews, political opponents, ethnic minorities, homosexuals, and gypsies. The mystery of how such evil took hold of human beings and disposed them to such conduct remains unsolved. However, such blatant disregard of the most basic human values made it morally impossible for the Allies to permit people like Göring to return quietly, without retribution, to the coziness of his home.

Although the Allies agreed that some type of retroactive justice was necessary, they disagreed over what form the punishment should take. As soon as an Allied victory became likely, dissensions emerged within the Allied camp regarding the proper response to Nazi atrocities. As early as 1942, the British Foreign Office circulated a memorandum opposing a proposal to try offenders such as Himmler, on the grounds that the guilt was so pronounced in these cases that it was beyond judicial process.[2] In their view, the major war criminals should be shot upon identification. This stance apparently influenced the 1943 Moscow Declaration, in which the foreign ministers of the United States, Britain, and the Soviet Union agreed that the major war criminals would be punished only by a joint decision of the Allies. Meanwhile, a United Nations War Crimes Commission was established in London. Included among its representatives were the governments-in-exile and the Allies. This commission proposed the inclusion of crimes against humanity — those committed against any person because of race or religion — among the list of crimes for which Nazi officials could be tried. However, the British insisted that the commission confine itself to war crimes.

At the Yalta Conference in 1945, Churchill favored the summary execution of major Nazi criminals, but no conclusive decision was reached. By the time the United Nations Conference on International Organizations met in San Francisco in April of that year, the United States had voiced strong support for using the judicial process. By then, however, many Nazi criminals had already committed suicide or been killed. This, and the difficulty of identifying the class of criminals who would be executed, prompted the British to change their position the following month.

The Nuremberg tribunals were a vision of the U.S. War Department and — after his appointment as chief prosecutor for the United States — of Associate Supreme Court Justice Robert H. Jackson. The Nuremberg tribunals were charged with applying international law not only to war crimes but also to the crime of waging an aggressive war and to crimes against humanity. In addition, the tribunal's charge included the crime of conspiracy to commit the above crimes, which facilitated the indictment of Nazi organizations. This vision was carried to the International Conference on Military Trials, convened by the Allies in London on June 26, 1945. There, heated negotiations ensued, prompted by political mistrust as well as by clashes among the various legal cultures. Finally, on August 8, 1945, the London Charter was signed.[3] The charter determined that the tribunal would be composed of eight judges, two from each of the four Allies, one with the right to vote and the other as an alternate. The trials were to be carried out in Nuremberg, a symbolic site, since the anti-Semitic laws of 1935 had been enacted there. The first series of trials would address the major criminals and would be followed by trials against other offenders.

Once the Allies determined the structure of the tribunal, they had to designate defendants and decide on the accusations. This task engendered new dissension concerning who to include among the list of defendants. For example, should industrialists who helped to build up the Nazi war machine be subject to Nuremberg's jurisdiction? In the end, twenty-four individuals were named as defendants, as well as several Nazi organizations which, if declared criminal, could facilitate indictment of their members. Given the suicide of Hitler and Joseph Goebbels, the highest-ranking defendant was Hermann Goering, followed by Rudolf Hess. Other defendants included Joachim von Ribbentrop, Robert Ley, Alfred Rosenberg, Hans Frank, Ernst Kaltenbrunner, Wilhelm Frick, Julius Streicher, Wilhelm Keitel, Walter Funk, Hjalmar

Schacht, Alfried Krupp, Erich Raeder, Karl Doenitz, Baldur von Schirach, Fritz Sauckel, Albert Speer, Martin Bormann, Franz von Papen, Alfred Jodl, Constantin von Neurath, Arthur Seyss-Inquart, and Hans Fritzsche.

The first Nuremberg trial began on November 20, 1945. Justice Jackson of the United States, along with lawyers from the four Allied powers, led the prosecution team. The defense team, comprised of German jurists, was appointed by the defendants. One of the greatest practical problems of the trial was translation, mainly that of translating into German the great mass of evidentiary documentation produced by the prosecution.[4] Another problem was the Continental lawyers' lack of familiarity with Anglo-American procedure, especially methods of cross-examination.

The accused were indicted on four separate counts:

> 1. conspiracy to wage a war of aggression or a war against international treaties;[5]
> 2. planning, preparing, and initiating a war of aggression or a war against international treaties;[6]
> 3. war crimes, defined as violations of the laws and customs of war, including murder, ill-treatment, subjection to slave labor, and deportation of civilians and prisoners of war;[7]
> 4. crimes against humanity, defined as murder, extermination, enslavement, or any other inhumane act committed against any civilian population before or during the war, as well as persecution based on political, religious, or racial grounds, in the execution of or in connection with any crime within the jurisdiction of the tribunal, regardless of whether the accused had violated the domestic law of the countries where the deeds had been committed.[8]

In the prosecution's opening statement, Justice Jackson passionately highlighted the exceptional character of the trials, mainly because such extremely evil acts on the part of the vanquished were being judged by the victors: "Unfortunately, the nature of these crimes is such that both prosecution and judgment must be by victor nations over vanquished foes. . . . If these men are the first leaders to be prosecuted in the name of the law, they are also the first to be given the chance to plead for their lives in the name of the law."[9]

During the trial, the prosecution flooded the court with evidence supporting the specific charges, called witnesses, and cross-examined the defendants. The defense employed a variety of strategies. The day before the opening session they presented a joint memorandum challenging the tribunal's jurisdiction to deal with anything but war crimes. The court rejected this challenge, relying on the London Charter's affirmation that neither the prosecution nor the defense could object to the tribunal's jurisdiction.

The defendants also challenged the charter itself, focusing on the issue of retroactive application of penal laws. For instance, Dr. Hermann Jahrreiss, who spoke on behalf of all defendants on questions of law and fact, said that none of the defendants could have known of the principle they were supposedly violating when the offenses were committed. Dr. Robert Servatius, representing Sauckel, maintained, for example, that much of the Hague Convention, which regulates land warfare, is esoteric. Furthermore, some of the war crimes for which the defendants were indicted, such as the prohibition against deportation or forced labor, are not explicitly prohibited in the Hague Convention. Dr. Otto Kranzbuehler, representing Doenitz, objected to article 8 of the charter, which established that obedience to a superior's order should be considered only as a mitigating circumstance but not as a defense to the charges. Kranzbuehler argued that if the defendant did not know, or had no basis for knowing, that the order was unlawful, he should bear no liability. Göring, during his deposition, acknowledged most of the atrocities, defending them in the broader context of Nazi ideology.

The tribunal's decision was delivered on September 30, 1946.[10] After delineating the historical and procedural backdrop to the Nuremberg trial, the tribunal addressed legal issues, emphasizing the importance of international conventions. Relying on pre–World War II treaties condemning war of aggression, the tribunal rejected the charge that it was applying ex post facto criminal laws. The tribunal further defined the crimes for which individual defendants bore responsibility, restricting the conspiracy charge to crimes against peace and further circumscribing to include only those acts close to the object of the conspiracy. The tribunal also restricted the pre-war meaning of "crimes against humanity" to those connected with the waging of a war of aggression. As a consequence, the tribunal ruled that it had no jurisdiction over the atrocities committed in Germany prior to the invasion of Poland in 1939. The decision then identified those organizations which it considered criminal, primarily for purposes of subsequent punishment.[11]

The sentences for the accused were announced on October 1, 1946. Goering was found guilty on all four counts and sentenced to death by hanging. Hess was found sane and sentenced to life imprisonment. Ribbentrop, Keitel, Kaltenbrunner, Rosenberg, Frank, Frick, Streicher, Jodl, Seyss-Inquart, Sauckel, and Bormann were also sentenced to death by hanging. Funk, Doenitz, Raeder, Speer, Neurath, and Schirach were sentenced to different prison terms. Von Papen, Schacht, and Fritzsche were acquitted, over the dissent of the Soviet voting judge. The defendants appealed some of the sentences to the Allied Control Council, specifically contesting the means by which the death penalty was to be executed. The appeals were rejected on October 11, 1946. The hanging of those sentenced to capital punishment took place on October 16;

Goering, however, was found dead on that same day after having swallowed a cyanide capsule that he had managed to retain throughout the trial.

The impact of the trial on the German public is a matter of controversy. In a poll asking whether they thought that national socialism was a good idea, though badly implemented, 53 percent responded yes immediately before the trial; as the trial progressed and crimes became known, the affirmative response dropped to 40 percent. In 1947, however, the affirmative response recovered to its pre-1946 level, and the response for 1948 was 55.5 percent.[12] This limited data does not sustain an enthusiastic judgment about the trial's impact on German citizens.

The initial trial was followed by twelve other Allied trials in Nuremberg, as well as by separate trials conducted by each of the occupying powers. Subsequently, the responsibility for persecuting Nazi criminals was left to the German authorities. These efforts were to little avail. The occupying powers themselves confronted strong pressure to parole most of those convicted, especially industrialists who had profited from slave labor. The German courts were quite lenient and extremely sensitive to legal issues, such as double jeopardy, which impeded trial of those who had been pardoned by the Allied courts, or retroactive application of laws, questioning why members of the Nazi regime should be tried under a set of laws that were not in effect during their implicated conduct. Domestic trials continued in Germany until the late 1950s, when they eventually languished.

At the end of that decade, however, there was a resurgence of interest in assigning Nazi responsibility, probably, in part, because of the pressure from the newly founded state of Israel and the concomitant upsurge in Jewish consciousness in the United States and elsewhere. The British Parliament, for example, extended the statute of limitation for Nazi crimes twice and finally abrogated it. Despite these efforts, the results were not dramatic. According to John H. Herz, in the more than 1,000 cases tried between 1959 and 1969, fewer than 100 of the convicted Nazi criminals received life sentences and less than 300 received limited terms.[13] In the following twelve years, there were 6,000 convictions, but only 157 were for life imprisonment. Despite the fact that Nazi judges imposed 26,000 death sentences for "crimes" such as making an anti-Nazi joke, not one judge was convicted for those bloody penalties, imposed often without any procedural guarantees.

Some believe the legacy of nazism was more satisfactorily discharged through reparations.[14] Germany made extensive indemnification of material damage and restitution of property. In addition, Germany restored citizenship, academic degrees, and some professional positions to individuals who had been persecuted during the war.

Although the Allied powers launched an extensive denazification campaign, aimed at purging from public positions those connected with Nazi activities, the results of this campaign were limited. Ex-Nazis found ways to escape detection and the authorities evinced an increasing tendency to "turn their backs" on the evidence of a Nazi past.

SEQUELS TO NUREMBERG

Following Nuremberg, further trials for massive human rights violations took place in the countries which had been allied with Nazi Germany, as well as in those invaded by it — Italy, Japan, Austria, France, Belgium, Hungary, Poland, and Czechoslovakia.

Austria. In 1938, the Anschluss effectively united Austria and Germany. This "unification" terminated the Patriotic Front's domestic dictatorship and established direct Nazi control. The Allies' 1943 Moscow Declaration proclaimed that an independent Austria would be recreated at the war's end, and in fact after Austria was occupied in 1945 it regained independence. Soon thereafter, Austria held free elections under the reinstated Constitution of 1920. Nonetheless, the Allied tutelage continued until the Treaty of 1955 and the incorporation of the country into the United Nations system.

The Allies encouraged denazification in Austria, though they let the Austrian government carry out the necessary measures. To this end, the Austrian government passed a statute that divided the approximately half-million members of the Nazi Party into categories according to whether they were strongly or weakly implicated in the regime. Those strongly implicated — numbering around 40,000 and consisting of members of the Gestapo and the SS, recipients of party medals, and beneficiaries of economic advantages — were heavily fined. Other members of the Nazi Party lost public positions and even their homes. For example, half of the judges from the Nazi period were replaced or not reappointed; under pressure from the Allies, those more heavily involved faced criminal charges. During the first three years of the Second Republic, People's Courts tried 17,500 individuals for war crimes; however, only 43 were sentenced to death, and only 29 were eventually executed. The denazification process never touched many Austrian Nazis, for the government enacted an amnesty for those "less" implicated just in time for the election of 1949.[15] In 1957 the Austrian government enacted a general amnesty for all members of the Nazi Party.

Italy. Nazi Germany's closest ally was fascist Italy. Unlike the case of Germany and even Austria, the Allies believed that Italian "defascization" was mainly a domestic issue. The Badoglio government, immediately after the armistice with the Allies, issued a wide set of decrees to purge the administration of fascists, establish principles for the prosecution of fascist crimes, and create a high commissioner for defascization. It appointed the republican Count Sforza to that position. A 1944 act further delineated the high commissioner's charge: punishing fascist crimes, purging the administration, confiscating fascist gains, and disposing of Fascist Party assets. In the section of the act dealing with criminalization, the Italian government conceded the need for ex post facto criminal laws, while avoiding their application by reinstating the previous liberal penal code that had been illegally abrogated under fascism.[16] The act's vague definitions of crimes, coupled with detailed descriptions of extenuating circumstances, reflected the high commissioner's charge to "hit high and forgive below." The act's enforcement was entrusted to a host of judicial and semijudicial agencies, including the High Court of Justice for trial of the top fascist officials for crimes committed against the state in bringing fascism to power, ordinary courts for trial of lower officials accused of similar charges before the armistice, ordinary and military courts for trial of those collaborating with the Germans after the armistice, and special commissions, formed by representatives of ministries, local administrations, and professional associations, for carrying out purges.

Because of practical difficulties in collecting evidence, this judicial-oriented approach to defascization became protracted.[17] As such, defascization engendered feelings not of justice but rather of hypocrisy. In the end, the office of the high commissioner was abolished and the minister of justice approved an amnesty law, making a travesty of the attempts at criminal prosecution. Only a few extremely "cruel tortures" were excluded from this amnesty law. Most of the public officials who had been purged were reinstated, and the confiscation of the fascists' economic profits came to an abrupt halt. On the other hand, private revenge was effective in Italy. The number of fascists who disappeared or were summarily executed in the weeks following liberation ranges from the official figure of 1,732 to the Neo-Fascists' estimation of 300,000; commentators reasonably estimate the number at 30,000.[18]

France. In 1940, France was invaded by Nazi Germany and an armistice was signed on June 22. It divided France into an occupied part, which included Paris, and an unoccupied part, headed by a domestic government in Vichy, which also controlled the colonies. In 1944 the Allies liberated France, and public sentiment, spearheaded by a fairly strong resistance movement, pressed for punishment of those who had collaborated with the Vichy government and the German invaders.

The Committee of National Liberation created a commission of prestigious jurists to delineate guiding principles for subsequent purges and criminalization. Article 75 of the French Penal Code, making treason an offense punishable by law, provided the legal mechanism for achieving retroactive justice. But the committee defined treason so broadly that virtually all who did not follow Gen. Charles De Gaulle into exile abroad or did not bear arms against Vichy, the Germans, or their paramilitary forces were susceptible to a treason charge.[19] The committee declared that Vichy was an illegitimate government and that the state of war with Germany had existed since 1939. Anyone who had dealt with Germany since the day of the armistice was thus considered a traitor. This broad definition of treason created a legal quandary.

To redress this problem, the French retroactively created a new offense, that of "collaboration." This offense, punishable by death, involved giving the enemy material or moral support, even indirectly, by helping the government of Vichy in domestic or foreign policy. Because this definition was also over-inclusive, a new crime for lesser offenders, "national indignity," was created retroactively. The crime of national indignity reached participation, in any form, in the Nazi or Vichy government from the armistice to the liberation, the production or distribution of propaganda on their behalf, participation in the Commissariat for Jewish Affairs, and participation or membership in any organization supporting collaboration. The French government, therefore, divided offenses related to the Nazi past into three categories: treason, collaboration, and national indignity.

The definition of these crimes led to judicial and semijudicial proceedings. At first, courts-martial and special tribunals of "urgency" dealt with many cases without many procedural guarantees. Administrative decisions led to the internment of approximately 120,000 to 150,000 persons, many of whom appeared on lists of collaborators and members of pro-Nazi organizations compiled by the Resistance and Gaullist groups. In time, the courts took responsibility for trying these offenses: the High Court of Justice tried the major criminals, the *cours de justice* tried lesser ones, and the *chambres civiques,* local courts, tried national indignity offenses. About 200,000 individuals were indicted, 100,000 were actually tried, and 65,000 were found guilty and remained in limbo until the promulgation of the amnesty law of 1953.[20] Marshal Philippe Pétain, the leader of the Vichy regime, and Pierre Laval, president of Vichy's Council of Ministers, were sentenced to death in 1945. Both sentences were later reduced to life imprisonment.

Instances of private citizens taking justice into their own hands were even more prevalent in France than in Italy. In 1944 alone, private citizens killed approximately 40,000 people accused of collaborating with the Nazis.

Belgium. The Allies liberated Belgium in 1944. Shortly thereafter, the Belgian Supreme Court validated the laws enacted by the government-in-exile during the Nazi occupation. The crime of collaboration was acknowledged in some of these laws. Nonjudicial agencies handled the purges against collaborators, while the military courts tried the criminal charges of collaboration. A full 400,000 individuals, 7 percent of the adult Belgian population, faced the prospect of trial. Tens of thousands were punished for acts of collaboration.

The crime of collaboration encompassed economic as well as political collaboration. The crime of economic collaboration was considered counterproductive, however, implicating many prominent members of the business community, as well as more than 60,000 workers who had volunteered to work in Germany. Therefore, in 1945 the Socialist government issued a law interpreting the collaboration statute to require proof of intent to help the German war machine before finding anyone guilty of economic collaboration. The government dismissed the charges against the workers.

Japan. Although the Japanese regime was highly authoritarian during World War II, its persecution of political opponents during that period was more subtle than that undertaken by its German and Italian allies. The government interpreted the 1925 Peace Preservation Act in increasingly broad terms in order to neutralize all those who could "upset" the existing order.[21]

Given the relative leniency of Japanese political persecution, the Supreme Commander of the Allied Powers did not attempt to punish crimes committed by the Japanese military against their fellow citizens. This stands in stark contrast to the zeal with which the Allies prosecuted Japanese war crimes. Allied military commissions tried more than 5,500 individuals for war crimes and issued 3,500 prison sentences, as well as 900 death penalties. In proceedings reminiscent of Nuremberg, twenty-eight Japanese leaders were tried for crimes against the peace before a special Military Tribunal for the Far East. After a protracted trial, seven defendants were sentenced to death, sixteen to life imprisonment, and two to lesser prison terms in November 1948.

The case of Gen. Tomoyuki Yamashita was especially interesting in legal terms. Yamashita was the Japanese occupation commander of the Philippines. When the North American troops landed, Yamashita ordered his troops to evacuate Manila. But the troops "disobeyed" him, killing and abusing more than 20,000 civilians. Given the enormous scope of the massacre, the prosecutor argued that Yamashita either intentionally permitted or secretly ordered the massacre. Defense counsel replied that the defendant could not have mitigated or prevented the attack because the lines of communication between the defendant and his troops were destroyed during the killing spree.

In its decision, the court admitted that a commander could not be convicted as a murderer or rapist just because one of his troops commits murder or rape. But when the murder and rape are brutal and take place over an extended period of time, and when the commander does not attempt to curtail and control the criminal actions, the commander could be held criminally responsible for the illicit acts of his subordinates. As such, Yamashita bore guilt and was sentenced to death.

Defense counsel appealed to the Supreme Court of the United States. A majority upheld the death penalty, arguing that international conventions had grounded responsibility of military chiefs on the acts of subordinates and that the tribunal had adequately discharged its duty to find such responsibility. The dissenters replied that the international conventions did not permit vicarious criminal liability and that it was absurd to convict the defendant of inaction when the American troops impeded such action. Justice Frank Murphy, one of the dissenters, emphasized that it is impossible to impute criminal liability without the requisite mens rea.

Some argue that the main purpose of the Tokyo trials was to publicize the war crimes of the Japanese leaders.[22] Whether the trials achieved this purpose, given that most Japanese citizens saw them as "victor's justice," appears questionable. For example, the ashes of the seven executed leaders were placed in a shrine, and in 1959 a leading statesman dedicated a stone to the "seven patriots."[23] Similarly, one war criminal sentenced to prison later became the Japanese foreign minister. In 1950 all the war criminals were freed and exonerated. Although the Allied command pressed heavily for extrajudicial purges, fewer than 6,000 were removed from office.[24]

EICHMANN'S TRIAL: RETROACTIVE JUSTICE
ON THE NATIONAL LEVEL

Retroactive justice also took place before national, rather than international, tribunals. The trial of Adolf Eichmann is the most prominent example.[25] The Israeli secret service kidnapped Eichmann in a suburb of Buenos Aires on the evening of May 11, 1960. This violation of Argentine sovereignty caused a significant uproar in Argentina, although the uproar was attenuated by the fact that Eichmann had entered the country under a false identity. The diplomatic incident between Israel and Argentina ended with a joint declaration on August 3, 1960, explicitly recognizing that Israeli agents violated Argentine sovereignty.

A Jerusalem district court tried Eichmann on April 11, 1960, charging him with fifteen separate counts under the Israeli Nazis and Nazi Collaborators Act of 1950. Among the charges were crimes against the Jewish people, crimes against humanity, and war crimes. All of these crimes were punishable by death.

The evidence convincingly proved that Eichmann was a primary architect of the "Final Solution" and bore responsibility for endless war crimes and crimes against humanity.[26] The trial court's decision was read on December 11, 1962. Eichmann was convicted of crimes against the Jewish people with the intent to exterminate the entire Jewish population by killing millions of Jews, placing them in conditions which would likely lead to their physical destruction, causing them serious bodily and mental harm, and banning births of Jewish children. He was also convicted of crimes against humanity, including genocide of non-Jewish peoples, mass murder, persecution of Jews on racial, religious, and political grounds, plundering of Jews' property, the expulsion of Poles and Slovenes from their homes, and the deportation of gypsies. Eichmann was also convicted of a variety of war crimes, as well as of membership in organizations deemed criminal in the Nuremberg trials. While the Israeli court recognized that Eichmann did not bear direct responsibility for most of these crimes, it ruled that in the case of such massive crimes, "distance" between the agent and the victims does not diminish responsibility. "On the contrary, in general the degree of responsibility increases as we draw further away from the man who uses the fatal instrument with his own hands."[27] Eichmann was sentenced to death.

The decision was appealed to the Israeli Supreme Court. The court confirmed the lower court's decision on May 29, 1962, rejecting the superior-orders defense. The court also dismissed Eichmann's contention that the fate of the Jews would not have changed had he never lived; the court reasoned that the Final Solution would not have acquired its infernal and fanatical zeal but for Eichmann and his accomplices. Eichmann pled for clemency to the president of Israel, who also received letters to the same effect from many prominent individuals, including Martin Buber, but the president rejected the plea on May 31. Eichmann was hanged that same day.

Prominent scholars, such as Hannah Arendt, objected to Eichmann being tried under a retroactive law before a victor's court. Arendt, however, believed that the Israeli court could respond as follows: first, the Nuremberg trials constituted precedent, and the Nazis and Nazi Collaborators Act of 1950 was based on that precedent; and second, this legislation differs from ordinary criminal statutes in that it deals with crimes that are much graver. Arendt also added that the principle of *nullum crimen, nulla poena sine lege* was violated formally, but not substantially, since the principle only applies to acts known to the legislator and not to crimes, such as genocide, which were unknown. According to Arendt, the key question was not whether legislation is retroactive but whether it is adequate.

Arendt also addressed the objection to the competence of the Israeli court but found it without merit. She analogized Eichmann's trial to similar trials in Poland and Hungary. The means by which the Israelis secured jurisdiction over Eichmann were of greater concern. While kidnapping constitutes a dangerous precedent, Arendt noted that there were extenuating circumstances in this case. Argentina was extremely reluctant to extradite Nazi criminals, making murder the only feasible retroactive alternative. This option, of course, carried problems of its own.

Arendt's objection to the trial was, in the end, more subtle. She argued that Eichmann should have been prosecuted for general crimes against humanity instead of crimes against the Jewish people. She believed that the extermination of Jews was a degradation of humankind and, as such, no domestic punishment carried enough deterrence. International law, she argued, would have been a superior means through which to redress these crimes.[28]

World War II introduced modern civilization to human rights violations that previously had been unimaginable. Yet in time Europe became the setting for a subsequent round of human rights violations. With southern Europe's transition to democracy in the 1970s, the new governments faced the issue of retroactive justice.

Post–World War II Europe
SOUTHERN EUROPE: DEMOCRATIC TRANSITIONS OF THE 1970S

As Spain, Portugal, and Greece underwent democratic transitions during the 1970s, each country grappled with retroactive justice for human rights violations. There were important differences between the experiences in southern Europe and Nazi Germany, and they help explain the different attitudes toward human rights abuses committed by the previous regimes. First, although southern Europe endured harsh dictatorships — totalitarian in the cases of Spain and Portugal, authoritarian in the case of Greece — the repression paled in comparison with that imposed by Nazi Germany. Second, the most severe human rights violations in southern Europe occurred significantly before the collapse of the dictatorships. In Spain and Portugal, the violations took place several decades prior to the dictatorship's collapse. Third, the persecutions in southern Europe targeted political opponents and, in some cases, terrorists, but not racial or religious groups. Fourth, in all three countries, the desire for retroactive justice, rather than being imposed by occupying foreign powers, had to come from within.[29]

In this contrast to Nazi Germany, the three southern European countries were similar. Yet their diverse experiences lent a unique flavor to each of their transitions and subsequent attempts to reconcile the future with the human rights violations of the past.

Spain. When Francisco Franco took power in Spain in 1939, he imposed a harsh totalitarian regime, founded on the principle of the *Falange* and centered on the personal rule of the caudillo. Franco abolished political parties and trade unions, confiscated their property, and either exiled or executed political and labor leaders. He established a highly repressive apparatus through use of Courts of Political Responsibilities and the Tribunal of Public Order, surveillance of public communication, and extensive purges in the administrative and educational systems. More than two hundred thousand Spaniards died in prison between 1939 and 1942.

While this repression subsided in time due to foreign pressure, it resurged in the late 1960s and early seventies in response to heightened political opposition, at times violent.[30] For example, the death sentences issued in the 1970 Burgos trials of Basque terrorists, sentencing ninety-eight to death for the alleged crimes of conspiracy and illegal propaganda, provoked international condemnation.[31] In 1974 two Basque terrorists were executed. Even the bishop of Bilbao was arrested for defending the use of the Basque language.

At the same time, however, Arias Navarro's party began negotiating a transition to a more democratic form of government. Franco's death in 1975 accelerated the rapprochement, which occurred under the auspices of Prime Minister Adolfo Súarez's government. Súarez promised not to purge Francoist officials accused of corruption and military and police personnel involved in the repression in order to placate those who favored the continuity of the regime.[32] The opposition pressed for a comprehensive amnesty of those accused of acts of political dissidence or of terrorism during the Francoist regime. In response, the Súarez government in October 1977 enacted a general amnesty of all politically motivated crimes. This amnesty covered offenses of which members of the opposition were charged, as well as abuses of human rights committed by state officials.

The gradual democratization process in Spain culminated with the 1978 Constitution, in many respects similar to the legal documents governing the Franco regime, and led to a general attitude of "let bygones be bygones." The fact that the most atrocious human rights abuses occurred several decades prior to Franco's demise, as well as a widespread fear of agitating the phantoms of the civil war, facilitated this approach. In the end, fear of the past, coupled with the peculiar dynamics between continuists, reformists, and rupturists, all of whom had "bargaining chips" to offer and to receive from the others, contributed greatly to the smoothness of the Spanish transition.

Portugal. Portuguese democratization differed significantly from the Spanish experience. The dictatorship commenced in 1926, after the military overthrew the republican government, and in the early 1930s Oliviera Salazar, a professor of economics, assumed control and imposed a corporatist state. At its inception, the regime was opposed to liberal democracy and communism, but World War II and the ensuing Cold War muffled state-sponsored opposition to democracy. Repression of opponents was similar to that carried out in Spain, including censorship, banning of political parties and trade unions, a demand for political loyalty in the educational system as well as in public administration, and the employment of special courts and police to deal with political "offenses."

But the downfall of the regime was quite distinct from the Spanish case. Salazar, who became incapacitated in 1968, was replaced by Marcelo Gaetano, university professor, jurist, and historian. While Gaetano liberalized the more repressive aspects of the regime, a severe economic crisis, coupled with the troubles of the colonial war in Africa — specifically in Angola and Mozambique — provoked a coup d'état in April 1974. A small group of middle-ranking military officers, radicalized during the war in Angola and Mozambique, carried out the coup. Post-coup instability was provoked by intramilitary conflicts between radicals, rightists, and moderates. The seizure of land and other resources by various social movements contributed to the unstable political climate. When the moderate Gen. Antonio Ramalho Eanes took power in November 1975, he managed to quell much of the unrest. The Constituent Assembly quickly produced a constitution that reflected compromises between liberal democrats and socialists. In the 1976 presidential and parliamentary election, the population reaffirmed its support for Eanes, electing him constitutional president and Mario Soares, a moderate socialist, head of government.

During the first two years following the elections, the government conducted purges and expulsions and even imprisoned some individuals connected with the old regime. However, these attempts at retroactive justice culminated in a truce between political groups. The spontaneous character of the Portuguese democratization process, coupled with the fact that the worst repression was a relic of a distant past, diverted attention from a potential systematic investigation and trial of human rights abuses.

Greece. Although the Greek transition from military dictatorship to democracy bears some similarity to other transitions in southern Europe, in fact that case more nearly approximates the South American experience that will be discussed later. There is one important difference: in terms of retroactive justice for the actions of a former dictatorship, the Greek case is lauded as a success.

The Greek military regime, established by a coup d'état in 1967, was led first by George Papadopoulos and subsequently by Demitrios Ioannidis, until it fell on July 23, 1974. Although the regime purported to be a temporary means of restoring parliamentary democracy, it instituted harsh repression of political opponents, mainly leftists. Systematic torture and bloodshed culminated in the massacre of students at Athens Polytechnic University in 1973.

Although the massacre prompted a period of liberalization, the regime's breaking point was linked to the disastrous results of the war with Turkey in Cyprus. When faced with a choice between a humiliating retreat from Cyprus or a full-scale war with Turkey, Ioannidis chose the second option. Senior military officers, who had previously supported the colonels' regime, thereupon pressured Ioannidis to abdicate. The president of the Greek Republic, Phaedon Ghizikis, then met with civilian leaders and decided to turn power over to a provisional government led by Constantine Karamanlis, a former conservative premier. Karamanlis immediately instituted political liberalization and granted amnesty for all political crimes except those committed by the dictatorship. A cease-fire agreement was reached with Turkey, displacing 180,000 Greek Cypriots. Karamanlis also reinstated the 1952 Constitution.

Karamanlis was given the onerous task of controlling the military. On August 11, 1974, he ordered the army to remove tanks from Athens, but his order was resisted until he threatened to mobilize the population.[33] Karamanlis took advantage of this temporary victory to purge the military. Nonetheless, the Greek population believed the transitional government was too slow to take action against those involved in the dictatorship. Many citizens initiated private legal actions against the military leaders for high treason and for systematic torture. As a result of these pressures, Karamanlis promulgated an act clarifying that offenses committed by the dictatorship were not covered by the amnesty and pledged to try such offenses in appellate courts under traditional due process rules. The military responded by plotting a coup, but the government countered by arresting several military officials and charging them of high treason. In November 1974, the public showed resounding support for Karamanlis's actions by electing him premier.

In 1975, Parliament declared that the 1967 coup had not been a revolution creating a new legal system and that the subsequent crimes of the dictatorship were not subject to the standard statute of limitations. The government indicted Papadopoulos, Ioannidis, other military leaders, political officers, and police officers accused of the torture of political prisoners for involvement in the coup, the student massacre at the Polytechnic, and systematic torture. During the trials, the military unsuccessfully attempted several coups, but Karamanlis responded with widespread purges of the army and security forces. He also developed a core of allies within the military who helped avert future incidents.[34] The trials began in July 1975 and received extensive press coverage.[35] The trial of the leaders of the 1967 coup ended with convictions of eighteen defendants. Papadopoulos, Nikolaos Makaresos, and Stylianos Pattakos were sentenced to death for mutiny and to life imprisonment for high treason. Eight other people, including Ioannidis and the former head of the central intelligence service, received ten-year prison sentences for mutiny and life imprisonment for high treason. The government reduced the death sentences to life imprisonment to avoid making martyrs of the convicted.

Victims of the military regime's human rights abuses pushed the matter further. In August and September 1975, they brought thirty-two former members of the military police to trial. The trial highlighted the military's systematic employment of torture to retain control. Three former commanders of the main detention center were given extended prison sentences, eight other officers received lesser sentences, and three officers were acquitted. Of the enlisted men on trial, five were sentenced to six years in prison and twelve were acquitted. All the enlisted men denied the charges on the grounds that they were obeying superiors' orders.[36] Subsequently, torture trials were held throughout Greece through 1976. Amnesty International estimates that there were anywhere from one hundred to four hundred torture trials in Greece.

The responsible military officials also faced trial for the student massacre at Athens Polytechnic. Ioannidis received another life sentence, Papadopoulos received an additional twenty-five-year sentence, and other defendants received lesser sentences. But the individuals indicted for having collaborated with the dictatorship were not tried for complicity, although some of them were tried for corruption.

Despite all these trials, the Karamanlis government faced criticism for inadequately punishing those responsible for human rights violations, failing to prosecute those against whom enough evidence had been collected, and allowing people to avoid prosecution by bargaining — giving evidence to the state.[37] Some saw the commutation of the death sentences as a capitulation to the army. Furthermore, torture victims were not compensated, although people who lost their jobs were reinstated. The government also faced criticism for relying on private prosecutions rather than actively prosecuting offenders. Nonetheless, scholars credit Karamanlis for punishing the dictatorship's worst offenders and purging the administration, mainly the army and the security forces, of their accomplices.

EASTERN EUROPE: EUROPEAN TRANSITIONS
OF THE LATE 1980S AND EARLY 1990S

Why an ideology such as marxism, which, unlike nazism, was openly rooted in the humanitarian ideals of equality and liberty, consistently led to massive violations of human rights and the imposition of totalitarian states comparable to that of Nazi Germany, is a question that has not satisfactorily been answered. Marxism illustrates the harmfulness of an ideology that is determined not solely by the ends it seeks to achieve but also by the process it employs for achieving those ends. Yet the elitist epistemology involved in the

Leninist notion of the "vanguard of the proletariat," which brought into being a party that scorned liberal-democratic constraints on the exercise of power, led to the establishment of regimes that required the highest degree of conformity to the dictates of a handful of "enlightened" leaders and that brutally suppressed dissent. Thus, from the Soviet Union to China, Cuba, and the countries of Eastern Europe, millions of people suffered several decades of systematic oppression and persecution. Once the Soviet empire collapsed in 1989, many Eastern European countries liberalized their political systems, though communism is still the excuse for state oppression in other parts of the world.

The human rights violations of the communist regimes were of massive proportions. For example, during the Soviet Union's Stalinist era, between seventeen and twenty million people were killed for political reasons, while unaccountable others were subject to the harshest conditions of imprisonment, deportation, and detention. According to Richard Pipes, Soviet human rights violations were based on explicit institutionalization of lawlessness, with expedience as the main political value.[38] While these massive human rights violations subsided with the end of the Stalinist regime, there were various waves of repression throughout Soviet history. Political repression and human rights violations were also characteristic of many Eastern European countries, especially those in which communist regimes were established in the wake of World War II.[39]

Once the communist regimes collapsed, the legacy of massive human rights violations had to be confronted. A lively controversy, which thrived in the midst of a newly acquired freedom, ensued. One of the most respected intellectual figures of the region, current Czech president Václav Havel, advocated forgiveness and tolerance. Another leading figure, Adam Michnick of Poland, editor of *Gazeta Wyborcza* and a member of Parliament, warned against unequal retroactive justice. While complete impunity seemed wrong, focusing on a group of scapegoats was tantamount to bolshevism. The widespread involvement of large segments of the population in activities which led to the violation of human rights, generally as informers, presented a formidable obstacle to imposing justice in anything but an arbitrary manner. Nonetheless, popular pressure for retroactive justice grew in light of economic hardship, heightened skepticism of democracy, and the realization that the bureaucrats of the former repressive regimes have been among the greatest beneficiaries of the new capitalism.

In confronting past human rights violations, Eastern European countries' responses ranged from revolutionlike violence, as in Romania, to restitution of nationalized property, as in Hungary. In Romania, for example, retroactive justice was apparently achieved through the summary trial and execution of Nicolae and Elena Ceauşescu in December 1989. The Rumanian government has pursued few subsequent trials and purges of former governmental officials and security agents suspected of human rights violations. Many suspect that the Ceauşescus' hasty trial and execution was, in fact, an attempt to silence those who desired further retroactive justice. The Bulgarian experience was similar. The country's former leader, Todor Zhikov, was, along with subordinates, convicted for embezzlement and given a hefty prison sentence. The Bulgarian government has not seriously pursued other ex-communist officials for their human rights abuses. Bulgaria and Romania seemed to achieve retroactive justice by concentrating guilt on a high-profile perpetrator, while ignoring the larger machinery that facilitated human rights abuses.

Other countries resolved to cast a wider net, but evidentiary problems hindered their efforts to achieve retroactive justice. A nonviolent "velvet revolution" overthrew the Czechoslovakian communist regime in November 1989. A legal regime was then instituted for the restitution of property that had been confiscated as punishment for political crimes. But "lustration," the process of screening public officials to determine whether they were collaborators or informers, dominated political discourse.[40] For this purpose, limited access was granted to the secret files of the State Security Police (StB). For a year, the interior minister held the files and refused to allow their examination. Thereafter, a commission of legal experts, appointed by Parliament to address the lustration issue, startled the country by recommending that all high public officials, including members of Parliament, be lustrated. Parliament, acting on the commission's recommendation, asked ten members to resign quietly after discovering that they were listed as informers. Ten other members refused to resign, alleging that the files were false.

Popular demand for lustration grew and, despite the misgivings of President Havel, the Law of Lustration 451 was enacted in 1991. It provided for the dismissal of communist, military, and security officials who had served at a certain minimum level, as well as of certain collaborators. The Lustration Law created two collaboration categories — secret collaborator and conscious collaborator — and rests on a presumption that the StB materials are reliable. The contents of the StB files can only be made public by decision of the Interior Ministry or by the person implicated.

Despite widespread agreement about the pervasive harmfulness of the collaborators' and informers' activities during the communist regime, many doubt that lustration achieves justice because of the questionable reliability of the StB files. These critics claim that the files contain names of those blackmailed into joining the network of informers, while excluding the names of the top Czechoslovakian and Soviet agents.[41]

The former Democratic Republic of Germany faced similar problems in carrying out extensive purges in public sectors such as education. German reunification in October 1990 complicated the legal issues involved in retroactive justice. Although unification generally extended West Germany's laws to East Germany, crimes committed in East Germany prior to unification were handled as follows: First, the defendant was judged under the law in force when the crime was committed. Then, the defendant was judged under the law of the Federal Republic when the crime was committed. The different outcomes were compared, and the milder penalty was applied. This legal regime gave rise to many problems. Because many East German leaders and members of the secret police (Stasi) committed acts that were not criminal when perpetrated, these individuals avoided prosecution. Some notorious leaders were prosecuted for relatively "petty" crimes. For example, the mastermind of the Stasi, Erich Mielke, was prosecuted for the murder of two policemen in 1931. Erich Honecker and several guards were prosecuted for killing those attempting to leave the country. The Federal Supreme Court rejected the guards' superior-orders defense on the theory that it provided no defense when those orders command violations of fundamental human rights, and found all defendants guilty. But the penalties were quite mild.

To complement the penal system, the government established a legislative commission, led by the highly respected human rights activist Rainer Eppelman, to carry out an exhaustive investigation of the communist regime's human rights violations. A January 1992 law addressed issues related to the Stasi files, creating an agency charged with making files available for legal, historical, and political uses.

The Czech and German attempts to achieve retroactive justice by conducting widespread purges have been frustrated by the questionable reliability of the evidence in the state security files. Likewise, in Poland, the lustration process is still a matter of debate, since the archives of the Department of Internal Affairs, including names of collaborators and informers, are considered highly unreliable.[42]

One of the most heated debates in Hungary centered on the relationship between the statute of limitations and the human rights abuses of the communist regime. Some scholars argued that there was a continuity between the legal system that existed when the acts were committed and the current legal system. They emphasized that the acts were legal when committed, that the criminal code prohibits retroactive changes in the standards by which acts are judged, including alterations in the statute of limitations, and that the perpetrators therefore should not face criminal prosecution. Other scholars asserted that although the constitution proscribes retroactive alteration in the definition of crimes and or the ensuing punishments, it does not proscribe retroactive modification in the "conditions of judgment." Therefore, modification of the criminal code's statute of limitations does not explicitly violate the constitution, although it may be inconsistent with the spirit of the document. Still another scholar, Csaba Varga, an advisor to the prime minister, argued that the law should not be viewed positivistically but rather as reflecting the demands of justice and the need to preserve national integrity in extraordinary circumstances; as such, the statute of limitations should be relaxed to facilitate prosecution of human rights violations.

Parliament enacted the "Zétényi-Takács law" on November 4, 1991, providing that the statute of limitations for the crimes of treason, murder with premeditation, and injuries causing death, committed between December 21, 1944 and May 2, 1990, did not begin until May 2, 1990. The law also provided that the punishment for these crimes could be imposed without any limit as to time. The lawmakers argued that statutes of limitations presuppose the state's claim of punishment; when there is no such claim of punishment, since the crimes themselves were an instrument for consolidating the government's tyrannical control, the statute of limitations becomes an evasive tool through which the perpetrators escape justice.

The law created considerable controversy, and President Arpád Göncz refused to sign it, submitting it instead to the Constitutional Court. The court declared the law unconstitutional, stating that it was not willing to sacrifice the rule of law to political justice. The court recognized the full continuity of Hungary's current legal system and the system of the communist period and thus believed there was no reason to lift the statute on murder and treason. But the main reason for striking down the statute was its unwillingness to accept "political reasons" as a rationale for failing to prosecute. The court believed that political reasons were too vague and, given the imprecision of the definition of the crime of treason, could lead to political manipulation.

In Russia, political instability has aggravated attempts at retroactive justice. For example, dismantling the power of the infamous KGB, the Committee for State Security, has proved quite difficult. Despite swift reorganization of the KGB in the wake of the attempted coup in August 1991,[43] many believe that the KGB has retained significant power and has merely been transformed into a tool which President Boris Yeltsin may utilize in the future to further authoritarian ends.[44] The KGB archives, containing evidence of many criminal acts, have not been significantly pierced, since only two parliamentary committees have access to the archives, and even their access is rather limited.[45]

The trial of the Communist Party in Russia was of great significance. At the beginning of 1992, thirty-seven communist deputies asked the Constitutional Court to declare unconstitutional President Yeltsin's decree of November 9,

1991, outlawing the Communist Party. Fifty-two Yeltsin supporters counter-petitioned, claiming that the Communist Party was an unconstitutional criminal organization that was not really a party but rather an instrument for the unbridled exercise of state power. On May 26, 1992, the chief justice of the Supreme Court, Valery Zorkin, decided to try both petitions simultaneously.

Communist Party supporters such as Viktor Zorkaltsev, a deputy in the Russian parliament, argued that the party had consolidated society and battled fascism; the party was outlawed merely because it had the bad luck of losing power after the coup. The democrats, on the other hand, had destroyed the national economy and jeopardized the union. Another party representative, Dmitri Stepanov, argued that the Communist Party was never as brutal as the United States Army in Vietnam. Yeltsin's leading advocate, Sergei Shakhrai, provided a historical account, arguing that the Communist Party never was, either de jure or de facto, a real party but merely an organization for monopolizing state power.

Each side presented witnesses. Those opposing the Communist Party presented victims of repression, including Lev Razgon, a writer who had spent more than ten years in Stalin's labor camps; Vladimir Bukovsky, who, following a period in Leonid Brezhnev's labor camps, had been traded to the West for the head of the Chilean Communist Party; and Gleb Yakunin, a dissident Orthodox priest who had been imprisoned for practicing his faith. Proponents of the Communist Party presented witnesses such as Yegor Ligachev, second in command of the party; Valentin Falin, head of the party's international division; and Nikolai Ryzhkov, prime minister for five years under Mikhail Gorbachev.

While the trial initially aroused public interest, even inciting public demonstrations, it ended amid public indifference.[46] The court issued a Solomonic judgment on November 30, 1992, upholding Yeltsin's decision to outlaw the Communist Party's leadership apparatus and to confiscate party property, but declaring unconstitutional Yeltsin's ban on grass-roots party cells.

The situation in the former Yugoslavia is in the most fluid state. With the downfall of the communist regime, the union between the ethnic provinces, consolidated after World War II under the strong leadership of Marshal Tito, began to collapse. On June 25, 1991, Croatia and Slovenia proclaimed independence; two days later the Serbian-controlled federal army intervened in Slovenia. On July 3, 1991, the Serbian and Croatian militias began fighting. When the provinces of Bosnia and Herzegovina, heavily populated by Muslims, declared independence, leaving only Serbia, Montenegro, Vojvodina, and Kosovo as part of the former Yugoslavia, the war between the Serbs and the Bosnian Muslims also began.

In Bosnia-Herzegovina, Serbs, Croatians, and Muslims lived among each other in towns and villages, provoking concentrated hostilities when the accumulated hatred erupted as each group feared being dominated by another. The Serbs advanced in Bosnia, conquering most of the province and displacing much of the population. In August 1992, the United Nations, which had already sent peacekeeping forces to the region, held an international conference on the former Yugoslavia led by a UN envoy, Cyrus Vance, and a representative of the European Community, Lord David Owen. The Bosnian participants were Mate Boban for the Bosnian Croats, Radovan Karadzic for the Bosnian Serbs, and Alija Izetbegovic for the Bosnian Muslims. The conference set forth a peace plan for the region, calling for Bosnia's division into ten provinces, a peace settlement, and the outline of a future Bosnian constitution. The Muslims rejected the plan because it would have validated many of the Serbian conquests. In late 1995, another peace initiative, this time spearheaded by the United States, was more successful.

Extensive human rights abuses have occurred during the war. Many were the consequence of Serbian president Slobodan Milosevic's policy of "ethnic cleansing," carried out by the leader of the Bosnian Serbs against the Bosnian Muslims. The result was indiscriminate killings of unarmed civilians, some of them as atrocious as running over children with trucks; the massive and systematic raping of thousands of women; torture and humiliation; displacements of entire populations; and destruction of property.

These atrocities provoked an international response. On February 22, 1993, the UN Security Council, by Resolution 808, established an international tribunal for the prosecution of perpetrators of human rights violations in the former Yugoslavia. The French, Italian, and Swedish representatives to the tribunal presented reports dealing with problems endemic to such tribunals: applicable law, jurisdiction, definition of the crimes, and procedure. According to these reports, the Nuremberg and Tokyo precedents, which allegedly had overcome the problem of retroactive penal laws, lent legitimacy to an international ad hoc court. On May 25, 1993, the Security Council, acting under chapter VII of the UN Charter, established an international court of eleven members to redress the violation of international humanitarian law in the former Yugoslavia. The wheels of justice have begun to turn.

Human Rights Violations Outside Europe
HUMAN RIGHTS ABUSES IN ASIA

The human rights violations perpetrated by the United States military in Vietnam are paradigmatic of what can happen when a powerful country gets entangled in a distant war. The abuses imputed to the United States Army are similar to those of which France was accused in Algeria or the Soviet Union in Afghanistan. As an example of the limits of retroactive justice in such cases, let us concentrate briefly on the United States in Vietnam.

Michael Walzer writes, "The American war in Vietnam was . . . carried out in so brutal a manner that even had it initially been defensible, it would have to be condemned, not in this or that aspect but generally."[47] Even though Walzer's statement has gained acceptance not only among intellectuals and radicals but also throughout much of the country, there has been no serious attempt to assess responsibility before the courts. By way of example, I would like to refer to the My Lai massacre and to the subsequent investigation and trials. I choose this particular incident because it was the worst atrocity committed during the war and the one that provoked the greatest public condemnation and demands for justice. But there were others. Joseph Goldstein, Burke Marshall, and Jack Schwartz write, "One need not accept every allegation of the antiwar literature to conclude that American soldiers in Vietnam committed numerous war crimes beyond those at My Lai, even though there is no hard evidence of any other such crimes of comparable magnitude."[48]

In March 1968, U.S. Army troops massacred a large number of noncombatants, almost exclusively old men, women, and children, in My Lai, Vietnam. Among the crimes committed were between 175 and 400 killings; individual and group maimings; rape; sodomy; and assault and mistreatment of prisoners. The American soldiers also destroyed property, killing livestock, destroying crops, closing wells, and burning houses.

Despite these atrocities, the matter would not have been investigated had it not been for a Vietnam veteran's 1969 letter to the secretary of defense. On November 29, 1969, the secretary of the army and the chief of staff issued an order to investigate the massacre and its cover-up. The investigation, conducted by Lt. Gen. William Peers, was completed by March 1970 but remained confidential until 1974.

The Peers report detailed the atrocities described above. Col. Frank Barker, who later died in action, ordered the assault on the village, thinking that it harbored the Vietcong command. He ordered the village burnt, the livestock and foodstuff destroyed, and the noncombatants held, although there was no evidence that he ordered the killings. Cloaked with these instructions, Capt. Ernest Medina ordered the destruction not only of houses and food but also of the inhabitants, who were deemed the enemy. On March 16, 1968, several platoons commanded by Lts. Thomas Willingham, William Calley, Jeffrey La Cross, and Steven Brooks carried out the brutal assault on the village. Some opposition to the operation was voiced, but it was obviously insufficient to derail the operation altogether.[49] The Peers report also discovered an extensive cover-up of what had occurred.[50]

Following the release of the Peers report, thirty alleged perpetrators were brought to trial before U.S. military courts, but Lieutenant Calley was the only one convicted.[51] Three were acquitted. Charges against twelve others were dismissed before the trial. Captain Medina was acquitted for lack of evidence. The course of the proceeding against Calley was torturous. A military court first sentenced him to confinement for life with hard labor as punishment for three premeditated murders and one assault with intent to commit murder. A reviewing military court later reduced this sentence to twenty years of confinement. Calley then sought a writ of habeas corpus from a federal district court, claiming that he had been denied due process. The district court agreed. It held that publicity, statements of government officials, and paucity of evidence had biased the original trial. The court viewed Calley's conviction as a catharsis of the national conscience. The Court of Appeals reversed this decision in September 1975. It held that obedience to superior orders is not a defense if the soldier knowingly followed an unlawful order or if a man of ordinary sense and understanding would have known of the illegality even if the actual perpetrator did not.[52]

Asian governments also perpetrated human rights violations against their own populations. A striking case is Cambodia. When the Khmer Rouge guerrillas entered Phnom Penh in April 1975, ending five years of civil war, they ordered the evacuation of the cities populated by people they viewed as enemies and class exploiters.[53] During this period the Khmer Rouge government violated the most basic human rights of the Cambodian population. The Khmer Rouge curtailed all freedom of religion, expression, and movement. All marriages required approval by the authorities. The Khmer Rouge systematically killed anyone who had served the previous government or who was educated, or even slightly "suspicious." Between 105,000 and 300,000 Cambodians were summarily executed, and the intelligence service tortured at least 20,000 others. The apex of the terror occurred in 1978 in an area bordering Vietnam. In that event, which has become known as the "eastern zone massacre," the Khmer Rouge killed over 100,000 people, or one-seventh of the population, including Khmer Rouge cadres themselves. The Khmer Rouge's atrocities ended in 1979, when Cambodia was invaded by Vietnam.

These human rights abuses received very little international attention. As early as 1975, the Ford administration expressed some concern for the killings. Two influential books published in 1977 instigated U.S. congressional hearings and a French presentation in the United Nations.[54] In 1978, the Carter administration condemned the Khmer Rouge regime and called for a

UN Human Rights Commission investigation. That same year, Amnesty International, the United Kingdom, Norway, and Canada released reports documenting the human rights violations. But these efforts dissipated when Cambodia was invaded by Vietnam. The government of Vietnam was primarily provoked by Khmer Rouge attacks on Vietnamese villages, but also used the human rights violations to justify the invasion. The Western powers muffled their concern for the atrocities, and some even openly supported the Khmer Rouge as the legitimate government of Cambodia; indeed, the Khmer Rouge was allowed to hold Cambodia's United Nations seat. Realpolitik overshadowed concerns about massive human rights violations.

The case of the Philippines is more analogous to the South American cases than to the other Asian cases. During Ferdinand Marcos's first presidential term, beginning in 1965, the Phillipines entered a deep socio-economic crisis. In 1969, Marcos was reelected.[55] His second term was marred by a worsening of the economic crisis, social protests, and a growing political opposition. In the 1972 parliamentary elections, the opposition won many seats and planned to draft a new constitution that would preclude the reelection of Marcos. Marcos countered by proclaiming martial law on September 21, 1972, giving him full control of the country until 1978. The police and armed forces persecuted the government's opponents, using torture, imprisonment, and executions. Marcos dismissed Congress. The Marcos government also banned activities of political parties; prohibited public meetings; instituted extensive censorship; enacted a curfew; and conducted extensive purges of the administration. From 1978 on, Marcos hid his authoritarian rule behind a democratic cloak. Although he organized elections, they were completely controlled. Marcos lifted martial law in 1981 but still retained essential control. He gave members of his direct family, including his wife, Imelda, important official positions; he absorbed legislative and executive functions; and he exerted the authority to arrest opponents through presidential detention orders.

During the Marcos years, the government committed unaccountable human rights violations. Although the most well known is the murder of opposition leader Benigno Aquino, over 2,500 political murders have been documented.[56] In addition, there is evidence that 132 massacres took place, 550 people disappeared, 70,000 were imprisoned, and hundreds were tortured by military and police officers. The judiciary also became one of Marcos's tools. The judges, many appointed by Marcos, declared martial law to be constitutional and thereby legitimated these human rights violations. Military courts often tried civilians. The judiciary frequently invoked the political-question doctrine to avoid awkward confrontations with the regime. Under this doctrine, courts can decline to address legal issues that are politically sensitive.

Eventually, Marcos's regime faltered. Bowing to national and international pressures, he called for "snap" elections in February 1986. The opposition unified behind Corazón Aquino, the wife of the murdered leader. The elections were fraught with violence and fraud. While the National Assembly proclaimed Marcos president, Mrs. Aquino organized her own victory rally in Manila, gathering over a million supporters. Meanwhile, the military, who had been solidly behind Marcos, formed a reform movement, furthering popular mobilization. On February 25, 1986, the Marcos government collapsed and he went into exile in Hawaii.

Mrs. Aquino was sworn in as president and assumed responsibility for the government. She purged the armed forces and began investigating the allegations of human rights abuses. Following the example of Argentina and Chile, she established a Presidential Commission on Human Rights to carry out the investigations, to report to the president, and to recommend punishment for the perpetrators and compensation for the victims. The commission, led by former senator Jose W. Diokno, one of the Philippines' most prominent human rights lawyers, consisted of seven members. Aquino also ordered the military to free all political prisoners. The military began to resent the Aquino government and the commission for not extending the amnesty to members of the military. This tension sparked confrontations between the government and the military. The military attempted seven coups d'état, one of which might have succeeded if it had not been for an explicit show of U.S. military force in support of Aquino.

The criticisms that Aquino's human rights policies received from the right-wing opposition combined with the abuses committed by her own armed forces, which had received more and more power to fight subversion, altered Aquino's resolve to investigate human rights violations. She began to speak of the need to forget and pardon and acceded to military demands that the communists' human rights violations also be investigated. While Aquino reported that the Commission on Human Rights had investigated 2,165 human rights violations and filed 707 complaints in 1988 alone, not one prosecution or conviction followed. In fact, a February 1992 Amnesty International report, "The Killing Goes On," linked the failure to investigate the Marcos years with the current abuses.

HUMAN RIGHTS ABUSES IN AFRICA

Whether the transition to democracy is peaceful or violent determines how emerging African democracies coped with human rights violations.[57] Where the transition was smooth, as in Benin, Niger, and Togo, the new governments generally granted some sort of immunity to the leaders of the previous regime in order to further democratic consolidation. For example, Mathieu Kerekou, the president of Benin, obtained immunity from prosecution before being defeated in the 1991 elections.

In other African countries, however, such as Uganda, Chad, and Ethiopia, the transition to democracy has been the violent result of civil war. In Uganda, the regimes of Idi Amin and Milton Obote killed approximately 800,000 after independence in 1962. Although President Yoweri Museveni, who took over in 1986, promised to respect human rights and establish the rule of law, an undisciplined army continued the killings and tortures in a war against subversives in the north and east of the country.

Museveni established a Human Rights Commission in 1986 to investigate past human rights violations and serve as an educational institution. The commission held public hearings and secured cooperation of witnesses. Even President Museveni testified that he had been involved in abuses against Muslims when leading an anti-Amin guerrilla group in western Uganda. The commission's work has been quite slow, however, due largely to lack of funding. The commission's report was released in October 1994 — eight years after the commission began its work — and recommended prosecutions as well as administrative measures to prevent the recurrence of human rights violations.

The Hissein Habré government in Chad, overthrown by armed opposition on December 1, 1990, was the most repressive in the country's history. Scores of people had been executed without trial, secretly detained, and tortured, and Habré himself was directly involved in many of these activities. Thousands died of starvation in detention centers, one of which was close to the United Nations office.

The new Chadian president, Idriss Deby, accepting the advice of Amnesty International, created a commission to investigate the Habré regime's human rights violations. The government also established a high court to try Habré, who had fled to Senegal with members of his government. The commission's work was hindered by limited resources and intimidation. While some commission members gave up, others endured. The commission's May 1992 report documented over 40,000 killings, systematic detentions, and extensive use of torture. According to the report, these human rights violations were sometimes carried out under the direct supervision of Habré. The report also alleged that the United States, which had given significant monetary aid to the Habré regime, trained the security service personnel.

Some scholars claim that the Chadian commission was the first to identify persons who violate human rights and even to publish their photographs. Yet no prosecutions have taken place. The commission also made recommendations designed to guarantee the future protection of human rights, proposing that the commission become a permanent body with the power to denounce violations and promote educational activities. However, because human rights violations are increasing also under the new government, many doubt whether this government will institutionalize measures that further protection of human rights.

In Ethiopia, the military, led by Col. Haile Mariam Mengistu, violated human rights as it attempted to repress opposition among three groups: the officials of the former regime, sixty of whom were killed immediately after the Dergue took power; the political opposition, mainly the Ethiopian People's Revolutionary Party (EPRP), against which the Dergue organized the "red terror," killing over 25,000 in Addis Ababa alone; and members of the nationalist movement in Eritrea, as well as Tigres and Oromos, who suffered killings, displacement, torture, and detentions.[58] The army and security forces were not the sole perpetrators of these massive human rights violations; they enjoyed the active collaboration of large portions of the civilian population.

In 1991, the Ethiopian People's Revolutionary Democratic Front (EPRDF) overthrew the Dergue government and established a new government in Addis Ababa. The EPRDF disbanded former military and police forces and detained more than 10,000 persons who had participated in the Dergue terror. Most have been freed, but the several hundred who remain detained presumably will be prosecuted and tried in the courts. The accused receive medical attention and legal counsel. The government created a special prosecution office to facilitate investigation, and the discovery of the security and intelligence files will further this effort.

RETROACTIVE JUSTICE IN THE DEMOCRATIZATION OF SOUTH AMERICA

South American countries have suffered many interruptions in democratic rule, during which violations of human rights have been prevalent. Governments persecuted, murdered, and tortured political opponents; the army and security forces, especially during military regimes, frequently abused the poor and petty criminals. In the past, when returning to democracy, South American governments have not investigated human rights abuses committed during the authoritarian period, sometimes granting an explicit amnesty, sometimes ignoring the past altogether. These responses were inevitable given the intrinsic weakness of South American democracies, which were under constant surveillance and pressure from their armed forces. Politicians were so content with the respite from direct authoritarianism that they did not risk debilitating confrontations. Often, the politicians leading these new democracies had participated in the human rights abuses of the authoritarian regime, further impeding efforts to achieve retroactive justice. This paradigm changed significantly during the 1980s as several South American countries underwent democratic transitions.

In the seventies, highly organized military dictatorships dominated the continent.[59] The military coups took place under the guise of "national security." In the face of violent left-wing guerrilla movements, in some cases supported by Cuba, the military displaced weak and corrupt civilian governments. These military regimes differed in their approach to economic issues. Brazil, for example, imposed trade barriers to encourage import substitution, while Gen. Augusto Pinochet in Chile employed the free market to rectify the country's economic problems. Yet the regimes were similar in one respect: To consolidate their rule, they denied their citizens the most basic human rights. These military regimes harnessed the state's repressive apparatus to create a pervasive sense of terror; they employed torture, imprisonment without trial, outright murder, and forced disappearances to combat violent political and intellectual opposition.

During the eighties the continent turned toward democracy and, in a break with earlier traditions, there was a belief that human rights violations of the dictatorships should be explicitly confronted, maybe even in civilian courts. This new attitude can be traced to the breadth of state-sponsored terrorism, an international climate less tolerant of human rights violations (mainly due to the U.S. State Department's new human rights policy), and increasing awareness among South America's political and economic elites. While these desires for retroactive justice were nonexistent in most Central American countries, as well as in Peru or Paraguay, they were a defining part of the transitional process to democracy in Brazil, Uruguay, Chile, and Argentina. The results, as we shall see, were quite different in each country. I shall briefly discuss the first three cases before turning at length to Argentina in the next chapter.

The Brazilian military coup occurred on April 1, 1964. In the first period of military governance, between 1964 and 1968, Gen. Castello Branco maintained a semblance of political openness, although the repression of political opponents gradually increased. This repression provoked opposition and even urban guerrilla activity, instigating more repression, which in turn culminated in a comprehensive dictatorship sanctioned by Institutional Act No. 5. When Gen. Emilio Medici took office on October 30, 1969, the harshest repression began. With the creation of independent security organs, thousands were killed and tortured. This extensive and systematic repression subsided when Gen. Ernesto Geisel replaced Medici in 1974, launching a gradual liberalization process. Gen. Joao Baptista Figuereido, Geisel's successor, began to negotiate with the increasingly strong political opposition. Although human rights abuses subsided during the period of political opening, beginning in 1979, they did not cease altogether. During the negotiations, General Figuereido promulgated a "mutual amnesty" covering those accused of political crimes, as well as state security agents who had violated human rights. The amnesty even precluded investigation of human rights violations committed between 1964 and 1979. Nonetheless, private groups assumed responsibility for spreading knowledge of such violations. The most prominent was an organization led by the archbishiop of São Paulo, Cardinal Páolo Evaristo Arns, and the head of the Brazilian Presbyterian church, Jaime Wright. As Lawrence Weschler recounts in *A Miracle, a Universe,* this investigation was risky.[60] The publication of the report, which contained extensive data, was delayed until the inauguration of the civilian president, José Sarney, in 1985. Entitled *Brasil: Nunca Más,* the report was released on July 15, 1985, and soon became an unprecedented bestseller. The report documented 144 political murders, 125 disappearances, and 1,843 incidents of torture. In November of the same year, the organization published a list of 444 people implicated in the human rights violations.

According to Weschler, the Brazilian democratic transition was possible because the civilian politicians respected the amnesty. Although the report "was a definite snag in the coverup," it did not fundamentally alter the politics that facilitated the amnesty.[61] Such a compromise was possible because the human rights violations, although prevalent, did not affect as much of the population as in Uruguay and Argentina, the disappearances were less common, and the worst excesses had occurred in the distant past. However, the publication of *Brasil: Nunca Más* was beneficial, stirring popular sentiment and prompting President Sarney to sign the United Nations Convention against Torture in 1985.

Until the sixties, Uruguay was a model of South American democracy, enjoying relative social equality, moderate wealth, and political tranquility. As the import-substitution-based economy faltered during the sixties, political violence emerged. Terrorists known as Tupamaros, or the Movement for National Liberation, under the leadership of Raúl Sendic, turned to kidnapping and murder to voice their opposition.

The civilian governments began to react harshly, inviting the military to intervene. In 1969 President Jorge Pacheco Areco asked the military to suppress strikes. Torture and maltreatment of prisoners became widespread. Pacheco then asked the military to combat the Tupamaros. Juan Maria Bordaberry, Pacheco's favored successor, won the presidency in the March 1972 election. He immediately suspended most civil rights, freeing the military for an all-out battle against the Tupamaros. By 1973, the military had brutally and effectively emasculated the Tupamaros, incarcerating and torturing many suspected members of the movement.

Protests concerning the military's methods permeated Uruguay. The military used these protests as an excuse to combat subversion in the universities, the educational system, public administration, the professions, and the political class. Bordaberry suspended the remaining civil liberties on June 1, 1973, without congressional approval. On June 27, 1973, the military suspended Congress itself, created a Supreme Military Council, and reduced Bordaberry's role to that of a figurehead.

Uruguay suffered greatly under the military. According to Weschler, more than 10 percent of the population went into exile between 1970 and 1985; of those remaining, one in fifty was detained and one in five hundred was subject to a long prison term.[62] Some of the worst human rights violations against Uruguayans were committed in neighboring Argentina due to cooperation from its military regime.[63] The military classified the entire Uruguayan population into three categories according to the degree of risk the individual presented to the regime.

When the Uruguayan military thought they had gained complete control of the economy and the country, they sought to legitimate their regime with a 1980 plebiscite on a draft of a new constitution. To their surprise, the military lost the plebiscite by a margin of 57 to 43 percent. The military reacted with anger and the repression continued. At the same time, the economy began to spiral out of control. In November 1982, the military sanctioned internal party elections, which were won by candidates antagonistic to the regime. Again, the military reacted with more repression, primarily targeting protesting students, several dozen of whom were arrested and tortured in June 1983. Still, widespread demonstrations increased, including the famed protest of the Montevideo housewives. There was also a hunger strike by priest Luis Pérez Aguirre and some nuns. Soon the military began negotiating with civilian politicians, concerned mainly with avoiding investigation and trials for human rights abuses in light of what was happening to their colleagues in Argentina. In June 1984 the military began formal talks with the remaining parties in the Naval Club.

The Naval Club agreement provided for elections in November 1984. The winner, Julio María Sanguinetti, took office on March 1, 1985. A week later he granted an amnesty to all political prisoners, but explicitly excluded the members of the military who had violated human rights. Private citizens began filing complaints against perpetrators for specific human rights violations.[64] The military resisted these judicial subpoenas, and the issue reached the Supreme Court. In September 1986, the president's party proposed a blanket amnesty for all the military. This initiative was defeated. As the Supreme Court began sending cases to the civil courts, military resistance grew more open and widespread. On December 22, 1986, the two major parties proposed a law of caducity, which ultimately gained congressional approval.

In February of the following year, a group of victims organized to fight this grant of amnesty. They called for a plebiscite to overturn the law, demanding more than half a million signatures. After an unprecedented mobilization and public debate, the group obtained more than six hundred thousand signatures.[65] Gen. Hugo Medina proclaimed that if the amnesty was overturned, the country would be threatened. Lawyers argued that the principle of non-retroactivity of the penal law would protect the military. The referendum took place on April 16, 1989. Eighty percent of the population voted; 53 percent of the voters favored maintaining the amnesty law, while 41 percent favored overturning it.

Despite the disappointing results of the plebiscite, the referendum spurred debate and private investigation of the military regime's abuses, which were documented in the book *Uruguay: Nunca Más*.[66] However, it is unclear whether this confrontation with the past reduced the military's hold on public life. In the early 1990s, newspapers contained reports of military pressure on President Luis Alberto Lacalle's government.[67] In 1995 Sanguinette began a second term as president and assured the military that the human rights issue was over and would not be reopened.

In Chile, Salvador Allende, the Socialist Party candidate, was elected president in 1970 with less than 30 percent of the popular vote. Despite this slim majority, he sought to deepen the social transformation begun by his predecessor. Allende's support from the poor, intellectuals, and students was not sufficient to override the strong opposition from the socioeconomic elites and the judiciary, as well as countervailing foreign pressures, mainly from the United States. When the social and political climate deteriorated in 1973, the military, led by General Pinochet, deposed Allende's government through a violent coup.

The military junta, with Pinochet at the helm, established a harsh police state, with widespread detentions and executions, as well as extensive purges throughout the public administration, the educational system, all carried out by the state's terrorism and surveillance unit, the National Direction of Intelligence (DINA). Many others disappeared or were subjected to systematic torture. Scores of people went into exile.[68] Some, who were considered politically dangerous, were killed while in foreign countries. The former head of the army, Gen. Carlos Prats, was murdered in Argentina in September 1974, and the former foreign minister, Orlando Letelier, was murdered in Washington, D.C., in 1976. The junta also instituted a strict system of press censorship.

After the first wave of repression, which quelled the public unrest notwithstanding deepening poverty among the poorest sectors of society, the government's policies of monetary adjustment, privatization, and openness to foreign investment began producing economic successes. In 1978 an amnesty was conferred on almost all the earlier abuses, and in 1980 Pinochet legitimated his power by drafting a constitution that then was approved by a plebiscite.

In the early 1980s, especially after a downturn in the economy, the population began to press for democratization. Human rights organizations, such as Vicaría de la Solidaridad of the Catholic church, became increasingly vocal in denouncing the regime's abuses. Following 1983, the economy once again recovered and the reign of terror lessened. In 1988 Pinochet offered, as provided for in the constitution, to hold a plebiscite on whether he should remain president. After heated debates, various opposition parties decided to participate in the plebiscite, seeing it as the only chance to end military rule. This difficult decision implied acceptance not only of the 1980 Constitution but also of the 1978 self-amnesty law. The opposition's gamble paid off: In October 1988, a majority of the population rejected the continuation of Pinochet's presidency.

As provided for in the 1980 Constitution, after the ruling in the plebiscite Pinochet called for open elections. He nominated a protégé to run for president. The opposition parties formed a broad coalition that supported Christian Democrat Patricio Aylwin. Retroactive justice was one of the most prominent campaign issues, but only in a limited way. The opposition believed that it was too risky to ignore the 1978 self-amnesty law and merely promised to work toward its abrogation. Even this compromise was unacceptable to Pinochet, who immediately declared that he would end democracy if any of his men were prosecuted. Under the 1980 Constitution, even after the defeat in the plebiscite, Pinochet continued as commander in chief of the army.

Aylwin won the 1989 elections and, in his first speech, confronted the issue of past human rights violations, declaring that the government must chart a cautious equilibrium between morality and prudence. While he hoped for trials and subsequent pardons, the amnesty law became an impenetrable obstacle. Not only did Pinochet remain head of the army, but the government did not control the Senate. Nine of the thirty-five members of that body were, under the 1980 Constitution, appointed by Pinochet or by institutions he controlled.[69] Moreover, the ultimate interpeter of the amnesty law, the Supreme Court, bore Pinochet's imprint: He had appointed almost all of the justices.

The government ultimately decided to create a Commission of Truth and Reconciliation, a close parallel to the National Commission for the Disappearance of Persons created earlier by President Raúl Alfonsín in Argentina.

The Chilean commission was an executive, rather than legislative, body comprised of distinguished personalities with different ideological bents. The commission was charged with the duty of providing a comprehensive overview of the regime's human rights abuses, including their methodology and overall policies; writing a history of the reactions among different social sectors; explaining the causes of such violations; and recording the personal and societal consequences of the violations.[70] The commission was also charged with compiling a case-by-case account of the killings and disappearances to achieve some moral vindication among the victims. In addition, the commission investigated those killed by left-wing terrorism.

After nine months of highly professional work, the commission presented its report to President Aylwin, who released it to the public on March 4, 1991. The report verified the killings and disappearances of a large number of people, although it could not established the fate of many who were missing. The report also contained moving testimonies by the victims. The commission, however, chose not to list the names of individuals responsible for the violations, seeing this as a task for the courts. The report served as official acknowledgment of the truth, contributing to prevention of future violations by raising social consciousness and recognizing, both monetarily and symbolically, the great harm that the military regime had inflicted on so many people.

Some of the Chilean report's impact was reduced due to the contemporaneous murder of right-wing senator Jaime Guzman by leftist terrorists, shifting the public's attention to the resurgence from the left. Nonetheless, the public generally remained committed to some measure of retroactive justice. The courts are beginning to interpret the amnesty law liberally as merely preventing punishment but not trial. This stance of the judiciary is creating some uneasiness in the armed forces, which have flexed their power on numerous occasions by, for example, parading in combat uniforms on May 28, 1993 in downtown Santiago. The armed forces' steadfast leader, General Pinochet, continues to press for an extended amnesty.[71] On August 3, 1993, President Aylwin initiated proceedings to assess responsibility for human rights violations not covered by the amnesty law — specifically, against two individuals responsible for the murder of Orlando Letelier in Washington, D.C. Two years later, the conviction of those persons — one the head of Dina — was affirmed by the Supreme Court and they were finally imprisoned. Pinochet fumed but did no more.

These brief case studies, although far from a comprehensive picture of human rights violations throughout the century, illustrate the obstacles that emerge when investigating and punishing state officials for massive human rights violations. Some problems stem from power relationships, since those who perpetrate the violations frequently retain influence and access to the coercive apparatus. Other problems surface when the world view under which the abuses were committed and justified is inferior to the world view under which the punishments are assessed. There are practical difficulties in defining the group of culpable perpetrators, requiring the prosecutors to forge a delicate balance between widespread, but burdensome, prosecutions and unjustly focusing all guilt on a few individuals. Reintegrating sectors that had previously been hostile toward each other into democracy, or at least peaceful coexistence, presents other difficulties. Retroactive justice raises legal questions concerning retroactivity of penal laws, statutes of limitations, procedure, the object and limits of the punishment, and the scope of universal jurisdiction.

I will discuss these problems further after analyzing the Argentina case study at greater length. For the moment, it is important to emphasize how rare retroactive justice is when crimes committed by state agents are in question. Inaction, amnesties, and pardons are the norm. Attempts at legal prosecution often have targeted those with mere ancillary responsibility for the human rights abuses. Of course, exceptions to these generalizations have occurred. When a state was defeated in an international war and a foreign army supported the trials, as in Western Europe and Japan after World War II, prosecution was used to achieve retroactive justice. Domestic courts frequently tried and punished the perpetrators, as in France or Belgium, but only when the group accused of collaborating with a previous foreign invader could easily be circumscribed. The violent or peaceful nature of the democratic transitions has a high correlation to the viability of retroactive justice. In this respect, the case of Greece stands out as exceptional, since, even though they lost a war, an invading army was not present to facilitate their trials.

But even when the perpetrators of human rights violations are prosecuted, widespread criticism typically surfaces. Some people are disappointed at the contrast between the expectations of justice and the limited results of the strenuous proceedings. Others feel guilty about the omissions, recognizing that the ensuing power relations were responsible for the trials' shape. Still others feel great hypocrisy when those integrally involved in the abusive regime escape punishment, even retaining important public positions, or when those who were silent in the past suddenly become vociferous advocates of retroactive justice. Some grieve for victims of human rights abuses who were not sufficiently compensated, rehabilitated, or acknowledged. Others feel resentful when the victorious foreigners form tribunals that are biased, or when those foreigners press for rigid standards of justice which their own societies

Retroactive Justice in Argentina

The Historical Background

Argentina's history can be divided into three periods. The first was from independence from Spain in 1810 — officially declared in 1816 — and the final constitutionalization of the country in 1860. During these fifty years, there were frequent civil wars between Buenos Aires and the interior provinces. This period was notorious for the preeminence of popular caudillos, Juan Manuel de Rosas's bloody dictatorship from 1828 to 1852, and failed attempts to establish liberal constitutions.[1] This shaky beginning may have had a permanent influence on Argentine culture. For instance, skewed land distribution, which to this day deeply affects social structures, was largely determined during this period, as the wealthy took advantage of legislative loopholes and the corruption of public officials.[2] Justo José de Urquiza, who led the army that overthrew Rosas, spearheaded the constitutionalization process. Urquiza convened a constitutional assembly in 1853 to enact the constitution that remains in effect to this day.[3]

The second period of Argentine history lasted from 1860 to 1930. It began when the Buenos Aires army triumphed over the provinces and forced the enactment of some constitutional amendments. The period was characterized by political tranquility amid restrained democracy; two conservative parties repeatedly vied for power in fraudulent elections. This pattern persisted until the electoral law was changed, and the Radical Civic Union, with support from the middle class and immigrants, won the 1916 elections.

Also during this period, the country experienced considerable social and economic progress. Immigration led to unprecedented population growth. The export-based economy, rooted firmly in grain and beef exports to Britain, boomed, making Argentina the seventh-largest economic power in the world. In 1928, the country had more automobiles per inhabitant than Great Britain! There was also considerable social reform, with a universal public education system that raised literacy rates to a par with the most advanced countries of the world. University reform, begun in 1918, not only opened universities to the middle class but also improved academic quality. Argentine scientists won several Nobel Prizes.

Despite these achievements, some authoritarian tendencies were evident during this period. Various elements of participatory democracy were curtailed. More disturbing, however, was the appearance of some repressive measures. For example, the government suppressed anarchist and socialist labor agitation during the so-called Tragic Week of January 1919. Instead of countering such measures, the courts became a legitimating force, upholding, for instance, the laws of de facto governments and endorsing many questionably constitutional policies.[4]

The third period began in 1930 with a coup by a nationalistic civic-military movement, and ended in 1983 with the democratization process that will be the focus of this chapter. The 1930 coup was the outgrowth of social, economic, and political unrest during the early twentieth century. In the period leading up to the 1930 coup, anarchist and socialist groups incited strikes and violence. The establishment's fear of social revolt, combined with nationalist sentiments, heightened the attractiveness of xenophobia and fascist ideology. A strong popular movement, led by the Radical Civic Union Party, pressed for changes in the electoral laws to prevent fraud and promote higher voter turnout. In 1912, the conservative establishment enacted universal, secret, and compulsory suffrage which, once applied, greatly weakened conservative parties' chances of winning in clean elections. The 1930 coup facilitated the displacement of popular government by the conservator sectors, a phenomenon which was to be repeated in the 1955, 1962, 1966, and 1976 coups.

The coup of 1943, which was inspired by a pro-fascist nationalist military, cleared the path for Juan Perón's election as president in 1946. Perón consolidated a populist dictatorship, with some democratic trappings. His popular support was bolstered by constitutional amendments enacted in 1949. Perón improved the living standards of the poorest Argentinians by nationalizing most public enterprises, commencing a concerted industrialization process, shielded by high tariff barriers, and institutionalizing a welfare state. At the same time, however, he created a police state, with widespread persecution of political opponents. Perón's government detained, or forced into exile, legislators in opposition parties. Some opponents were killed, while many others were tortured. Corruption ran rampant in Perón's regime.

Deposed by the military in 1955, Perón went into exile in Spain, but he maintained significant influence over Argentine politics from Madrid. Perón infiltrated the trade union movement and the left-wing guerrilla opposition. When the violence escalated, the military allowed the Peronists to compete in elections, although Perón himself was not permitted to run for office. In 1973, a Peronista, Hector Cámpora, won the presidential election. He followed independent left-wing policies, however, and Perón withdrew his endorsement, forcing Cámpora's immediate resignation. An election was called and Perón won. A few months later, Perón died and Isabel, his third wife, assumed presidential duties. Isabel was profoundly influenced by her minister of welfare, José López Rega. A former policeman with mystic inclinations, López Rega created a right-wing terrorist group, the Argentine Anticommunist Alliance (AAA), to combat left-wing guerrilla activity.

Amid an economic crisis, allegations of corruption, and mounting violence, the military overthrew Isabel Perón on March 24, 1976 and institutionalized the most repressive authoritarian regime in Argentine history. Popular indignation with the regime's massive human rights violations, coupled with the military's defeat at the hands of the British in the Malvinas (Falklands) War and economic disaster, forced the military to call free elections in 1982. President Raúl Alfonsín won and assumed office in December 1983.

The period from 1930 to 1983 was somewhat similar to the first fifty years of Argentine independence: a cycle of relative anarchy, dictatorship, and restrained democracy. Argentina's economic potential, as well as its social and cultural standards, declined sharply during this period. Firm adherence to an import-substitution policy to spur industrialization and a dependence on agricultural exports forged linkages between economic and political cycles. A rise in internal consumption, usually prompted by popularly elected governments, heightened demand for imported primary goods. To garner the foreign currency to pay for these imports, Argentina had to promote its agricultural exports by devaluing the currency. Military governments, which were not directly accountable to the population, would institute such devaluations, which in turn would curtail consumption by making imports more expensive. This slowdown in consumption produced the popular discontent that ultimately forced democratization. The whole cycle could then begin again.

Recurring Trends in Argentine History

During these three historical periods, four recurring dynamics emerged — ideological dualism, corporatism, anomie, and concentration of power — that help explain the massive human rights violations we will discuss later in this chapter.

Ideological dualism, perceptible from the beginning of Argentina's history, involves a clash between two world views.[5] On the one hand, the liberal tradition is founded on the universalist principles of secularism, merit-based advancement, critical assessment of traditions, and skepticism of the legitimacy of corporatist groups — the military, the church, and the unions. On the other hand, the conservative tradition favors a closed, organic social framework that defends traditional social institutions.

The tension between these two world views has been played out in many forums. For instance, during the Constitutional Convention of 1853, traditionalist groups pressed for constitutional recognition that Catholicism was the official religion of the country, while liberals argued that equality among different religions should be guaranteed in the constitution. A compromise between these factions resulted in the provision in article 2 for state "support" to the Catholic church and the stipulation that the president should belong to the Catholic faith.

In my view, resolution of this ideologic dualism is becoming more difficult and tortuous in Argentina than in many other parts of the Western world because of the way in which liberalism has historically been defended. Liberals were not democrats. Many liberals were elitist in their disregard for mass participation of those whom they thought too uncultivated.[6] As a result, liberals did not engender support among the interior and less "sophisticated" areas of Argentina. Both supporters and enemies identified liberalism with the defense of capitalism, with minimal concern for the rights of the weakest sectors of society. Liberals also entered into compromises with conservatives on questions of personal autonomy. For instance, liberals agreed to the Catholic church's constitutionally granted special status, raising questions regarding their commitment to personal autonomy. These contradictions in the liberal concept of society gave credence to the conservative view. Many believed that traditionalism was more democratic, more sensitive to the interests of the interior, more committed to social justice, or equally indifferent to personal autonomy.

Present in almost all pluralist societies, ideological debate of this type is invaluable, for the positions reflect different yet genuine values that must be voiced in democratic societies. But in Argentina, the confrontation between liberals and conservatives was so intense that it endangered and sometimes toppled the democratic framework designed to contain and promote such debate. Traditionalism led to military dictatorships which favored corporatism, and homogeneity led to populist regimes which carelessly ignored the strictures of democratic processes and respect for civil liberties. Liberalism also had its dictatorships. The liberal vision of a cosmopolitan country, integrated into the world through free trade, led to military dictatorships under the pretext of constructing a true liberal democracy, which in fact persecuted those who opposed the liberal view.

The conservative view of an organic polity became deeply rooted in Argentina's state apparatus as fear of communist revolution swelled. This fear generated authoritarian measures designed to control subversive movements, to develop an intelligence network, to limit the influx of foreigners, to support rightist groups, and to control the private habits of citizens. Fear of communism also explained the adoption of protectionist trade policies, since import substitution, as well as a strong welfare state, were thought to respond to social discontent.[7] This fear even shaped Argentina's pro-Axis sympathies during World War II.

Argentines' endemic fear of social revolt was magnified by the Cold War, which gave rise to an ideology — the "doctrine of national security" — that was used to legitimate the massive human rights violations of the 1970s. Supported by domestic partisans as well as by American and French military advisors, the doctrine envisioned a "total war" in which the whole population was embroiled; according to this view, the enemy, communist agents, had thoroughly infiltrated the population, primarily in the educational system, the professions, and the trade union movement. The enemy conducted war through intellectual agitation and arbitrary terrorist acts. The doctrine of national security, and the concomitant image of total war, took firm root in those sectors which had been most influenced by the conservative, organic conception of society.[8]

The second trend, *corporatism,* is often misunderstood. Guillermo O'Donnell astutely notes that corporatism's distinguishing feature in Latin America is *bi-frontality.*[9] It is a means of controlling sectors of society through the state apparatus, and also a way in which different interest groups voice strident opinions inside the state apparatus to influence its decisions and garner special protection.[10]

Latin American corporatism can be either inclusionary or exclusionary, depending on whether the working class, represented by the trade union movement, is among the corporatist constellation.[11] Argentina has oscillated between inclusionary and exclusionary corporatism. The military regime that emerged from the 1930 coup d'état was exclusionary; the military coup of

1943, which was similarly nationalist and pro-fascist, produced an inclusionary corporatist system supported by a trade union movement. Although Perón's quasiconstitutional regime was inclusionary, the coups that countered Peronist governments in 1955, 1966, and 1976 were clearly designed to reestablish exclusionary corporatism. The present government of President Carlos Menem clearly has strong corporative leanings, but it is the first Peronist government to be decisively exclusionary. Argentine corporatism was a tool of both military regimes and populist democracies. Despite the differing manifestations of corporatism, the key members of the corporatist constellation — the military, the Catholic church, and entrepreneur groups — have remained constant.

The military, especially during the first and third historical periods, gained a preeminence stemming partially from the conservative conception of an organic society that views the military, together with the church and other corporatist groups, as part of the "real" fabric of society.[12] Of course, when the doctrine of national security further radicalized this ideological camp, the military was seen as the savior of a nation facing a pervasive threat of subversion. The military's privileged position, therefore, has been seen as instrumental to its role as custodian of national values. The military has thoroughly infiltrated civil society; many public services, such as meteorological forecasts, civilian airports, civilian aviation, and even some secondary schools, have been controlled by the armed forces. The military has enjoyed a veto, even under civilian governments, over many issues of internal security and intelligence. Traditionally, all members of the military have been exempt from common prosecution for crimes committed in connection with military service. Members of the military also have enjoyed a wide range of fringe benefits, including subsidized housing, access to special clubs and vacation resorts, and early retirement. Over the years, their salaries have been relatively high, and the military's budget has traditionally consumed a disproportionate percentage of public expenditures.

The Catholic church has enjoyed a privileged status. The constitution mandates that the church receive state "support," which most legal scholars have interpreted as being limited to financial support. As such, the state has provided concessions for church sites, subsidies for Catholic schools, and priests' salaries. More fundamentally, however, the church has been conceived as a guardian of national values. As a result, the church has held veto power on issues related to education, the family, contraception, abortion, and sexual habits.

The trade union movement has enjoyed a privileged status since the first Peronist government, which granted the Confederation of General Labor (CGT) a monopoly over working-class representation. The CGT's financial power was also greatly enhanced when it was given control over the whole social security and health assistance system. On the other side, certain economic groups and entrepreneurs' associations became beneficiaries of the import-substitution policies. Large landowners, the primary producers of agricultural exports, received most foreign currency. Whenever it became necessary to increase exports to meet trade deficits, the landholders received benefits in the form of currency devaluations, tax exemptions, and tax restitutions. The industrial sector was the beneficiary of most protectionist laws — customs barriers, tax exemptions, and special credits. Moreover, by granting concessions for public works or by granting contracts with state providers of public services to a few, megaeconomic groups, Argentine governments have further ingrained their privilege and buttressed their control over the economy.

The third dynamic, *anomie,* consists of a disregard for social norms, including the law. Anomie is a legacy from the colonial period, when local officials frequently proclaimed: "Here the law is respected, but not obeyed."[13] During the first fifty years after independence, Argentina failed to enact a constitution (which the dictator Juan Manuel de Rosas scornfully dismissed as "that little notebook"). Fledgling pieces of legislation, such as the law of land colonization enacted in the 1820s during the presidency of Bernardino Rivadavia, enabled those with connections to acquire large tracts of land at no charge; this land has effectively served to entrench their social and economic power throughout Argentine history. During the second period (1860–1930), electoral fraud was a potent example of institutional anomie. During the third period (1930–1983), anomie was evidenced by the prevalence of coups d'état as a means of obtaining political power and the use of unconstitutional mechanisms to enhance the president's power.

Judicial recognition of the legitimacy of coups d'état and the regime's ensuing laws is perhaps the clearest example of institutional anomie. Argentine judges have developed the doctrine of de facto laws to legitimate laws enacted by the military governments. In a 1868 decision (*Martinez*), the Supreme Court endorsed a presidential decree that approximated a legislative act. After the 1930 coup, the court officially recognized the new regime as the legitimate government, given that it controlled the state's coercive apparatus and was capable of maintaining law and order. In 1947, the court expanded the doctrine of de facto laws, declaring that decrees promulgated by a military government were valid even after the military left power as long as the constitutional government did not explicitly abrogate the law. Subsequent decisions conferred even greater legal powers on military governments. This process culminated in 1976 when the court recognized the military's authority to modify and suspend the constitution.

As we shall see, in 1984 this doctrine radically shifted when the Supreme Court, in the *Videla* case, declared the military's amnesty law invalid because of its origin and its content. The court ruled that military decrees were valid only if they were explicitly or implicitly ratified through constitutionally mandated processes. Unfortunately, President Menem's 1990 expansion of the court resulted in a reversion to the old doctrine; his court declared that, despite the "ideological or affective evaluation of democracy," the laws enacted by a military regime are as valid as those enacted by Congress.

Aside from these institutional ramifications, anomie is a widespread societal, as well as political, phenomenon. The black market flourishes in Argentina. Tax evasion, although more controlled over the last few years, has been rampant. Private citizens partake in many corrupt practices, ranging from smuggling to bribery. Traffic regulations, such as those setting speed limits, are seldom followed. Argentine folklore and music, including the tango, manifest distrust of the law and justice, which are instruments of oppression by the powerful.

I believe that this widespread anomie results from the problem of coordinating collective action.[14] Everyone would be better off if the laws were obeyed, but no single individual is motivated to do so. The inefficiencies driving anomie, such as quasimonopolization of land ownership, corruption, and low productivity, may help explain the ostensible reverses in Argentina's social and economic development. Anomie is also related to corporatism. The highest expression of a law-abiding society is the rule of law, which entails the universal and impartial application of legal norms. Corporatism, which is grounded in granting particular groups special privileges, defies the rule of law and therefore encourages anomie.

The fourth defining characteristic is *concentration of power*. The highly centralized Spanish colonial regime bestowed this legacy upon Argentina. Throughout the first fifty years following independence, conflicts arose as to the proper distribution of power between Buenos Aires and the rest of the provinces. The ensuing constitution, as amended in 1860, institutionalized a weak federal system, with Buenos Aires as the country's capital. Its residents enjoyed privileged use of government facilities, and to bolster their privileged position, powerful groups supported government initiatives to increase public expenditures in Buenos Aires. Now, more than a third of the population lives around Buenos Aires, while large areas of Argentina remain deserted.

Concentration of power not only manifests itself in the balance between the federal government and the provincial and municipal governments. Within the federal government itself, power has been concentrated in the presidency at the expense of the legislative and judicial branches. The result has been a *hyperpresidential* system of government. The founder of Argentina's constitution, the jurist Juan Bautista Alberdi, explicitly emulated the Chilean Constitution of 1828.[15] Alberdi believed that Argentine history demanded an elected king, a government democratic in its origin but not in its exercise. Accordingly, the constitution granted to the president the following powers which are absent in its American counterpart: appointment of cabinet members and other executive officials without Senate confirmation; unilateral enactment of state-of-siege legislation when Congress is in recess; the ability to detain and displace people during a state of siege; and, arguably, the ability to remove elected provincial authorities during periods of internal or external strife.

More important than the constitutionally sanctioned powers are the de facto presidential powers that have evolved. Specifically, the president has acquired, through implicit delegation, many legislative powers. Likewise, the president has acquired power to usurp legislative prerogative when the issues involved are "necessity and urgency." The executive can veto part of a congressional enactment and personally promulgate the rest, molding the legislation so as to best suit his or her own tastes. Despite the fact that the constitution suggests otherwise, the president has also assumed the power to pardon defendants on trial but not yet convicted. The president has the power to create, via decree, quasi-executive agencies, such as the Central Bank, which are directly controlled by the president.[16]

The military experiences complemented and contributed to the concentration of power in the federal government and, more specifically, in the executive branch. During military regimes, power rested wholly within the federal executive. The juntas exercised control over day-to-day governmental functions. The military president enacted legislation — constitutionally congressional terrain — as well as executive decrees. The military has typically dismissed the Supreme Court justices, along with other politically "obstructive" judges, and appointed puppet-judges who would ultimately approve doctrines that facilitated the military's control. The military president also dominated the provincial governments, since the governors of the provinces were directly accountable to the president. The military president became the natural center of Argentine power.

In my view, these four phenomena — ideological dualism, corporatism, anomie, and concentration of power — set the stage for the massive human rights violations sanctioned and perpetrated by the military government between 1976 and 1983. The attempt to punish such abuses by the civilian government that took power in 1983 should be conceived as part of a general strategy to counteract these trends.

Political Polarization and Escalating Violence, 1960–1976

Although the third historical period, which began in the 1930s, was unstable, the atmosphere did not become violent until the 1960s. Before the 1960s, dictatorships, coups d'état, and political clashes resulted in death and varied human rights violations, but these remained rare and isolated incidents. From the mid-sixties on, however, Argentina became embroiled in bloody left- and right-wing terrorism, as well as state repression. This spiral of violence culminated in the massive human rights abuses of the 1970s.

The first signs of violence were perceptible as early as 1959–1960, with the ultimately frustrated guerrilla movement known as Uturuncus. In 1962 a Trotskyist group blew up an apartment building in Buenos Aires. In August 1963, the Tacuara Revolutionary Nationalist Movement robbed a clinic, killing two guards. In 1964, a revolutionary arm of the Peronist movement, supported by Perón himself, was established. In 1966, Peronist factions, led by Gen. Juan Carlos Onganía, deposed President Arturo Illia of the Radical Party. The regime established in its place was a highly repressive bureaucratic-authoritarian state: The universities were purged of dissidents; opponents were detained under a state of siege; and the government, inspired by right-wing sectors of the church, established strict standards of private morality. The regime also commenced a capitalist-oriented, or "neoliberal," economic plan that redistributed income from workers to capital holders, and from small national firms to large, transnational ones.

Against this backdrop, the major guerrilla groups emerged. The People's Revolutionary Army (ERP), founded as a Guevarist faction, began its terrorist activities in 1969. Among its most prominent terrorist activities were the 1971 kidnapping of a British honorary consul, Stanley Sylvester, and the 1972 killing of Oberdan Sallustro, general manager of the Fiat car factory. The Peronist Armed Forces (FAP) was formed in 1968 under the leadership of Envar El Kadri and Carlos Caride; by 1971 it had receded into the political background when its top leaders were imprisoned. In 1967, the Revolutionary Armed Forces (FAR), originally inspired by Che Guevara and now led by Carlos Ernesto Olmedo and Roberto Jorge Quieto, began persistent urban terrorist activity, including the bombing of a supermarket chain owned by Nelson Rockefeller. The FAR merged with the Montoneros, a faction of the Peronist movement, in 1973. The National Revolutionary Army (ENR), associated with the weekly *El Descamisado,* assassinated two important Peronist trade union leaders, Augusto T. Vandor and José Alonso, before joining the Montoneros in 1970.[17]

The Montoneros were the most steadfast of the leftist guerrilla groups. Formed by a small group of Catholic students from upper-middle-class families who had originally been attracted to nationalist right-wing ideology, the Montoneros quickly turned toward the left.[18] The Montoneros, like the other urban guerrilla movements, adopted a cellular, militaristic structure, with grades and hierarchies. Its members believed that the movement embodied the Peronist doctrine of "national socialism" in its purest form.[19] While Perón was in Spain, he supported and encouraged the Montoneros. The Montoneros leveraged the increasingly popular discontent with the miliary government's economic, social, and educative polices, climaxing in the "Cordobazo," a 1969 violent street protest in Córdoba which was ultimately repressed by the armed forces.

On the first anniversary of the Cordobazo, the Montoneros abducted, and later assassinated, former military president Pedro Eugenio Aramburu, in revenge for the execution of Peronist military rebels in 1956. The Montoneros suffered great losses when, in succeeding operations, such as the occupation of La Calera in July 1970 and the Bank of Galicia robbery in September of the same year, its leaders were killed. Many of those who survived were tried and convicted for participation in these acts. Nonetheless, the Montoneros endured as an active part of the Peronist movement, within which they fought for Perón's return.

The increasing deterioration of the socio-economic climate prompted the armed forces to replace Onganía with Gen. Alejandro Agustín Lanusse, who planned to legalize the Peronists' call for elections. Meanwhile, guerrilla operations continued, and the military responded with repression—death squads, bombings of the offices of lawyers who defended terrorists, torture, imprisonment—although in a somewhat lesser degree than during Onganía's regime. I remember, for example, an incident when five heavily armed policemen came to my law office, asking for my partner. Although the military never pursued the matter, we were quite intimidated. In August 1972, many high-ranking ERP, FAR, and Montoneros guerrilla leaders who had been imprisoned in Rawson attempted to escape through Trelew. Although some succeeded, others were recaptured and ultimately murdered by military guards in what is known as the Massacre of Trelew.

In light of the upcoming elections to be held on March 11, 1973, in which the Peronist party could legally participate for the first time since the downfall of Perón's regime,[20] the Montoneros curtailed their terrorist activity and instead began political work with the Youth Branch of the Peronist Party. When

Perón's delegate, Héctor Cámpora, became president on May 25, 1973, imprisoned guerrilla members were granted amnesty and immediately freed by a large mob of sympathizers. The ERP, led by Mario Roberto Santucho, continued guerrilla operations, but the Montoneros and other Peronist groups "came up for air," taking advantage of close contacts with some ministers in the Cámpora   government and their power within the University of Buenos Aires.[21] Perón, annoyed by gestures of independence by Cámpora, forced Cámpora to resign forty-nine days after assuming office. New elections, in which Perón was a candidate, were called for September 1973. When Perón returned to the country on June 20, 1973, outbursts of violence between the leftist (including the Montoneros) and rightist Peronist factions occurred amid the millions of people who awaited Perón at the Ezeiza Airport in Buenos Aires.[22]

Perón won the election and assumed office on October 12, 1973. The Peronist armed groups refrained from most violence, hopeful that Perón would carry out their revolutionary policies. Instead, Perón ushered through Congress harsh criminal legislation aimed at subversive activity. On Workers' Day, May 1, 1974, he spoke to a crowd of about a hundred thousand in Plaza de Mayo. Infuriated by leftist chants, Perón praised the loyal trade union movement and criticized the leftist protesters as "infiltrators" and "beardless fools." The Montoneros and the Peronist Youth left the plaza.

The tension between Perón and the Montoneros had no chance of deepening because Perón, at age seventy-eight, died of a heart attack two months after the Plaza de Mayo confrontation. Perón's third wife, Isabel, replaced him. It was immediately obvious that her administration would be dominated by López Rega, who used the death squad he had created, the AAA, to do battle with the left. Composed of retired policemen, the AAA murdered scores of leftists, not only members of guerrilla organizations but also priests, intellectuals, lawyers, and politicians. Among its victims were Silvio Frondizi, the intellectual; Father Carlos Mugica; Gen. Carlos Prats of Chile; and Atilio López, the former vice governor of Córdoba. By September 1974 the AAA had killed approximately two hundred people.[23]

In response, the Montoneros turned again to subversive activity, denouncing Isabel's Perón's government as anti-Peronist. With more than five thousand members at its peak in 1975 and with an infusion of funds from a lucrative kidnapping,[24] the Montoneros began stepping up its military activity, mainly against police targets. The assassination of the chief of the Federal Police, Alberto Villar, a cooperative effort between the Montoneros and some Marxist groups, was the most spectacular of these activities. In October 1975, the Montoneros attacked a military garrison in Formosa. In December 1975, the police and armed forces arrested one of the Montoneros chiefs, Roberto

Quieto, while he was playing on a beach with his family. Immediately afterwards, the military raided guerrilla bases, resulting in many disappearances, a strong indication that Quieto had succumbed under torture. He was sentenced to death by a revolutionary court.

On December 23, 1975, the ERP mobilized its forces to attack the army in Monte Chingolo in the province of Buenos Aires. Apparently, some information was leaked to the army, which successfully repelled the attack. Most of the ERP attackers were killed, fatally wounding the ERP organization.

Casualties mounted. According to the *Buenos Aires Herald,* there were 200 political deaths during 1974, 860 during 1975, and 149 in the three months prior to the 1976 coup.[25] The *Herald* also reported that of the 705 political deaths between July 1, 1974 and September 12, 1975, 248 were members of leftist groups, 131 died in gunfights, 41 were members of rightist groups, 75 were police, 34 were members of the army, 19 were businessmen, 35 were people without a political orientation, and 122 bodies could not be identified at all. According to the security forces, between May 1973 and March 1976, the 1,358 terrorist-related deaths included 445 subversives, 180 policemen, 66 members of the military, and 677 civilians. Amnesty International estimated that right-wing violence resulted in 1,500 deaths in an eighteen-month period.[26]

Meanwhile, military repression increased. In February 1975, the army fought the ERP in Tucumán. In May 1975, President Isabel Perón, by decree, authorized army intervention to counter subversive forces in Tucumán. In July 1975, the army, together with the trade unions, forced López Rega's resignation. In August 1975, Gen. Jorge Rafael Videla became commander in chief of the army, and in October of that year the army became part of an internal security council, led by the president. Soon the police force was subsumed into the army. The army began to press for Isabel Perón's resignation. In June 1975, a presidential decree authorized the army to aggressively fight subversion throughout the country. Amid widespread violence from the right and the left, a deteriorating economy, and pervasive corruption, the armed forces decided to take control of the government. On March 24, 1976, the military deposed Isabel Perón. The darkest period in Argentine history was about to begin.

The Military Dictatorship, 1976–1980

The military junta, led by General Videla, Adm. Emilio Eduardo Massera of the navy, and Brig. Orlando Ramón Agosti of the air force took control of Argentina's government. At the same time, Videla was appointed president of the nation. The junta immediately issued an "Act Fixing the Purpose and

Basic Objectives for the Process of National Reconstruction." That act said that the objectives of the junta were to further the primacy of the state (and ensure national security), promote morality (including Christianity), eradicate subversion, and further economic development.

The same day, the junta promulgated "regulations" delimiting its functions, along with those of the executive, and establishing an advisory commission for legislation (formed by delegates of the three forces). The junta was the supreme organ of the state; its members, the commanders of the three armed forces, held three-year terms. The president, a member of the junta and appointed by it, was in charge of the executive power. The executive could enact laws which the advisory legislative commission did not classify as important. Those laws which were deemed important were promulgated directly by the executive, unless the president disagreed with that classification, in which case the junta would resolve the conflict.

The junta also immediately curtailed civil liberties. The military suspended article 23 of the constitution, which guaranteed to those arrested under the state of siege the right to leave the country. Congress was dissolved. Supreme Court justices, as well as other politically sensitive judges, were dismissed and replaced by individuals whom the military trusted. Many provincial governors and legislators were also dismissed. The military purged the universities. Members of the military seized control of public radio and television. In the following days, harsh criminal legislation establishing the death penalty as punishment for subversive activity was promulgated. Military courts gained jurisdiction over civilians charged with committing subversive acts. The junta prohibited political and trade union activity, and a law was enacted that allowed the government to dismiss officials suspected of subversion. Habeas corpus remedies were curtailed.

The junta appointed José Alfredo Martínez de Hoz as economic minister. He initiated a five-year stabilization plan, approved by the International Monetary Fund, which was designed to encourage fiscal austerity, eliminate trade barriers, force devaluation of the currency, and promote foreign capital flows. The austerity plan resulted in deindustrialization, a sharp decrease in workers' salaries,[27] and the accumulation of an external debt which, by the end of the military regime, totaled more than forty-five billion dollars. Popular opposition to such measures was quashed.

The military's control led to unprecedented violence. The armed forces systematically organized repression among themselves, forming task forces responsible for abducting "subversives," torturing and interrogating them, hiding them in clandestine places, and killing them in a variety of ways, primarily by throwing them from airplanes over the sea. A few of those who "disappeared" were subsequently released, most often on the condition that they leave the country; others became official prisoners, subjected to the whims of an officer who held great power under the state of siege or to trial before military or civilian courts.

Task forces wearing civilian clothes and driving cars without license plates carried out the abductions; local police were ordered not to intervene. Normally, the victim's home was ransacked and destroyed at the same time that the abduction took place. Perpetrators robbed for personal gain. Children of abducted parents were either given to neighbors, taken by the members of the task forces, or abducted along with their parents. Persons who were seized by the security forces were transported to more than three hundred clandestine detention centers, such as the ESMA (the School of the Navy Mechanics), the Automotores Orletti, the Club Atletico in Buenos Aires, or La Perla in Córdoba. At the detention centers, the victim was subjected to torture, humiliation, and sexual abuse. The military utilized techniques such as electric shocks, immersion in cold water, and placing prisoners in pens with violent dogs. Rapes occurred in front of close relatives. Jewish victims were subjected to especially harsh treatment and further humiliated by frequently being placed in rooms decorated with Nazi insignia.[28]

The following stories, which are, of course, a very narrow selection of the brutal experiences suffered under the military regime, illustrate the depth and severity of the repression. On May 14, 1976, at five in the morning, five armed men stormed Emilio Mignone's apartment in central Buenos Aires. Several armed vehicles were waiting on the street, preventing pedestrians from passing. The area was declared "free," that is, free from local police intervention. The intruders, although dressed in civilian clothing, claimed to be members of the army. They asked for Mignone's twenty-four-year-old daughter, who was doing volunteer work in shanty towns. The abductors claimed to be taking her to the Patricios regiment to interrogate her about a friend and further claimed that she would return in a few hours. Even though Mignone was a prominent member of Argentine society and had served as an undersecretary of education under the previous military regime, he was not able to discover the whereabouts of his daughter. The family never saw her again.

Mario Villani, a physicist of the National Institute of Industrial Technology, was kidnapped on November 18, 1977. He spent four years in clandestine detention in the Olympus Camp, where he was savagely tortured. Eventually, he became the camp "journalist." In 1981, after four years of incarceration, he was released under supervision, and later he became one of the chief witnesses in the trial of the junta members.[29] Ramón Mirailles told his story to the National Commission on Disappeared Persons (CONADEP).[30] It included "unspeakable tortures" and the abduction of his entire family,

Testifying in front of CONADEP, Susan L. Caride claimed that she had been kidnapped in July 1978.[31] She was subjected to a myriad of torture techniques, including simulated execution, electric shocks, beatings, and the "cleansing" of wounds with salt water. Her captors wanted her to reveal the whereabouts of the judicial officer Guillermo Diaz Lestrem, who subsequently disappeared. Pedro Miguel Vanrell testified that the Jewish inmates were forced to shout, "I love Hitler" and paint their bodies with swastikas.[32] One Jewish inmate named "Chango" was ordered to imitate a dog and lick the guards' boots.

Prof. Alfredo Bravo, a prominent member of a teachers' union who later became undersecretary of education under Alfonsín's government, was kidnapped in September 1977 and tortured in order to obtain information about the unions. Subsequently, he became a legal detainee under the state of siege and still later was released on surveillance.[33]

The military employed methods other than disappearances. Many well-known activists were summarily executed in the streets and countryside. Collective executions and massacres, such as the March 1978 massacre of two hundred prisoners in the prison of Villa Devoto, have been documented.[34]

Although government officials denied knowledge of any atrocities, they came close to justifying such measures publicly. This was a "dirty war" against an enemy without uniform or flag. Because this enemy did not follow the rules of war, the government claimed it was justified in resorting to extraordinary measures to repel aggression. Gen. Roberto Viola, commander in chief of the army and president, declared that war, injury, and death go hand in hand. Gen. Leopoldo F. Galtieri, who later would become president (and launch the Malvinas War), said that the military could not explain the unexplainable, nor could they give reasons for the irrational; to obtain the prize of glory, zones of darkness and mud had to be crossed first.[35]

Gen. Tomás Sanchez de Bustamante, who later became a judge on the military court first given jurisdiction to try those responsible for the atrocities, declared that this type of struggle demanded complete secrecy; therefore, a cloud of silence must loom over the press.[36] Gen. Ramón J. Camps, chief of police in the province of Buenos Aires, explicitly stated to *Clarín* on January 20, 1984, that "we had to extract information before 24 hours. Of course, it was preferable to act without tortures and cries of pain, but this is not always possible, and sometimes it is necessary to save the life of honest citizens playing against time."[37] In private conversations, some high-ranking military officials argued that if five of every hundred abducted were terrorists, the repression would be justified.[38]

While the junta authorized repressive tactics, lower-level military officers willingly carried out the orders.[39] Of the lower-level officers, the one who acquired greatest notoriety was Lt. Alfredo Astiz. He was accused of shooting and abducting a Swedish girl, Dagmar Hagelin, in January 1977; of helping to abduct the French nuns Sister Alice Domon and Sister Léonie Duquet in December 1977; and of facilitating the abduction of one of the leaders of the Madres de Plaza de Mayo.[40] Witnesses before CONADEP testified that doctors and priests, such as Christian von Wernich, participated in the torture sessions.

While many of those who were killed or who disappeared were members of left-wing guerrilla movements, many others were merely relatives or friends of those involved in such activity. Others were lawyers who filed habeas corpus petitions for those illegally detained, journalists who complained of the regime's abuses, psychoanalysts and writers considered dangerous, members of human rights groups, trade unionists (such as Oscar Smith) who opposed the regime's economic policy, and politicians who were deemed dangerous. Héctor Hidalgo Solá, who had been Argentina's ambassador to Venezuela, was abducted in the center of Buenos Aires on July 18, 1977. Similarly, Edgardo Sajón, press secretary to former military president Alejandro Lanusse, disappeared. The "Night of the Pencils" is a poignant example of how repression unjustifiably targeted innocent citizens. On September 16, 1976, eight adolescents between fourteen and eighteen years old were kidnapped from their homes, taken to various clandestine detention centers, tortured, and ultimately killed because they were active in a secondary-school student movement demanding student discount tickets for public transportation.[41]

Eventually, this harsh repression effectively neutralized left-wing terrorist activity. The ERP suffered crippling losses in the four months preceding the coup and became virtually paralyzed in the four months after.[42] The ERP's leaders, Mario Roberto Santucho, José Benito Urteaga, and Domingo Menna, were murdered on July 19, 1976.

The Montoneros were also greatly weakened by the killing of hundreds of its members, including such prominent leaders as Carlos Caride and Miguel Zavala Rodriguez. At first they continued carrying out many terrorist operations. Among these operations were Ana María González's killing of the Federal Police chief, Gen. Cesáreo Cardozo, on July 18, 1976; the July 2, 1976 bombing of the police department, killing twenty-five people and wounding sixty; a car bombing on September 12, 1976 that killed eleven policemen and two civilians; the bombing of the provincial police headquarters in La Plata on November 9, 1976, killing one and injuring eleven officers; the explosion at Metropolitan Airport in February 1977 as a plane carrying Videla passed by some meters above; the bombing of the Condor Building of the Air Force Command; and the bombing of a platform on which Videla had been speaking some moments before.

The military reacted harshly to such operations. By August 1978, the Montoneros estimated their post-coup fatalities at forty-five hundred.[43] Many members, including leaders such as Mario Firmenich and Fernando Vaca Narvaja, emigrated and began asking the world for support. The year 1978 was relatively quiet because World Cup Soccer, centered in Buenos Aires, inevitably attracted foreign visitors, including the media. In 1979, however, the Montoneros attempted to reinvigorate their activities, targeting members of the economic ministry, injuring the family of Coordination Secretary Guillermo Walter Klein, and attempting to kill Treasury Secretary Juan Alemann. In return, the military heightened their violence and killed leading members of the Montoneros. This violence provoked internal dissent within the Montoneros, and many of the leaders who remained alive emigrated. In the meantime, many terrorists detained in clandestine centers collaborated with their captors, divulging the identity of their compatriots and even participating in the abductions.[44]

In the end, the whole leftist movement proved to be an insignificant threat to an armed forces of 130,000 members. The military even admitted, in response to the report of the Inter-American Commission on Human Rights, that the number of victims of leftist terrorist activity was only one-eighth of the official number of disappearances. Leftist terrorist activity became a useful pretext for "disposing of" numerous individuals considered threatening to the consolidation of the military's political, social, and economic power.

Amid such repression, the justice system was powerless to contain the abuses. Emilio Mignone, who, in response to the disappearance of his daughter, became the leader of an active human rights group, estimates that approximately eighty thousand habeas corpus petitions were filed during the military's tenure.[45] Most of the petitions were summarily rejected, following orders from the Ministry of the Interior. The petitioner bore judicial expenses. Even those few habeas petitions granted were practically nullified because, according to Law 21,312, enacted in February 1976, relief was suspended pending appeal. While the Supreme Court generally rejected habeas petitions, there was a prominent exception. A group under the command of General Camps abducted the journalist Jacobo Timerman in April 1977. Some time later, his arrest was legalized under the state-of-siege provisions. Attorney Genaro Carrió, who would become chief justice of the Supreme Court during Alfonsín's government, filed a habeas petition on behalf of Timerman. The Supreme Court accepted the petition, although it seemed that the military would not comply with the order of release. Apparently, however, Videla insisted upon Timerman's release, and the junta finally complied with the order, expelling Timerman from the country and taking away his citizenship.

Toward the end of the military regime, the Supreme Court seemed to change its practice. On several occasions, the Court consolidated various petitions of habeas corpus in order to make general, potentially precedential statements. In the *Hidalgo Solá* case, the Court instructed the judges to release the petitioner. In the *Perez de Smith* case, the Supreme Court addressed the executive, noting that the internal situation had become grave and ordering it to take the necessary measures to insure the freedoms recognized by the constitution.

The Argentine press, suffering from the disappearance of many journalists, was not a particularly outspoken defender of human rights. With few exceptions, the most notable being the English daily the *Buenos Aires Herald,* the independent press remained silent in the face of the abuses; the official press actively justified the repression. Likewise, many priests, religious, ethnic, and professional associations remained indifferent to the human rights abuses. The Buenos Aires Association of Lawyers was a notable exception. Scientists and writers also remained silent. Again, there were some exceptions, such as the writer Ernesto Sábato.

The most insistent and effective domestic protesters were, of course, the relatives of those who disappeared, who aligned with various individuals to form advocacy groups. The oldest of these groups, the Liga Argentina por los Derechos del Hombre, was active in providing legal assistance after 1975. The Asamblea Permanente por los Derechos Humanos was a convergence of religious and political leaders, and at one time was cochaired by Raúl Alfonsín. The Servicio de Paz y Justicia was created in 1974 by Adolfo Perez Esquivel, who, after being detained for two years, received the Nobel Peace Prize. The Centro de Estudios Legales y Sociales (CELS), officially founded in 1980 by Emilio Mignone and Augusto Comte, became an outspoken critic of human rights violations in judicial and administrative forums.

The world-renowned Madres de Plaza de Mayo, led by Hebe de Bonafini and comprised of mothers whose children disappeared, emerged in 1977 as a silent protest.[46] Every Thursday, the mothers, with their white head covers, marched silently around the pyramid of Plaza de Mayo, demanding that their children be returned alive. Such demonstrations continue to this day. The Abuelas de Plaza de Mayo, a splinter group, investigated the disappearance of more than two hundred children born to those in captivity.

The military continually harassed these advocacy groups. For instance, Azuzena Villaflor de Vicenti, one of the leaders of the Madres, was abducted in December 1977, taken to the ESMA, and never heard from again. The abduction was orchestrated by Lt. Alfredo Astiz, who had infiltrated the Madres under the pseudonymn of Gustavo Niño, claiming that his sister had disappeared.

International opposition to the human rights abuses was quite effective in attenuating the repression after 1979. The Inter-American Commission on Human Rights, which had been prevented from conducting an on-site visit in Argentina for some time, was permitted to enter Argentina in December 1978 thanks to increased U.S. pressure. After conducting a thorough on-site visit in 1979, the commission published a report that contained a serious indictment of the Argentine military regime.[47] The commission concluded that, through action and omission, the Argentine state, along with its agents, had violated many of the fundamental human rights recognized in the American Declaration of Rights and Duties of Man, including the rights to life, personal freedom, personal integrity and security, and judicial trial. The commission focused on the disappearances, noting that they had diminished since the commission's visit. The Argentine government refused to publish the report in Argentina without its own refutations. Nonetheless, the report piqued the interest of President Jimmy Carter of the United States. The undersecretary of state for human rights in the U.S., Patricia Derian, as well as Tex Harris of the American embassy in Buenos Aires, applied increasing pressure on the military regime to curtail its human rights abuses.

The Transition to Democracy: Phase One, 1980–1983

During 1980, the military dictatorship began to lose steam. International pressure forced relaxation of repression and censorship. Some journalists began criticizing the government. Even the issue of disappearances began to enter the public realm. The strongest force behind the deterioration of the government was the faltering of Martínez de Hoz's economic plan, evidenced by the bankruptcy of the Banco de Intercambio Regional. Nonetheless, the government refused to consider any type of political compromise or diminution in its power. After his five-year term expired, Videla was replaced on March 29, 1981, by Gen. Eduardo Viola, the commander in chief of the army. Viola began speaking with civilian politicians and also experimented with radical economic measures. But the socioeconomic situation deteriorated so much that the junta on December 22, 1981 replaced Viola with General Galtieri, who had succeeded Viola as the commander in chief of the army.

By the time Galtieri assumed office, public opinion had already turned against the military regime. On March 30, 1982, trade unions and political parties joined to denounce publicly the social and economic policies of the regime; the demonstration, gathering tens of thousands of people in the Plaza de Mayo, was the largest demonstration staged in opposition to the regime. I attended this demonstration with my wife, Susana, and some university colleagues. We had some moments of fear when the mounted police began to charge the crowd and spray tear gas.

In response to such opposition, Galtieri sought drastically to change the government's image. Two days after the demonstration, on April 2, 1982, Argentina invaded the Malvinas (Falkland) Islands, which had been held by Great Britain since 1830. Plaza de Mayo again filled, but this time in nationalistic support of Galtieri's invasion. (Some of my colleagues attended once more, but this time we were not united by feelings of brotherhood.) The Malvinas War ended, however, in disgrace for Argentina, which was forced to surrender on June 14, 1982. This defeat was the beginning of the end for the military regime. Galtieri resigned under pressure from the armed forces, and the junta was dismantled because of dissension among the armed forces. Gen. Reynaldo Benito Bignone became president on June 22, 1982. Leaders of various political parties, forming the "Multipartidaria," convened to demand the lifting of the state of siege, the legalization of political activity, and elections. Bignone reluctantly promised to allow gradual political opening.

The military regime hoped to negotiate the terms of democratization. However, the parties did not want to negotiate openly with a regime that was falling apart. Instead, they proposed a general election for October 30, 1983. In response, the government set forth fifteen conditions, including the "nonrevisability" of the "dirty war against subversion" and of deeds of corruption, as well as preserving the continuity of the judicial system. The parties dismissed these conditions, while forging ahead with the electoral campaign. Excavations of mass graves, alarming press reports, and widespread clamoring for retroactive justice fueled the campaign.

It was at this time that a group of colleagues from the Law School of the University of Buenos Aires and the Argentine Society of Analytical Philosophy, Genaro R. Carrió, Eugenio Bulygin, Eduardo Rabossi, Jaime Malamud Goti, Martín D. Farrell, Ricardo Guibourg, and myself, began meeting to discuss ways of facilitating the democratization process. After deciding to contact Radical Party leaders, we met with Raúl Alfonsín in Juan Gauna's home. We were impressed by Alfonsín's commitment to principles, readiness to discuss ideas, and warm personality. He seemed to be attracted by our group and began calling us "the philosophers," an epithet which would later seep into the press. We began holding meetings in his law office with his partner, Dante Giadone, his general secretary, Dante Caputo, and two other colleagues.

While the various political parties were bickering over the intricacies of the democratization process, the junta reconstituted itself. On April 23, 1983, the junta issued the "Final Document of the Military Junta on the War against Subversion and Terrorism" — the so-called Final Document. In this statement, the military assumed historical responsibility for the war, but claimed that the military's actions were a direct consequence of Isabel Perón's and Italo Luder's 1975 decrees. (In 1975 Luder, as acting president, signed a decree giving the military freedom to crack down on leftist guerrillas.) The junta admitted that the techniques employed in the "dirty war" were unprecedented, but argued that the nature of the conflict demanded such a response. The military also admitted that some mistakes, including violations of human rights, may have been committed in the passion of combat, but argued that they must be left to the judgment of God. To preserve military jurisdiction and lay a foundation for the defense of obeying orders, the Final Document also stipulated that all actions conform with plans approved by the superior commands. On the same day that the Final Document was released, the junta ratified an institutional act which declared that "all the operations against subversion and terrorism carried out by the security forces, the police and the prison guards, under operational control, in compliance with Decrees 261/75, 2770/75, 2771/75 and 2772/75, were executed in conformity with plans approved and supervised by the superior organic commands of the armed forces and by the military junta since its constitution."

Many groups rebuked the Final Document and accompanying institutional act. Even the Catholic church — which, except for such valiant bishops as Jaime de Navarez, Miguel E. Hesayne, and Justo Laguna, had remained silent or indifferent during most of the repression — declared, through the Executive Commission of the Episcopate, that the junta's statements showed insufficient remorse for its mistakes, especially with regard to the children who had disappeared, and paid inadequate attention to reparation.

In response to the Final Document, Raúl Alfonsín, who was the Radical Party's candidate in the elections, issued a statement entitled "It is Not the Final Word." He promised to employ the civil justice system to try those who had committed illegal acts. Alfonsín also declared that violations of nonresisting persons' right to life and personal integrity were illegitimate functions of the armed forces. As such, civilian judges, rather than members of the implicated military, should decide whether defenses such as due obedience, error, and coercion applied.

At the same time, Jaime Malamud, Martín Farrell, and I had begun working with Alfonsín and Caputo to design strategies for dealing with past human rights abuses. Alfonsín also asked us to begin drafting a legislative package to ensure future protection of human rights. The three of us began to have frequent working lunches in the Association of Judges, just in front of the Palace of Justice in Buenos Aires, with friends and colleagues from the Law School, such as Ricardo Gil Lavedra and Andrés D'Alessio, who would become judges on the court that tried the commanders, as well as Enrique Paixao, who would become minister of justice.

In articulating a program for redressing human rights violations, Alfonsín identified three categories of perpetrators: those who planned the repression and gave the accompanying orders; those who acted beyond the scope of the orders, moved by cruelty, perversity, or greed; and those who strictly complied with the orders. Alfonsín believed that while those in the first two categories deserved punishment, those in the third group should be given the opportunity to reincorporate themselves into the democratic process.

Alfonsín first articulated these distinctions publicly in a lecture at the Argentine Federation of Bar Associations in August 1983. In that lecture, he also set forth five basic philosophical tenets concerning human rights:

> 1. Every human being enjoys human rights, regardless of race, nationality, or gender.
> 2. Human rights assure that people are not used as mere instruments for the sake of collective objectives.
> 3. Human rights can be violated by omission as well as action.
> 4. Governments' legitimacy is intimately linked to the preservation and promotion of human rights.
> 5. As a concern of the international community, the defense of human rights transcends national frontiers.

Alfonsín's position on human rights and the remedies for violations was generally well received, although its unintentional ambiguity neutralized controversy. Alfonsín's distinctions among the various categories of perpetrators were rather vague. What acts were "beyond the scope" of the orders? Those that were not part of the operational plans, such as robberies or rapes that had historically been a part of military activity? Or acts that were excessive, whether or not the object of orders, by virtue of sinister motives? The latter definition was more acceptable to human rights groups.

Around this time, Farrell, Malamud, and I met with Caputo in the Perú Street offices. We learned that Alfonsín wanted to try the commanders and high-ranking officers, although he was skeptical about trying too many lower-ranking officers, fearing a dangerous reaction among the armed forces. Our task was to devise some type of legal mechanism to facilitate Alfonsín's wishes. We recognized the difficulties embedded in this task, but nevertheless began to study alternatives.

At a subsequent meeting, with Alfonsín, Raúl Borrás, Horacio Jaunarena, and Dante Giadone in attendance, we presented a proposal, which I wrote and which Horacio Verbitsky later published in *Civiles y militares*.[48] It attempted to delineate and distinguish among Alfonsín's three categories of perpetrators. The proposal distinguished the first category by virtue of its constituents' deliberative capacity, factoring rank and command into the calculus. We distinguished the second and third groups, by examining and dissecting the due-obedience defense. We allowed the due-obedience defense with torture. While it is true that due obedience is not a viable excuse when referring to abhorrent acts such as torture, we acknowledged that in this particular historical context, an exception should be made. Such abhorrent acts were being committed within a climate of compulsion and amid an intense propaganda campaign that aimed to legitimate the violence. Accordingly, there were compelling prudential reasons to restrain punishment to those who acted outside certain boundaries and grant to others—those who followed orders—the opportunity to cooperate in the democratic reconstruction. This distinction was especially relevant if punishment was not viewed as retributive but rather as protecting the future social order.

We believed that the distinction between those who exceeded the bounds of superior orders and those who complied strictly with superior orders should be decided within the military in a hearing that was to be conducted by officers who retired prior to 1973. A perpetrator could not be punished unless such a body determined that the individual officer acted beyond the scope of his orders, say, for greed or some personal motive. That body would determine the advisability of punishment, not the legality of the underlying act. This distinction preserved an equality among offenders, since no judgment was made concerning legality—all had engaged in illegal conduct, but prudential considerations led to limiting the punishment to some.[49] Alfonsín appeared interested in our ideas, listening carefully to the proposal while, as always, pacing the room frantically.

It was widely believed that the junta would soon enact an amnesty law to protect itself from subsequent prosecution. On August 19, 1983, there was an important popular demonstration, with more than forty thousand in attendance, in opposition to any amnesty proposal. Many young people chanted slogans like "There were no mistakes, there were no excesses, all the participants of the process are just murderers."[50] The main presidential candidates sent contingents to the march. My wife and I, along with several of our closest friends, attended the demonstration. After so many years of silence and repression, we could not help but be moved by the joyous upsurge of expression we were witnessing.

On September 23, 1983, only five weeks before the elections, Bignone signed Law 22,924, known as the "self-amnesty law." He claimed that the law would establish the foundation for national reconciliation, pacification, and reconstitution. He also insisted that the armed forces had fought in the name of human dignity; the cruel and sinister terrorist methods demanded a response, however, which was unfortunately incompatible with that overarching purpose. The first article of Law 22,924 granted a blanket amnesty for all subversive and countersubversive acts that had taken place between May 25, 1973 and June 17, 1982. The amnesty extended to anyone who had aided or abetted such subversive or countersubversive activity, as well as common or military crimes. The second article excluded from its protection all those members of terrorist associations who were not residing in Argentina at the time of the law's enactment. This article also excluded those who, by their actions, evinced continued association with such terrorist groups. Other articles of the law excluded from the amnesty those who already had been sentenced, as well as those accused of "economic subversion." Finally, the law prohibited courts from issuing a subpoena against or interrogating those for whom a prima facie showing that amnesty was applicable could be made; the law also created a summary procedure for obtaining from courts of appeals the definitive dismissal of any penal charge. The law precluded civil compensation for those acts covered by the amnesty.

The amnesty law created a new legal obstacle to the trial of human rights abuses. Almost all political factions, except those on the far right, in particular the UCEDE (Union of the Democratic Center), led by Alvaro Alsogaray, rejected the amnesty law and human rights groups were among the most outspoken opponents. Alfonsín, believing the law was spurious and immoral, publicly advocated its nullification. Other politicians, most notably the Peronist candidate Italo Luder, a distinguished constitutional lawyer, opposed the law but believed that abrogation would not, by virtue of article 2 of the Penal Code, prevent judges from giving it some force. Article 2 guarantees defendants the benefit of the most favorable law existing from the time of the crime to the sentencing, and the article could not be abrogated without violating article 18 of the Constitution, proscribing retroactive penal legislation.

Genaro Carrió, Jaime Malamud, Eduardo Rabossi, Jorge Bacqué, and I published a letter in *La Nación* refuting Luder's argument. We maintained that validity is an evaluative concept which is integrally linked to morality. The self-amnesty law should not be automatically deemed valid but rather should be scrutinized in terms of morality. We questioned the morality of the law using two lines of argument. First, we employed a constitutional argument, developed by Carrió, rooted in article 29 of the Constitution, which prohibits granting the executive extraordinary powers. Because the self-amnesty law prevented the judiciary from investigating the decisions of an executive that had already absorbed legislative functions, we believed the self-amnesty law violated article 29.

I developed the second line of argument in an article, "Hacia una nueva estrategia para el tratamiento de las normas de facto," published in the legal daily *La Ley*.[51] I advocated the abandonment of the doctrine of de facto norms on the grounds that it was based on a naturalistic fallacy, so characteristic of positivism. In determining the normative binding force of legal norms, empirical facts such as normative efficacy and the distribution of power to enact such norms inform evaluations. Once the evaluative character of validity is acknowledged, I argued, it logically follows that, given the epistemic character of the democratic process, only norms with democratic origin enjoy a presumption of moral acceptability.

During the final days of the military government, some judges refused to apply the self-amnesty law, deeming it void and unconstitutional. Among them there were Jorge Torlasco and Guillermo Ledesma (two judges who would later be promoted to the Federal Court of Appeals of Buenos Aires, which tried the junta members). The military was not concerned about this defiance because they assumed that, as most polls indicated and most of the people believed, the Peronist candidate would win. Because the military was certain of a Peronist victory, they did not try to coopt the Radical Party, as they had with the Peronist Party. However, Alfonsín gained popularity by denouncing what he termed the "trade unionist–military pact" to preclude human rights trials under a Peronist government.[52]

As the election approached, large sectors of society enthusiastically embraced Alfonsín's campaign. He held successful rallies in boxing and soccer stadiums. On October 26, 1983, around one million people gathered in the Avenue 9 de Julio to hear Alfonsín speak about human rights. He emphasized the need for truth and justice and reiterated his three categories of responsibility. The Peronists held a similar rally, although it was met with much less enthusiasm, most likely because the Peronist candidate, Luder, lacked charisma and because the thuggish, right-wing Peronist candidate for governor of the province of Buenos Aires, Herminio Iglesias, burned a coffin on the podium with the figure of Alfonsín inside. The people had endured violence in the recent past; Iglesias's sinister gesture evoked unpleasant memories.

Alfonsín won the presidency with 52 percent of the votes, garnering the support of a wide constellation of groups with different expectations. This marked the first time in Argentine history that the Peronist Party had been defeated in a clean and open election. While we celebrated the election results in Caputo's home, we were fraught with concern over what the future would bring. We all knew that no democratic government had completed its term since the presidency of Marcelo T. de Alvear in 1928. Our work had just begun.

President Alfonsín, 1983

As soon as Alfonsín was elected, he began to establish clear parameters for what must be done. First and foremost, there must be an unrestrained search for the whereabouts of those who disappeared. With regard to punishment, Alfonsín set forth three guiding principles:

1. Both state and subversive terrorism should be punished.
2. There must be limits on those held responsible, for it would be impossible effectively to pursue all those who had committed crimes.
3. The trials should be limited to a finite period during which public enthusiasm for such a program remained high.

Alfonsín also set some forward-looking goals, hoping to institutionalize legal changes designed to prevent violations of human rights in the future.

During this period, Jaime Malamud and I, along with Radical politicians who were given cabinet positions, began working on the details of the human rights program. We first completed the forward-looking measures with help from D'Alessio, Gil Lavedra, and Paixao. Then we turned toward the more difficult issues of retroactive justice.

Assuming that the tenure of the present members of the judiciary would not presumptively be respected, since the judges had sworn by the statute of the military, Malamud began reforming the federal judiciary. He proposed new justices for the Supreme Court; Carrió was immediately accepted as chief justice. Judges on politically sensitive courts, mainly the Federal Criminal Court of Appeals of Buenos Aires, which would play a crucial role in responding to human rights violations, were replaced.

We also had several meetings with Antonio Troccoli, who would become the minister of the interior; Raúl Galván, who would become undersecretary of the interior; and Horacio Jaunarena, who would become minister of defense. Jaunarena held the narrowest view of retroactive justice, conveying the impression that only the junta members should stand trial. Galván, Malamud, and I believed that the trials should be wider in scope. Troccoli took a more neutral position, although he often sided with Jaunarena.

This working group drafted a law, which Alfonsín eventually approved, designed to limit responsibility based on deliberative capacity and a reinterpretation of the due-obedience clause in the military code. We also began discussing the possibility of forming a commission to investigate the fate of the disappeared people; human rights groups believed that it should be a bicameral commission of Congress, but Alfonsín was of a different mind.

Jurisdiction for trials remained a point of controversy. Malamud and I believed that the civil courts should govern the trials or, alternatively, that the military courts should retain jurisdiction only over pretrial hearings. Borrás,

Jaunarena, and Troccoli favored the military jurisdiction. A crucial meeting, chaired by Alfonsín, took place on December 6, 1983, in the Panamericano Hotel. In attendance were Borrás, Troccoli, Jaunarena, Malamud, and I. We began by presenting the forward-looking legislative proposals concerning human rights. They were all approved. When we broached the issue of trials, the main point of contention remained jurisdiction. The idea of pretrial hearings appeared cumbersome. Alfonsín concluded the meeting by tentatively endorsing the civil courts as the appropriate forum. We arranged to meet again the following day.

In the meantime, *La Razón*, an evening newspaper allegedly linked with the intelligence services, published most of the content of our meeting. Malamud and I were quite concerned. We knew that a participant in the meeting must have been an informer, and we feared that Alfonsín would suspect us because we were the least closely related to his administration. The following morning, we raised the subject. He directed us to the window, pointed out to the other side of the wide avenue, and stated that our conversations were being recorded with a directional microphone which detected the window vibrations. By this time, the police had already installed a device to prevent further interception.

At this meeting, Alfonsín retreated from his previous position and endorsed the use of military courts in the first instance with a broad right of appeal before the civilian courts. We believed that his was a good compromise. He asked us to finalize the project.

We did not know what positions, if any, we would hold in the future government. When I returned from an academic trip to Mendoza on December 8, Malamud told me that Alfonsín wanted to appoint us his advisors. So, with great joy and emotion, we were appointed to that position the day before Alfonsín's inauguration as president. During the ceremonies on December 10, we were frantically working on the legislative projects and the decrees necessary to begin the prosecutions.

In Alfonsín's inaugural address before the legislature, he advocated, in general terms, an inquiry into the fate of those who had disappeared. He also spoke of the need to provide the judiciary with the means to distinguish among the three categories of responsibility. On December 13, when all the legislative projects were complete, President Alfonsín set forth his human rights program over all radio and television stations. He emphasized that his overarching goals included the reinstatement of the rule of law and the prevention of such human rights violations in the future. Impunity was incompatible with these principles. While the pursuit of truth would be unrestricted, the punishment would be limited, based on deterrent rather than retributive considerations and on the need to incorporate every sector in the democratic process.

The president then announced his forward-looking package, which included:

> •repealing all draconian laws against subversion enacted by the previous Peronist and military governments. In their place, laws supporting democracy would be enacted; they would criminalize acts, especially by the army or security forces, that jeopardized the constitutional system.
>
> •enacting a law punishing torture in the same way that murder was punished. This law would hold prison directors, police chiefs, and members of military garrisons responsible for acts of torture committed within their jurisdiction.
>
> •abolishing military jurisdiction for civilians.
>
> •reforming the federal criminal procedure code, limiting the duration of trials and making parole easier to obtain.
>
> •enacting a law that would prohibit public and private discrimination.
>
> •ratifying several international human rights treaties, including the American Convention on Human Rights (which entailed accepting the obligatory jurisdiction of the Inter-American Court of Human Rights), the United Nations Covenant on Civil and Political Rights, and the United Nations Covenant on Economic and Social Rights.
>
> •reforming the Military Code to abolish, in effect, military jurisdiction over common crimes committed in connection with acts of service.

Alfonsín then announced his backward-looking program. It included:

> •establishing a habeas corpus remedy through which civilians sentenced by military courts could have their convictions reviewed by civil courts.
>
> •enacting a law that shortened prison terms for those detained for exaggerated security concerns.
>
> •nullifying the amnesty law. The president concluded that the amnesty law violated equal protection principles of article 16 of the Constitution; granted the executive extraordinary powers, in contravention of article 29 of the Constitution; and, as a morally unacceptable de facto law, lacked the presumption of binding validity.
>
> •modifying the Military Code so as to acknowledge military jurisdiction, but also to provide federal appeals courts with broad powers of review.
>
> •modifying the Military Code provisions that granted impunity to officers obeying orders. A rebuttable presumption was to be created for those who followed orders that ultimately violated human rights and erred about the legitimacy of the orders. This presumption was not to be available to those who had decision-making capacity.
>
> •issuing the decrees necessary to begin the prosecution of the leaders of the subversive guerrilla movements, and also the members of the three military juntas.[53]

After the speech, all of the members of the cabinet signed the executive orders and proposed pieces of legislation. I was surprised by the content of some of these — in particular, the lists of those targeted for prosecution were shorter than Malamud and I had expected. I was also concerned that those who hoped for strong retributive measures would be disappointed by the speech. In fact, I was hesitant to attend a birthday party for Carrió because I feared that many of the guests' hopes would be crushed and that the party would turn into a session of bitter criticism. In the end I attended, and everybody greeted me with great enthusiasm. This was the first indication of the difficulties Alfonsín would have in conveying to the public his intention to restrict the scope of the trials.

In the wake of the president's speech, a strategy was devised for dealing with certain legal obstacles to the prosecutions. The first obstacle arose from article 2 of the Penal Code, which, in turn, could not retroactively be abrogated without violating article 18 of the constitution. Article 2 gave the defendant the benefit of the least harsh law in effect. This obstacle was surmounted by formulating a new theory of de facto laws that permitted nullification ex nihilo of the amnesty law, refuting its binding force from its inception.

The second obstacle involved the impossibility of retroactively modifying the military jurisdiction in the face of article 18 of the constitution, which proscribes ex post facto laws. This obstacle was overcome by invoking article 95 of the constitution, which prohibits the president, and the courts dependent on him, such as the military one, from trying people and imposing punishment. To satisfy these two conflicting constitutional provisions, we compromised, recognizing military jurisdiction in the first instance and establishing a broad appellate review in the civilian courts.[54] Other modifications to the military's procedure were not considered retroactive *in malam parte,* since they expanded due process guarantees.

The third obstacle was the retroactive modification, without violating article 18 of the constitution, of the provisions of the Penal Code and Military Code that provided for a broad defense of due obedience that could cover practically all human rights abuses. This difficulty was resolved by reinterpreting, rather than modifying, the existing due obedience laws for the period March 24, 1976 to December 10, 1983. As already recognized by most scholars, even those attached to the military, the due-obedience defense was triggered only when there was a mistake about the legitimacy of the orders. The proposed reinterpretation created a rebuttable presumption that, unless the agent held decision-making authority, all those invoking the defense of due obedience either mistakenly believed that the orders were legitimate due to intense propaganda or, alternatively, were subject to an overall climate of compulsion.

In addition to these three legal obstacles, Alfonsín had to determine how to limit the duration and scope of the trials. To limit their duration, the president looked to the Military Code's summary procedure guidelines; the time limits for appellate proceedings were also fixed at short intervals. With regard to the scope of responsibility, Alfonsín sought a two-tiered approach. First, he believed that he could rely on the military courts to act swiftly against a small group of people who committed the cruelest acts as a means of purifying themselves and recovering their social credibility. Second, reinterpretation of the norm of due obedience left those falling in Alfonsín's first two categories of responsibility exposed to prosecution. The first category, recall, included those who had had decision-making capacity, including all members of the juntas and all those who had commanded operational units. The second category included all those subordinates who had complied with orders but, in so doing, had acted in such a cruel and perverse way that a judge could impute from the nature of the act a presumption that there was no mistake about the legitimacy of the orders received; in other words, no reasonable person could believe that an order allowing the most atrocious acts could possibly be legitimate.

This political strategy of concentrating guilt in a small group of people who had promoted and conducted state terrorism, as well as those who had executed the most cruel and perverse acts, became the focal point of opposition and distrust for many human rights organizations and leftist political groups. These groups apparently believed that the policy exempted too many from responsibility and that in the end only the members of the junta would be held responsible for the human rights violations. On the other side, the military and right-wing groups also opposed Alfonsín's policies, believing that because hundreds would be subject to criminal prosecution for their participation in the repression, the integrity of the military would be threatened. I always believed that if the far right and left had met and discussed their concerns and the government had explained that its intention was to try dozens, rather than either a handful or hundreds, the process that ensued would have been much smoother.

Alfonsín immediately sent the legislative package to Congress. He also informed the Supreme Council of the Armed Forces of the content of Decree 158, initiating the prosecution of the nine members of the juntas from 1976 to 1983. Likewise, Alfonsín notified the new attorney general, Juán Gauna, of Decree 157, which called for the prosecution of the leaders of the subversive movements.

The president also began reconstituting the courts that would be most closely involved with issues concerning human rights violations, notably the Supreme Court and the Federal Court of Appeals of Buenos Aires. The reconstituted Supreme Court was comprised of Genaro R. Carrió as chief justice and Carlos Fayt, José Severo Caballero, Enrique Petracchi, and Augusto Belluscio as associate justices. Ricardo Gil Lavedra, Andrés D'Alessio, Carlos Arslanián, Jorge Valerga Araoz, Jorge Torlasco, and Guillermo Ledesma became the new judges on the Court of Appeals.

Despite the fact that judges on the key courts were close friends of the administration, the two courts retained a high degree of independence. Carrió was deemed an extremely thoughtful jurist, and his sole political experience was a short tenure as Undersecretary of the Interior Aramburu's military presidency; Petracchi, though a friend of Malamud, was a Peronist with strong connections with Lorenzo Miguel, the metallurgic trade union leader; Fayt, a former president of the progressive Association of Lawyers of Buenos Aires, had deep-seated socialist affiliations; Belluscio, a well-known jurist on civil matters, had some Radical connections; and Severo Caballero, related to the vice president, Victor Martínez, was connected to the right wing of the Radical Party. All were confirmed by the Senate, dominated by Peronists and their allies. In the Federal Court of Appeals, the only judges with clear Radical sympathies were our friends Gil Lavedra and D'Alessio, who also had had judicial functions during the military regime; Arslanián, who had been a judge previously and was a Peronist (he even became minister of justice under Menem); and Torlasco, Ledesma, and Valerga Araoz, were career members of the judiciary, with a strong sense of esprit de corps and political neutrality, but had acted valiantly during the dictatorship.

Once the judiciary was reconstituted, Alfonsín began concentrating on proposals for a commission to investigate the disappearances. The president rejected proposals to create a bicameral congressional commission, advocated by human rights groups and the Peronists. He believed that a commission linked to Congress would give legislators an unhealthy opportunity to compete in lambasting the military, and as a result create an extremely tense situation. Instead, on December 15, 1983, Alfonsín promulgated a decree that created the National Commission on Disappeared Persons (CONADEP).

CONADEP was an executive commission linked to the Ministry of the Interior. It was charged with investigating the fate and whereabouts of those who had disappeared. CONADEP was given 180 days to fulfill its mission and was expected to present the president with a report at the end of this period describing, in detail, the methodology used to conduct the investigation. CONADEP had jurisdiction to hear complaints from victims and pass them on to the judiciary, to receive voluntary testimony and documentation from private citizens, and to demand written testimony from any public official or member of the armed services. CONADEP was also given immediate access to anyone incarcerated in special prisons, military garrisons, or police precincts.

Even though CONADEP exercised some quasijudicial functions as an executive commission, it abstained from issuing judgments on facts and issues that were within the exclusive competence of the judiciary.

The members of CONADEP included Ernesto Sábato, a famous writer and one of the few prominent figures in Argentina openly to oppose the human rights abuses; Magdalena Ruiz Guiñazu, a Catholic radio journalist who had also spoken out against the abuses; Ricardo Colombres, a justice of the Supreme Court during Frondizi's government; René Favaloro, a famous surgeon who subsequently resigned; Hilario Fernández Long, a former director of the University of Buenos Aires during Illia's presidency; Carlos T. Gattinoni, a Protestant pastor committed to the defense of human rights; Gregorio Klimovsky, a philosopher and mathematician; Marshall Meyer, a rabbi of American origin who was very active in the defense of human rights; Jaime de Nevares, a Catholic bishop who was extremely courageous in his defense of human rights; and Eduardo Rabossi, a philosopher, lawyer, and president of the Argentine Society of Analytical Philosophy. Six deputies and senators nominated by the two houses of the legislature would also serve on CONADEP.

I played an active role in defining CONADEP's membership. While Malamud was working with Minister of Justice Raúl Alconada Sempé on the appointment of judges, I worked with José Ignacio López, a Catholic journalist who was Alfonsín's spokesman, on the formation of the CONADEP. I suggested Rabossi, Klimovsky, Fernández Long, and Meyer, as well as Colombres on the advice of Carrió. Although we wanted representation of the human rights organizations, these organizations were skeptical about the commission and ultimately refused to participate. As we shall see, the human rights organizations later cooperated intimately with CONADEP, once they recognized the seriousness with which it approached its tasks.

The Second Phase, 1984

In 1984, battles were fought on many fronts. To counteract the traditional autonomy of the military and thus facilitate retroactive justice, Alfonsín made each corps of the armed forces directly accountable to him, through his minister of defense, and changed the head of each branch from a commander in chief to an advisory chief of staff. The president also gave the Ministry of Defense, rather than the army and navy, jurisdiction over the Police of Frontiers and the Seas. Control over the production of armaments, an important source of income, was taken from the military and given to the minister of defense. President Alfonsín also reduced the military's budget by more than half, with a concomitant reduction of staff at all levels.[55]

In Congress, of course, the Radical government confronted the other parties, specifically the Peronists. The Radical Party had a majority in the House of Deputies, but the Peronists were strongly represented and were able to derail legislation by impeding the necessary quorum. In the Senate, the Peronists were an even stronger faction, capable of mustering an absolute majority when joining with representatives from the provincial parties normally allied with the Peronists.

Having learned the lesson of the 1983 election, the Peronists, in general, located themselves to the left of Alfonsín's party. They insisted on the formation of a bicameral congressional commission to investigate the fate of those who had disappeared, and when CONADEP was formed, they refused to take any of the seats reserved for legislators.[56] The Peronist legislators bitterly complained about Alfonsín's human rights policies, but in the end they provided the requisite quorum to approve the laws necessary to implement those policies, tacitly acknowledging that the issue was too delicate to interfere with the executive's program.

Congress's first decision was to nullify the self-amnesty law. Both houses, with the Madres de Plaza de Mayo in attendance in the upper balconies, unanimously approved Law 23,040, the nullification. Even Alvaro Alsogaray, a member of UCEDE and a retired military man, voted for this measure, acknowledging that society demanded knowledge of the truth. Deputies and senators from all the parties called for justice, opening the way for trials and, for the first time in Argentina's history, a new approach to de facto laws.

Congress smoothly passed most of the forward-looking package, except for the law banning discrimination and the law of conscientious objection to military service, which had been proposed to deal with Jehovah's Witnesses who were treated as deserters. The measure known as "Defense of Democracy and Constitutional Order" was enacted as Law 23,077. Law 23,097 modified the Penal Code regarding torture. The legislative proposal modifying the Federal Code of Criminal Procedure regarding the duration of trials and parole procedure became laws 23,050 and 23,042, respectively. Law 23,057 reformed probation procedures. The rules governing preventive detention were embodied in Law 23,070. Finally, Argentina ratified the American Convention on Human Rights in Law 23,054.

The more controversial reforms dealt with issues of jurisdiction and due obedience, upon which members of the legislature voiced a wide range of views. Several deputies from the left-wing and Peronist parties opposed the specifics of these reforms. These deputies insisted that trials should be given to civilian judges. The Peronist block, primarily Deputy Oscar Fappiano, defended Eugenio R. Zaffaroni's proposal that looked to the Supreme Council of the Armed Forces, reconstituted with civilian judges, as the appropriate forum for the trial of the human rights cases. Ricardo Balestra, a right-wing deputy, defended the conduct of the military. A Radical Party deputy, Juan Manuel Casella, believed that the presumption of due obedience could be rebutted by a judicial finding that the acts in question were atrocious or abhorrent.

Despite such varied views, the measure proposed by President Alfonsín was approved by the House of Deputies, with two modifications. One modification made the presumption in favor of due obedience discretionary by changing the law's wording from "it will be presumed" to "it may be presumed; the other placed a 180-day cap on the time allowed for the military court to decide human rights cases, and made the federal courts of appeals the default trial courts.

Opposition, however, was even stronger in the Senate, where the Radical Party did not hold a majority. There the Peronist leader, Vicente Saadi, opposed the definition of the role of the military court and the due-obedience provision. He deemed the latter a "covert amnesty." Senator Antonio Berhongaray of the Radical Party became the administration's chief defender in the Senate. In the face of Peronist opposition, however, negotiation with the provincial parties, in particular with the Popular Movement of Neuquén, became critical to the reform's success. Sen. Elias Sapag, who had a relative who had disappeared, pledged support for the administration's position contingent on the following conditions: that the law explicitly provide for Federal Court of Appeals jurisdiction in the face of the military court's undue delay or negligence; that the victim or relatives of the victim enjoy an appeal by right; and that the law explicitly provide that abhorrent or atrocious acts rebut the presumption of mistake about the legitimacy of the orders.

This last condition thwarted Alfonsín's strategy, transforming a narrow, implicit exception to a bright-line rule into a broader, explicit means to rebut the presumption. Immediately, human rights groups, left-wing groups, and the members of the military responsible for the worst deeds but desiring solidarity among all members of the military, argued that every crime could be considered atrocious and abhorrent. Could anybody deny that the kidnapping of unarmed civilians, detention of civilians in clandestine places, and the torture and murder of civilians were atrocious and abhorrent acts? Using such lines of argument, the legislators embraced Senator Sapag's position and passed Law 23,049 regulating the trials, which was signed by the president on February 13, 1993.

Andrés D'Alessio, who advised Senator Berhongaray and negotiated with Rodolfo Rivarola, an advisor to Senator Sapag, recounts that when he announced the compromise, I turned pale. Greatly agitated, I phoned Alfonsín and asked him to prevent a disaster. He responded rather fatalistically, saying that we should let things be and wait to see what transpired.

The battle for retroactive justice was also fought in the Supreme Council of the Armed Forces, an institution founded in 1895 as the highest court of military justice and, in 1984, led by Brig. Luís María Fagés.[57] Two of the members refused to try the human rights case against the junta, since they were members of the Videla government. Although President Alfonsín had the right to replace these members, he did not exercise this right so as not to be seen as meddling with the trial. Instead, by lot, Gen. Emiliano Flouret and Brig. Carlos R. Etchegoyen were nominated as associate members of the Supreme Council.

At this time, the Supreme Council was embroiled in another hot case: the trial, initiated by military president Bignone, for crimes committed in the planning and execution of the Malvinas War.[58] The Supreme Council asked the government to set a priority between the two trials, but Bignone had already agreed to place the Malvinas War trial on hold. Therefore, on December 29, 1983, the Supreme Council notified the members of the juntas included in Decree 158 that they were on trial for the human rights crimes.[59] (Others were identified for trial with the junta members.) Decree 280, of January 19, 1984, ordered that Gen. Ramón Camps, who was openly defending the military's action in the "dirty war," be subject to trial. He was immediately put under arrest. Similarly, the head of the ESMA, Adm. Rubén J. Chamorro, was indicted on February 21, 1984 and was arrested when he returned from a vacation in South Africa.

The accused were called before the Supreme Council, which was in possession of documents provided by the government, human rights groups, and individual victims. Videla declared his innocence, claiming that all his acts had been political and were thus nonjusticiable. He also argued that he had acted during a war of subversion and with the explicit support of many sectors of society. Videla denied knowledge of the executions and tortures. Massera, like Videla, proclaimed his innocence, but added that in 1978 he had promoted a process of pacification by, for example, publishing a list of guerrillas who had died or disappeared in the fight. The testimony of others was of the same tenor, although several commanders emphasized that the triumph of the armed forces in the war against subversion had facilitated free elections. Others argued that the trials were simply another stage in the "dirty war" and a means for taking revenge on the armed forces.

During April and May 1984, the Supreme Council began receiving testimony from victims as well as from civilians who could corroborate the evidence. On June 28, 1984, the six-month period granted to the Supreme Council in Law 23,049 lapsed. The Federal Court of Appeals of Buenos Aires, which was well staffed with newly appointed judges and ready with a prosecutor, Julio Strassera, discussed how to respond to the delay. The Supreme Council argued that it had been unable to reach a conclusion because of the complexity of the case. In reply, the Federal Court of Appeals asked to see the files for forty-eight hours and subsequently gave the council thirty more days to proceed. At the end of that period, the court would have to be informed about the trial's progress. The court also said that the trial should not last for more than ninety days.

After this episode, the members of the Court of Appeals and the Supreme Council, Malamud, and I surreptitiously attended a barbecue in the Police Club. The purpose of the gathering was to foster friendly relationships among the various trial actors and, on our part, to try to detect any leanings of the Supreme Council vis-à-vis the trial. The atmosphere was friendly, as in most Argentine barbecues. We perceived that the leader of the council, Gen. Sanchez de Bustamante, was a very articulate and good-humored man, and there were assurances that the council would go forward, though these assurances were a little too vague to be completely comforting.

Meanwhile, military unrest began to grow. Young officers met to decide how to defend the armed forces against the "aggression" of the trials and the curtailment in the military budget. The military accused President Alfonsín of being "red." In response, Alfonsín replaced army general Jorge Arguindegui with Gen. Gustavo Pianta. In Córdoba, several bombings took place when Maj. Ernesto Barreiro was detained. The former commander of the Third Military Corps violently threatened someone who confronted him when leaving a television station; his photo, with knife in hand, appeared on the front page of every newspaper and further turned public opinion against the military. At the same time, the members of the Supreme Council received daily anonymous letters enclosing a white feather, the military symbol of cowardice.[60]

Nevertheless, the government's pressure on the Supreme Council began generating results. On August 2, 1984, after Videla had reiterated his justification for the "dirty war," the council placed him in preventive detention, "believing him responsible for the deeds mentioned in Decree 158." On the same day, the Supreme Court rejected an appeal the commanders had taken questioning the constitutionality of the modifications to military procedure. Like Videla, Brig. Orlando R. Agosti was placed in preventative detention by the Supreme Council. When the thirty-day term expired, the council reported to the Federal Court of Appeals, which in turn granted the council still another thirty-day period. On August 30, 1984, Massera was placed in preventive detention. He accused leftist terrorists of orchestrating both the trial and a defamatory campaign against the armed forces. The president of the Supreme Council, Luís María Fagés, responded to Massera's statements in an apologetic tone, noting that although he agreed with Massera, he was bound by the decree.[61]

When the second thirty-day extension expired, the Supreme Council sent a report to the Federal Court of Appeals which dropped like a bomb. First, the council admitted that it would most likely not finish the trial in the ninety days allotted. Second, the council stated that the commanders could not legitimately be convicted without first making a determination of the crimes committed, the immediate perpetrators, and the victim of each crime. So far, the council added, all it possessed was general statements that lacked probative evidentiary value. Consequently, the council needed to investigate further the specific behavior of the defendants in the context of "the battle against terrorist delinquency which affected our fatherland." Only then could the council balance the need to respect military discipline against the needs of retroactive justice. The report concluded with the following highly provocative statement: "As a result of the studies performed to date, the decrees, directives, and operational orders that mandated the military activity against subversion are, with regard to their content and form, unobjectionable."

In response, the Federal Court of Appeals immediately ordered the Supreme Council to send the fifteen thousand pages of files to prosecutor Strassera. He then declared that the moment had come for the court to assert control over the trial under the provisions of Law 23,049. The court confirmed this view on October 4, 1984. This decision marked the failure of a key element in Alfonsín's strategy: using the military court as a filter to assess responsibility for human rights violations. The Supreme Council retained control over the other cases. But given the Supreme Council's inaction in those cases and the reluctance of most federal courts of appeals in the interior to intervene, this allocation of power would involve excessive extension of the trials and cause increasing military unrest. Nobody, except perhaps Alfonsín, knows why the military, through the Supreme Council, failed to purify itself and reestablish its social ascendancy. Maybe social pressure forced the council to renege on its previous promises.

The third forum in which the battle for retroactive justice was fought was CONADEP. The commission had begun its duties on December 29, 1983 by appointing Ernesto Sábato as president and designating five secretaries to handle specific tasks: Graciela Fernández Meijide became the secretary in charge of receiving denunciations, Daniel Salvador became the secretary in charge of documentation and processing data, Raúl Aragón became the secretary in charge of procedures, Alberto Mansur became the secretary in charge of legal affairs,[62] and Leopoldo Silgueira became the secretary in charge of administrative affairs.

CONADEP was given offices in the Cultural Center of San Martín, a municipal complex of theaters and museums in downtown Buenos Aires, where it began to receive a flood of complaints and allegations. Although the human rights groups first distrusted CONADEP, they soon realized the seriousness of CONADEP's mission and began collaborating with it. CONADEP's ability simultaneously to attend to the needs of the victims and placate the human rights groups was in itself an extremely valuable contribution to the government's general strategy. The need for such mediation was great. I remember a 1984 meeting between the leaders of the Madres de Plaza de Mayo, Alfonsín, Malamud, and me, at which we tried to explain to the Madres the government's general policy; they retorted that all those who had disappeared should be returned alive and that all the guilty should be punished. Hebe de Bonafini was particularly hostile toward Malamud when he began to explain some legal subtleties. Alfonsín lost his temper, stating that the Madres were confusing his government with the prior military governments.

CONADEP also received cooperation from the United Nations, the Organization of American States, and several individual countries, which sent experts to identify corpses. CONADEP was thus able to establish branches in some cities in the interior and to visit fifteen provinces, where it received 1,400 accusations. CONADEP also received testimony from members of the armed and security forces. It inspected 340 clandestine detention centers and visited morgues and cemeteries in order to identify corpses. CONADEP inspected registers of the police and of prisons. Members of the commission went to military garrisons, prisons, and mental hospitals that had been identified as places where some of those who had disappeared could be found; the results were always negative. Several of CONADEP's members traveled abroad to examine evidence and to receive charges from exiles, establishing permanent offices in some embassies. CONADEP sent 1,300 requests of information to the administration. With the cooperation of the Abuelas de Plaza de Mayo, CONADEP helped create a data bank in the Durán Hospital that would help identify and return to their relatives children born to women in detention. Those children had been "adopted" during the military regime.[63]

In the course of its proceedings, CONADEP received testimony covering fifty thousand file pages on seven thousand different cases. Certain testimony was extremely forceful and effective. For instance, the architect Roberto Omar Ramirez, who had been in different clandestine detention centers, described how such centers functioned.[64] Juan Carlos Torres testified as to how the corpses of executed people were burnt.[65] Andrés Castillo described the inner workings of the Information Center that Massera had established in Paris.[66] Dr. Norberto Liwsky, Carlos Enrique Ghezan, and Enrique Nuñez testified about systematic torture.[67] Various minors testified about the way in which they were raped.[68] Juan Matías Bianchi described various perverse sexual practices.[69] Santiago Burnichon and Lucio Ramón Perez described how the kidnappings had been carried out.[70] Federico Manuel Vogelius testified about the robberies conducted in conjunction with the abductions.[71] Sara Solarz de Osatinsky testified about the birth of children in clandestine detention centers.[72] Alicia Mabel Portnoy corroborated the story of the abduction of adolescents.[73]

The findings of the commission began with a description of the general process by which the military deprived civilians of their human rights: abduction, detention in clandestine centers, torture, and, in many cases, murder. Approximately 8,960 people remained unaccounted for, the report stated, and the violence touched not only alleged terrorists but also civilians unconnected to any terrorist activity. While the military government claimed that there were over 25,000 "subversives," only 350 were ever convicted in military courts. CONADEP labeled the acts of repression "systematic atrocities" rather than "excesses" and rejected the military's excuses based on "defense against terrorism." CONADEP also discovered that military president Bignone had ordered the destruction of the documentation of the military's program of repression. CONADEP concluded its report by recommending that the body replacing CONADEP continue filing cases in the courts and that the courts continue investigating the cases before them. Consistent with its mandate, CONADEP itself had presented 1,086 cases to the judiciary.[74] The commission also recommended that laws be enacted to assist economically the relatives of those who had disappeared, that the disappearances be declared crimes of *lesa humanitas,* that human rights organizations receive support, that human rights be taught in schools, that judges be given the means to investigate violations of human rights, and that remaining repressive legislation be abrogated.

CONADEP's report, along with the fifty thousand pages of files, was presented to President Alfonsín on September 20, 1984, during a moving ceremony. The president ordered publication of the report, along with an appendix listing the names of those who had disappeared. *Nunca Más* became Argentina's greatest bestseller and was translated to several languages.

There was considerable dispute within CONADEP regarding the publication of the names of members of the military identified in the testimony as perpetrators of human rights violations. In the end, CONADEP decided not to publish the list, to avoid any appearance of acting as a court. Nevertheless, the list of the thousand military members who had been identified was given to President Alfonsín secretly. A few days later, the list was published in *El Periodista,* probably a result of a leak by CONADEP staff affiliated with human rights groups.

Before its dissolution, CONADEP sponsored a television program to publicize its findings. This was of some concern to the government, since certain sectors thought that it would provoke military reaction. But Alfonsín approved the program, which included a prologue by Minister of the Interior Antonio Troccoli. When CONADEP was dissolved, the president created an undersecretary of human rights within the Ministry of the Interior. The undersecretary was charged with finishing CONADEP's work, as delineated in the recommendations, and Eduardo Rabossi was appointed to the position.

All in all, the work of CONADEP was extraordinary in its impartiality and thoroughness. Despite the differences among its members, the group and its staff remained unified and worked efficiently. Unlike the setbacks in Congress and the Supreme Council, Alfonsín's CONADEP strategy was entirely successful. CONADEP's efforts helped account for those who had disappeared, collected invaluable evidence for the trials, created a haven in the state apparatus for the victims and their relatives, and fostered good relationships with human rights groups.

The Third Phase, 1985

Although in 1984 the battle for retroactive justice was fought in the halls of Congress, the French-style mansion of the Supreme Council, and the modern cultural center where CONADEP had its offices, in 1985 the struggle switched to the old Palace of Justice in Buenos Aires. This was the year of the "big trial."

On December 27, 1984, the Supreme Court rejected the commanders' claim against the law nullifying the self-amnesty measure and establishing the jurisdiction of the civilian courts. The court unanimously confirmed, in a hundred-page opinion, the new approach toward de facto norms, holding that procedural norms can be changed when they do not adversely affect a proper defense and that the doctrine of "a natural judge" does not impede changes in jurisdiction. Justice Augusto Belluscio explicitly remarked that trial by a military court is an aberration which is incompatible not only with the goals of finality but also with the greater guarantees furthered by independent courts.

Around the same time, Alfonsín instructed Malamud and me to draft laws that would repair the damage caused by some of the measures Congress had passed regarding the trials and the Supreme Council. The president hoped to limit the length of the trials, to better define "atrocious and abhorrent" acts, and to identify those who had held "decision-making capacity." Our proposals modified the Supreme Council's procedure in order to expedite the remaining trials. We recommended that the council should now hear cases in panels and the trials were to be limited to three or six months (depending on whether the process began before or after the enactment of Law 23,049). We proposed laws imputing decision-making capacity to those who reached the rank of general or colonel, or their equivalent in the other forces, or to those who had had direct control over clandestine detention centers. "Atrocious or abhorrent acts," which excluded those that could be attributed to a mistake regarding the legitimacy of the orders, were defined as crimes of commission (as opposed to omission) of murder, serious assault, rape, torture, and aggravated robbery, but excluded the abduction itself. Finally, we recommended that when the competence of the civil judge was questioned on appeal, and when the prosecutor agreed with the appeal, the civil judge could not impose preventive detention.[75] In the end, Alfonsín decided not to send these proposals to Congress, on the theory that the benefits they might produce in assuaging the military were minimal and in any event did not justify the political cost.[76] Given the subsequent course of events, the wisdom of this decision may be questioned.

In any event, on February 4, 1985, the Court of Appeals of Buenos Aires held its first meeting regarding the case against the commanders. At the same time the prosecutor, Julio Strassera, with his assistant, Luís Moreno Ocampo, and his legal staff of fifteen, almost all young lawyers, began studying 670 of the abduction cases selected from the materials provided by CONADEP. On February 12, they requested that the defendants be cited; the Court of Appeals accepted this request on February 14 and proceeded to cite the defendants between February 21 and March 11. After the defendants presented their case, the court divulged the identity of the victims, clarifying the prosecution's claims, thereby expanding the grounds for preventive detention over that used by the Supreme Council and thus foreclosing appeal to the Supreme Court.

Also in early 1985, a new military crisis erupted when the Federal Court decided that the Supreme Council should try Lieutenant Astiz for the abduction of Dagmar Hagelin. The council dismissed the case in one day, holding that a previous military court decision barred rehearing. Raúl Borrás, the minister of defense, immediately instructed the military prosecutor to ask for nullification of that particular decision of the council and to bring the case before the Federal Court. President Alfonsín also dismissed several members of the army's and navy's high commands, including the joint chief of staff, Juan Torres, who was replaced by Brig. Teodoro Waldner.

The first public hearing in the "big trial" took place on April 22, 1985. The atmosphere was highly charged and emotional. Fifty thousand people demonstrated, in Buenos Aires as well as the cities in the interior, in support of the trial. Many people were moved when they saw the once all-powerful dictators stand as the six civilian judges entered the room. Hebe de Bonafini, Perez Esquivel, and Eduardo Rabossi attended the first hearing. The atmosphere was rather heated. When José María Orgeira, Viola's counsel, addressed the court in a disrespectful manner, the presiding judge, Arslanián, ordered his disciplinary arrest.

Italo Luder, who had run against Alfonsín in 1983, was the first witness; he asked about the decree he had signed in 1975, as acting president during the administration of Isabel Perón, ordering the annihilation of subversion. He declared that the decree had not called for the physical elimination of subversives but rather for the curtailment of their actions. Furthermore, he testified, an executive decree could not abrogate the basic constitutional principles. Several ministers of Isabel Perón's government corroborated these sentiments.

The following day, Theo Van Boven, who had served as director of the United Nations Human Rights Commission, testified that the UN had received numerous complaints regarding the human rights situation during Argentina's military regime. By way of defense, several members of the navy testified to their understanding of "annihilation" and denied accusations that people remained detained in the ESMA. Ramón Baldassini, a well-known trade union leader, also testified, claiming that when he was detained, he received excellent treatment. The testimony of Erik Stover, the director of the American Science Association, had a strong impact on public opinion because he identified the corpses of an entire family, including children, who had been shot. Clive Snow of Physicians for Human Rights corroborated Stover's testimony. The French admiral Antoine Sanguinetti recounted a meeting with Gen. José Montes, a foreign minister of the military government, during which he had inquired about the French nuns who had disappeared; Montes replied that it was strange to evince concern about those nuns when a manager of the Peugeot factory had been assassinated by the guerrillas. Several politicians, along with members of the final, or so-called fourth, junta, explained the "Final Document."

Robert Cox, former editor of the *Buenos Aires Herald,* testified that he had felt pressure not to publish lists of those who had disappeared. Adriana Calvo de Laborde, a physicist, told how she had given birth to her child while being abducted in a car amid the humiliating verbal abuse of her captors. Jacobo Timerman described his abduction and torture, including his interrogation by Camps regarding the banker Daniel Graiver, who allegedly had laundered money for the Montoneros. Domingo Moncalvillo testified about a group of young people who, having been kidnapped, managed to regain some freedom and even have contact with their families. However, they ultimately disappeared. Carlos Alberto Hours, a subofficial of the Buenos Aires police, described how policemen had murdered Edgardo Sajón. Former military president Gen. Alejandro Lanusse testified that there were illegal procedures and described the disputes he had concerning them with several military leaders, including military president Bignone, when he criticized those procedures.

Several witnesses described the kidnapping and torture of the members of the Grassi economic group. Rabossi described CONADEP's work. Emilio Gracelli, a priest who was a military chaplain, described the claims he had received about the disappearances. The former human rights coordinator for the United States Department of State, Patricia Derian, testified to her knowledge of the Argentine human rights violations, to the presentations she had made before the military government, and to the heated confrontations she had had with its members, such as Minister of the Interior Albano Harguindeguy. Several moderate journalists, such as Mariano Grondona and Magdalena Ruiz Guiñazú, testified to the climate of repression in which they had lived. Lt. Facundo Urién, who had been dismissed for refusing to participate in the program of repression, testified that several corpses had been unearthed in his garrison.

Several witnesses testified about the case of Amelia Insaurralde, who had been found dead on her bed in a cell of a clandestine prison. After that testimony, some officers suggested that suicide could account for the death, but a forensic physician stated that he believed the death was caused by hanging. Gustavo Adolfo Contemponi, who initially had been imprisoned in Córdoba for conspiracy as a member of the Montoneros and later became a collaborator of the military regime, described in detail the La Perla clandestine detention center in Córdoba. Sen. Hipólito Solari Yrigoyen, who had been abducted along with other members of the Radical Party, described the torture, and ultimate death, of some of his colleagues. Emilio Mignone testified to the abduction of his daughter. This list merely represents an illustrative cross-section of the 832 people who testified during the "big trial."

A group of well-known English-speaking moral and legal philosophers, Ronald Dworkin (who later wrote the introduction to the English version of *Nunca Más*), Owen Fiss, Thomas Nagel, Thomas Scanlon, and Bernard Williams, attended some of the hearings. In a rather Athenian climate, they discussed the legal and philosophical problems associated with retroactive justice. They also gave public lectures about abstract philosophical questions in the University of Buenos Aires and the Argentine Society of Analytical Philosophy.

Meanwhile, military unrest swelled; the trials were considered intolerable and characterized as nothing more than a leftist maneuver. The army's chief of staff, General Pianta, was replaced by Gen. Héctor Ríos Ereñú. At the end of June 1985, Ríos Ereñú stated that an amnesty law was the only way of making Argentina a great nation. On July 1, Minister of Defense Roque Carranza, who had replaced the late Raúl Borrás, declared that there would be no amnesty law. Former President Frondizi, who became very close to the military after being overthrown by them, called the trial a "political show." The military chaplain, Jose Miguel Medina, asked publicly if there was an underground force determined to dismember "my beloved armed forces and police." At the same time, labor unrest increased. In the course of the trial—specifically, on May 23, 1985—the General Confederation of Labor mobilized 120,000 people to demand economic reform.[77]

On August 14, 1985, testimony was completed, and on September 11 Strassera began summarizing the prosecution's evidence. He began by recognizing that at least 9,000 people had disappeared. He added that state terrorism must be understood within the context of a loss of legal consciousness. This method of state terrorism—which he deemed, looking at the commanders, as ferocious, clandestine, and cowardly—frustrated its own objectives by using the same unethical courses of action that it was fighting. Moreno Ocampo continued by saying that once the targets of the repression had been dehumanized, it was a short leap to seeking their annihilation by any means necessary.

After describing the facts surrounding the 709 cases in question, the prosecution explored the legal basis for punishment. In discussing principles of agency, making the commanders responsible for acts which they did not directly execute, the prosecution relied on the Yamashita case, in which the commander had been convicted for the acts of his subordinate, and theories by Roxin and other German scholars, according to which the "author behind the author" can be held responsible for a crime that utilizes an apparatus of power which he controls completely and an agent that is completely fungible.

The prosecution also claimed that the accused were responsible for murder and torture by acts of commission as well as omission. The prosecutors rejected the possible pleas of lawful defense, since there was no proportionality; of necessity, since the harm caused was greater than that avoided; of compliance with the law, since the law did not specifically authorize the acts; and of state of war, since there had been no such war, and even if there had been, the defendants should be considered war criminals.[78]

Strassera concluded his case by arguing that although the accused had committed crimes for which Dante, in the *Divine Comedy,* reserved for the seventh circle of hell, he was merely asking for punishment which, as Oliver Wendell Holmes, Sr., said, would give sufficient credibility to the preventive threats of the law. After asking for different penalties, ranging from life imprisonment for the members of the first two juntas to ten years for members of the last junta, Strassera concluded dramatically by repeating the phrase that belonged to the Argentine people, "Never again."

The defense began its summation on September 30, 1985. Videla's public defender, Carlos Alberto Tavares, began by questioning President Alfonsín's Decree 158, which he alleged assumed that the defendants were guilty. He also questioned Law 23,049 in terms of the principle of the "natural judge" and due process guarantees. Tavares dismissed the testimony given by people involved in CONADEP's investigation; he saw CONADEP as the true center for fabricating evidence. He asked for Videla's acquittal and application of the amnesty law. José María Orgeira, another of Viola's defense counsel, called the court an inquisitorial tribunal and dismissed the evidence as fabricated by those connected with leftist terrorism; he also argued that omission could not be a source of responsibility for these types of actions. Viola declared that he was being accused of something of which he was proud — the victory against leftist subversion.

Massera's counsel, Jaime Prats Cardona, claimed that the trial was part of a conspiracy to destroy the armed forces. He also dismissed the witnesses' testimony because he believed they were involved with terrorism and asked for

Massera's acquittal. Massera himself, during a subsequent deposition, stated that he would not defend himself, for no one had to defend himself for having won a war against subversive terrorism. The subversives had won the psychological battle, he added; that was why they were in court. But the armed forces would defeat them in the future as they had done in the past.

Bernardo Rodriguez Palma and Ignacio Garona, counsel for Brigadier Agosti, tried to distinguish the air force from the other branches of the military, as well as denying the accuracy of the direct accusations.

Enrique Ramos Mejía and Fernando Goldaracena, Armando Lambruschini's defense counsel, relying on Isabel Perón's and Luder's decrees of "annihilation," alleged that a state of war had in fact existed. Omar Graffigna's defense counsel, Roberto Calandra, argued that not one deed could be directly imputed to their client. Galtieri's defense team, led by Eduardo Munilla Lacasa, warned that measures like the trial would ultimately lead to situations like that experienced in Nicaragua. Jorge Anaya's defense team, led by Eduardo Aguirre Obarrio, alleged that by the time their client had taken charge of the navy, the repression had ceased. Miguel Marcópoulus, Lami Dozo's defense counsel, justified the war against subversion, quoting Napoleón's words: "He who saves the nation does not break any law." He also argued that the antisubversive battle had come to an end before Lami Dozo took power.

During these proceedings, a series of bombings took place in different parts of the country, including the homes of some military leaders. Only four hours after the defendant's case ended on October 21, 1985, presidential spokesman José Ignacio Lopez announced that President Alfonsín had declared a state of siege in response to the bombings. The state of siege was limited to the sixty-day detention of six members of the military and six civilians. Some judges began declaring the state of siege unconstitutional due to a lack of evidence connecting the bombings to those detained. The president revoked the state of siege a few weeks later. In a phone conversation with Alfonsín, I expressed disagreement with the action he had initially taken. To avoid a general state of siege, his declaration of a state of siege was in effect limited to a specific number of individuals, but I believed that generality was an implicit constitutional requirement.

Once the state of siege was imposed, the bombings ceased completely, but the military's anxiety increased as the Federal Court recessed to consider its decision. The government hoped that the court's decision would quell the fears of those who believed that liberal interpretation of the due obedience provision would engender widespread prosecutions. Accordingly, Alfonsín asked Malamud and me to organize a secret meeting with the members of the Federal Court to discuss the issue of due obedience.[79] The dinner meeting took place at my home in October 1985, attended by six judges, Alfonsín, who arrived in a car with tinted glasses, Malamud, my wife, Susana, and me. Over drinks and dinner, we did not discuss the trial, abiding by Alfonsín's customary respect for judges, which critics attributed to his being a small-town lawyer. Alfonsín called the judges heroes, adding that society would be forever grateful for their efforts. He also confessed that he often went to bed without knowing whether he would be abducted during the night. Over coffee, Alfonsín asked whether petty officers would, after ten years, be held responsible for their acts. Judge Ledesma replied that, in most cases, the individual perpetrators could not be identified. Other judges suggested that a six-month term could be established, at the end of which all those unidentified would be free from penal prosecution. Alfonsín remained unconvinced that such measures would adequately contain the trial. He finally asked whether the judges could define due obedience in their decision to effect such ends. They answered that it would be quite difficult to do so since they were dealing with those who had given the orders and, as judges, they could not make general statements. The judges departed. When Alfonsín was about to leave, his bodyguard warned that he could not yet leave since there was a small fire in a neighboring apartment and many people, besides firemen, were outside on the street. So the president had to wait with us; during this time we showed him a video of the trial that D'Alessio had given to me.[80]

On December 9, 1985, the Court of Appeals publicly announced its decision. It began by describing the general pattern of repression. From an examination of the evidence, the judges concluded that the measures undertaken by the defendants were radically different from those authorized by law:

> Lack of confidence in civilized methods to prevent the repetition of terrorist acts or to punish the instigators, the certainty that national and international public opinion would not tolerate a massive application of the death penalty, and the desire to avoid the public scrutiny that such a course of action would have entailed prompted the defendants to take the steps that were subsequently followed in the campaign against subversion. In essence, those steps consisted of kidnapping and then physically eliminating those who were identified — according to the judgment of those who executed the orders — as subversive criminals. That the system chosen to fight subversion departed from the rule of law — even from those laws of exception which are designed for times of emergency — is reflected not only in the violence characterizing the operations, but also in the measures which were taken for the purpose of concealing the arrests and the fate of the detainees, submitting them to unacceptable conditions of captivity. All the evidence which has been produced and evaluated in the preceding chapters confirms this assertion.[81]

Regardless of the prosecution's arguments to the contrary, the court refused to impute responsibility to the juntas themselves but rather insisted on assign-

ing responsibility to each commander in chief; notwithstanding the cooperation that from time to time one branch lent to another, "it does not follow that
the operations were conducted by a higher authority than that of each commander in chief." The court further asserted that the commanders must have
known the procedures their subordinates utilized, including kidnapping, torture, the seizure of property, and even murder, given the general pattern of
those operations and the control they wielded over their forces. The same,
however, could not be said of crimes concerning dispossession of real property, abduction of minors, and bribery. Because most of the orders were given
orally, it was not surprising that the Supreme Council found the written ones
"unobjectionable."

The court then discussed the crimes at issue. Relying on the definition of
deprivation of liberty found in article 144(b) of the Argentine Penal Code, the
court denied that such abductions were authorized by law. Torture had been
proscribed in article 144(c) of the code, as amended by Law 14,616. In some
cases, such as that of Jorge Anaya, the torture was aggravated when it caused
the death of the victims. According to article 80 of the code, the murders were
aggravated due to the cruelty by which they were committed. On the other
hand, the court did not find that the defendants had committed the following
crimes: concealment, reduction to serfdom, and insertion of falsehoods in
public documents.

The court then dealt with the various defenses. The defense of necessity was
rejected because the means used to combat subversion had been just as per-
nicious as the subversion itself; furthermore, some of the evils sought to be
prevented had not been imminent. The defense of acting in compliance with a
legal duty was rejected since the decrees in question should be construed in
harmony with the rest of the legal system. Lawful defense was also rejected
since the alleged defensive action had not been reasonably proportionate to
the aggression and since the abduction had terminated any threat. Nor could
defendants successfully argue that they had acted in mere "excess" of legitimate orders because most of the acts had been unnecessary in the first place.

The Court of Appeals discussed the state-of-war defense at length, high-
lighting distinctions between different types of wars and describing the stages
of the so-called revolutionary war. The court began with a disclaimer: There
was no single, defining characteristic of war. But, the court continued, even
during war, national and international rules govern, and the defendants had
not complied with such rules. Although the method they had used had accelerated the victory against subversion, this alone could not justify the excessive
use of force.

The next section of the opinion was devoted to the rules of agency and participation. The court held that the theory of "control of the act" (*dominio del hecho*), formulated by the German scholar Hans Welzel, should be the governing doctrine. The author of the crime is the one who controls the course of events. This notion comports with the Military Code, especially article 514 dealing with due obedience. The court stated:

> The indirect perpetrator is criminally responsible because he is in control of the perpetration of the crime. The indirect perpetrator controls the criminal act by controlling the will (*dominio de la voluntad*) of the person who actually perpetrates the crime. . . . In the opinion of this court, the defendants are responsible for the crimes committed by their subordinates independently of the criminal responsibility of the latter. The criminal acts perpetrated by the subordinate officers were always under the control of the defendants, hence they must answer as indirect perpetrators even if some of the direct perpetrators can be exempt from criminal responsibility on the bases of some grounds of justification. . . . Under these circumstances, who actually perpetrated the crimes is not so important. The control of those who headed the system was absolute. Even if a subordinate refused to obey, he would be automatically replaced by another who would conform to the directives.[82]

The court said that the defendants had contributed to the crimes not only by giving the directives but also by facilitating their execution.

In the next section of its decision, the court attributed liability to each of the defendants. For instance, Videla was found responsible for 16 counts of homicide aggravated by cruelty, 50 counts of homicide aggravated by cruelty, 306 counts of unlawful deprivation of freedom aggravated by violent threats, 93 counts of torture, four counts of torture followed by death, and 26 counts of robbery. He was acquitted of other charges.

The final section of the court's opinion contained the sentences. Videla and Massera received life imprisonment and permanent disqualification from holding public office; Agosti received four and a half years in prison and permanent disqualification; Viola received seventeen years in prison and absolute disqualification from any public post; Lambruschini received eight years in prison and absolute disqualification; Graffigna, Galtieri, Anaya, and Lami Dozo were acquitted. The opinion also included a point that would later become controversial. The criminal offenses that were discovered in the course of the proceedings were reported to the Supreme Council so that it could bring criminal charges against the superior officers who had been in charge of the relevant areas during the campaign against subversion.[83] Both the prosecution and the defense appealed the decision to the Supreme Court.

While some in the government were disappointed that the Federal Court of Appeals did not more decisively circumscribe the due obedience defense, the court's decision was undoubtedly the most successful component of Alfonsín's strategy. Despite the pressures from different sectors and the ostensible risks, the court had conducted the trial in an extremely dignified way and, in its sober and thorough decision, had set forth principles conducive to the reestablishment of the rule of law and elementary ethical principles in Argentine life. The moral consciousness of society seems to have been deeply affected by these trials. Even though the trial was not directly televised, the months of testimony regarding the atrocities made a perceptible impact on the minds of the people.[84]

The Fourth Phase, 1986–1990

During this period, public reaction began to thwart Alfonsín's original strategy, forcing measures to contain the punitive process. My connection to the events of this period was less intense, since on Christmas Eve 1985 the president appointed me coordinator of the new Council for the Consolidation of Democracy, an interdisciplinary and bipartisan advisory body charged with proposing structural reforms to rectify some of the endemic trends mentioned at the beginning of this chapter, especially concentration of power. Thereafter, I became less involved in the administration's program of retroactive justice.

In March 1986 there was another secret meeting between Alfonsín and some of the judges to discuss the problems of the trials, this time in the president's Olivos residence. Also in attendance were Malamud and I, Minister of the Interior Troccoli, the new minister of defense, Germán López, and the new secretary of justice, Ideler Tonelli. Although we did not reach a consensus about the course of action that should be taken, I had the distinct impression that the idea of stopping the trials was growing. Petracchi, a justice of the Supreme Court who had given Alfonsín Tonelli's name, was drafting a proposal that would shorten the statute of limitations. Although the proposal was opposed by some judges — especially Gil Lavedra, who proposed to accelerate the remaining trials — Alfonsín assured the judges that he would support it.[85]

The government first tried to convince the Supreme Council to accelerate the remaining trials. The government also tried to pressure the federal courts in the interior to take over the cases in their jurisdictions. Some officials, including Malamud, traveled to the interior to determine how the government could assist these courts. The courts, however, were quite reluctant to take over the trials, since the military pressures were stronger in the small provincial towns. The Córdoba court, which had to deal with Gen. Benjamin Menendez and the abuses in the clandestine center La Perla, was the most intransigent. It was likely that some of the court's members were connected to Menendez. On April

4, 1986, the Federal Court of Appeals of Buenos Aires decided to take over the trial of General Camps. The decision evinced implicit criticism of the interior courts that were allowing the statute of limitations to run out.

On April 23, 1986, Secretary of Defense Horacio Jaunarena called a meeting of Minister of Defense López, Secretary of Justice Tonelli, and the legal advisors of the armed forces. In that meeting a consensus emerged, based on a text prepared by Tonelli: The minister of defense should give instructions to the military prosecutors to accelerate those cases on trial in the Supreme Council in which the officers with decision-making capacity were defendants; the other defendants should be acquitted. When the draft proposal was presented to several people in the government, only Undersecretary of Human Rights Rabossi and Deputy Federico Storani expressed their opposition. The president approved the proposal on April 24, 1986.

At that time, Rabossi told me about the meeting and some members of the Federal Court of Appeals communicated serious concern. I spoke with Alfonsín, and he told me that the proposed instructions had been presented to the judges and that they were in agreement. The judges denied seeing the draft proposal. Alfonsín sent me to a meeting with Germán López, Jaunarena, and Tonelli. The meeting was quite heated. I argued that the proposal clearly contradicted the text of the law, but Tonelli responded that no serious jurist would interpret the instructions as I had.[86] I asked him not to personalize the discussion.

The instructions to the judges provoked considerable criticism among the press and the human rights groups. Judge Jorge Torlasco of the Federal Court resigned. President Alfonsín sent Tonelli to the court to avert additional resignations, but the judges reacted with hostility. Alfonsín then met with the judges on April 29, 1986, promising to clarify the instructions.

In his May 1, 1986 speech before the legislature, the president announced that he would give new instructions so that those who had had decision-making capacity or had committed atrocious or abhorrent deeds could not rely on the due obedience defense. Some sectors of the press still called for a cessation of the trials.[87] On June 11, 1986, the president, in a press conference, clarified the instructions, stating that the acquittals would not reach those who had committed abhorrent and atrocious acts.

Several courts responded by taking cases away from the Supreme Council. This occurred in the Federal Court of La Plata, in a case concerning Bignone and Rosario, and in the Federal Court of Buenos Aires in the cases concerning the First Army Corps. When learning that the court of Buenos Aires was going to take jurisdiction over these cases, Alfonsín held another meeting with the judges in order to avert such a course of action. He even asked Supreme

Court Justice Enrique Petracchi to intercede, but the judges were adamant in their decision.[88] Therefore, in the end the attempt to contain the prosecutions boomeranged.

The president's instructions had an effect in an odd forum. On August 18, 1986, the Supreme Council used the instructions to acquit General Menendez of the Third Army Corps in Córdoba. That same day, General Camps refused to testify before the Federal Court of Buenos Aires. The Federal Court of Córdoba finally took over the Menendez case, although it left the "La Perla" trial in the Supreme Council's jurisdiction. The Federal Court of Buenos Aires decided not to usurp the ESMA case from the Supreme Council, but the minister of defense asked the military prosecutor to pressure the council into taking action in this case. In response, several members of the council resigned.

The transfer of virtually all of the cases to the federal courts aggravated the armed forces. High officers met to discuss their concerns. Col. Jorge Eduardo Gorleri publicly announced that he would not allow any of his officers to be cited by civilian courts. Alfonsín immediately ordered Gorleri's dismissal. The situation became even more tense when the Federal Court of Mendoza ordered the preventative detention of Lt. Carlos Esteban Plá, who was accused of shooting two youths in the back of their heads. Plá garrisoned himself, refusing to obey the court's orders. His fellow officers expressed their solidarity. Ríos Ereñú, Jaunarena, and Tonelli searched for a solution. Initially, the Federal Court decided not to carry out the detention order. Later, the court set aside its initial order when it discovered that one of the witnesses had committed perjury. Meanwhile, Plá went on a mission to Spain. This episode revealed that attempts to detain inferior officers for subsequent trial would be resisted. At the same time, popular attention had already turned away from the trials toward the heightening economic crisis.

In October 1986, different sectors of the government again began looking for ways to contain the trials. Some thought that the Supreme Court should clarify the issue of due obedience, especially in light of Videla's pending appeal. Although Justice Petracchi was sympathetic to this idea, he retreated, arguing that the link between due obedience and the issues at hand was too tenuous. Minister Troccoli studied the due obedience project. It would eliminate the "abhorrent and atrocious acts" exception and turn the presumption of mistake into an irrebuttable presumption. Subsequently, Alfonsín asked Malamud and Ricardo Entelman to draft a proposal, based on Justice Petracchi's original idea to shorten the statute of limitations. The result was a proposal known as the "full-stop" law (*punto final*), imposing a cut-off date for all trials.

The Federal Court of Appeals of Buenos Aires continued hearing the Camps case and the Ricchieri case, as well as the cases of several military officers and policemen. On December 2, the Federal Court sentenced Camps to twenty-five years in prison, Miguel Etchecolatz, the chief of police, to twenty-three years, Gen. Pablo Ricchieri to fourteen years, Jorge Bergés, the police doctor, to six years, and Corp. Norberto Cozzani to four years.

Two days later, a serious military crisis developed. The Federal Court cited retired Gens. Jorge Róvere, José Montes, Andrés Ferrero, Juan B. Sasain, and Adolfo Sigwald, as well as Col. Roque Presti. When Minister of Defense Jaunarena relayed this decision, Héctor Ríos Ereñú, chief of the army, responded that such a decision would provoke a strong military reaction and would force his own retirement. As the tension heightened, Troccoli, Jaunarena, and Malamud went to Justice Petracchi's home to ask whether the judiciary could mollify the situation. Petracchi found a temporary solution: a policeman (Juan Antonio del Cerro) accused of torture had appealed to the Supreme Court on the ground that the Federal Court of Appeals had inappropriately taken jurisdiction of his case. Petracchi responded by calling for the files of the case. That had the effect of suspending the proceedings at the Federal Court, and since del Cerro's claim was similar to those of all the other officers just cited, those proceedings were stayed too. As a result, a crisis was temporarily averted.

Meanwhile, on December 5, 1986, the Federal Court of Buenos Aires acquitted Astiz, despite the kidnapping of Dagmar Hagelin, by applying the statute of limitations. On that very day, President Alfonsín sent the full-stop law to Congress. I attended a large meeting in Olivos to discuss the draft proposal. Troccoli and Dante Caputo defended it. I thought that the full-stop law was politically counterproductive. Later, I gave Alfonsín a letter, clearly stating my objections, while asking for a leave to teach at the Yale Law School. He put the letter in his pocket, hugged me while saying, "Let me try," and wished me good luck at Yale.

The full-stop law was designed to counter the uncertainty created by the lack of resolution in many cases. The law established a sixty-day limit for filing all claims based on criminal activity as defined in Law 23,049; otherwise all such claims would be extinguished. The same would apply to any person accused of violent political action prior to December 10, 1983. The law did not apply to the abduction of minors. Furthermore, preventive detention would no longer be necessary if the superior of the officer assumed responsibility for the accused's appearance in court. It also provided that the courts of appeals could order the Supreme Council to assess the progress of the cases within forty-eight hours.

The law was enacted by Congress on December 23, 1986, amid public opposition.[89] Guillermo Ledesma, another member of the Federal Court of

Appeals of Buenos Aires, resigned. On January 19, 1987, the Supreme Council acquitted fifteen admirals in the ESMA case. Alfonsín, deeply affected by the public reaction to the law, issued a decree on January 23, ordering the attorney general to give instructions to the prosecutors to bring charges against all who were covered by Law 23,049. Because the government handled information so poorly, the public did not realize that this was a push toward more prosecutions, rather than, as most sectors of the left-wing press and human rights groups believed, another attempt to avoid confrontation with the past.[90]

The Supreme Court revised the decision of the Federal Court of Appeals in the Videla case. The majority of the Supreme Court disagreed with the criteria the Federal Court had applied with regard to agency, stating that the theory of control of the action was too controversial. The Supreme Court was nevertheless prepared to consider the commanders' behavior as necessary complicity, which carried the same penalty. The Supreme Court added that the self-amnesty law should be invalidated because there was an abuse of power. In the minority, Jorge Bacqué[91] and Enrique Petracchi argued for a narrower approach to the validity of de facto laws. They also believed the defendants should be judged as authors of the crimes, rather than mere accomplices. Given the majority's analysis, however, the Supreme Court revoked the imputation of some crimes to Viola and Agosti, reducing the sentences of the former to sixteen years and of the latter to three years and nine months.

When the full-stop law became operative, courts all over the country, even those in the interior which had been rather dormant, became frantic with activity, even skipping the usual summer judicial vacation in January. While teaching at Yale, I read an editorial in the *New York Times* entitled "Justice Diluted in Argentina" that criticized the full-stop law as a concession to the military. My reply, entitled "Speedy Trials for Argentina's Military?" argued that the law in question would help accelerate the trials, for the number of cases currently in the Argentine courts had trebled.[92] When I returned to Argentina in the middle of March 1987, I learned that I had underestimated the law's effect: I had estimated the number of trials prompted by the law at 150, but in fact there were 400 — twenty times the number of defendants tried to date.

Moreover, because the courts believed the full-stop law had given them a small time frame to undertake the historical responsibility for punishing these crimes, they greatly accelerated their activity, receiving copious evidence from victims and human rights groups. Therefore, the full-stop law was having, like Alfonsín's instructions, a boomerang effect, provoking an outburst of judicial action.

The situation was initially stable, with the military retreating in the face of this judicial activism. At last justice seemed to have imposed itself! At that time, the Federal Court of San Marín convicted Firmenich, who was extradited from Brazil. Unlike the officers who were being tried by the reformed oral procedure in the military code, Firmenich was being tried by the ancient written procedure and was sentenced to thirty years in prison. At the same time, López Rega, who had been hiding in Florida and who was the object of an extradition request to the United States government, was brought to Argentina to testify about his crimes. Alfonsín even took to the pulpit. On April 2, 1987, during a mass in the National Cathedral for the victims of the Malvinas War, the military chaplain gave a homily denouncing corruption, injustice, and national disintegration. Alfonsín was in the audience, asked for permission to get up to the pulpit, and from there responded to the chaplain. Later that week, the Pope visited for a week, expressing hope that there would not be more disappearances and praising the bishops who had saved lives during the dictatorship. The government was still hopeful that the Supreme Court would define the limits of due obedience in a case involving subordinate officers that was pending.[93]

When Easter Week approached, the status quo seemed stable, and almost all the government officials, including the president, were ready to take a small vacation outside Buenos Aires. A personal anecdote illustrates this deceptive sense of calm. Three well-known scholars, Owen Fiss, Thomas Nagel and Antony Honoré, came to Buenos Aires for a conference on human rights, during which Rabossi was heatedly criticized by human rights groups for the full-stop law. Late in the evening of April 15, we were having coffee in the Recoleta district of Buenos Aires, where we met Robert Cox, the former editor of the *Buenos Aires Herald,* who was at the same conference. I said this was the greatest moment for the consolidation of democracy. We lingered a little longer, and then, on our way home, we passed by a newsstand and I bought them each a copy of *La Razón,* almost as a souvenir. The headlines seemed so hopeful for Argentina: "López Rega Brought to the Country," "Firmenich Convicted," "More Officers Cited to Testify in the Trials," "An Agreement Reached Regarding the External Debt," and "Conversations between the Government and the Trade Unions." When our guests flew to Salta the next morning, however, they perceived the first symptoms of what would be the beginning of the end.

On April 14, 1987, Maj. Ernesto Barreiro, cited to respond to accusations of torture, communicated to his superior in the Fourteenth Airborne Infantry Brigade in Córdoba, Lt. Col. Luís Polo, that he would not show up in court. Polo reported Barreiro's decision to the commander of the Third Army Corps. Gen. Antonio Fichera immediately traveled to Buenos Aires to interview the deputy chief of the army, Gen. Mario Sanchez. Sanchez told Polo that he should compel Barreiro to present himself in court. Polo refused. On April 15, Barreiro's resistance was leaked to the press, and when the time to appear in court arrived, he garrisoned himself in the officers' club. The Federal Court of Córdoba refused to grant a delay and asked the national government how it should proceed. In the end, the court declared Barreiro a rebel and asked the federal police to facilitate his capture.

Chief of Military Staff Ríos Ereñu met with the high command of the army to see whether they should send troops or police to capture Barreiro. That night, the government declared that it would respect the constitutional order. Major Barreiro also issued a communication adhering to his position, saying he would not show up in court. The offices of several newspapers received communications from officers throughout the country supporting Barreiro's stance. An officer in the regiment declared that an arrest order would be resisted.

The following day, April 16, news of the rebellion made early-morning press headlines and the population became seriously concerned. The rebels accused Ríos Ereñú of purposely aborting the negotiations with the army and asked for his resignation. They also asked for an amnesty. After meeting for two hours with the generals and ordering them to repress the rebellion, President Alfonsín called an urgent meeting of the national legislature, from which he made a televised speech. In a session attended not only by legislators but also by leaders from the political parties, trade unions, and entrepreneurial and professional associations, Alfonsín proclaimed that Argentine democracy would not be negotiated and that extortion was unacceptable. The officers of the armed forces had a duty to obey, and the decisions of an autonomous judicial power could not be negotiated. Alfonsín was widely acclaimed by everybody in the hall, as well as by those demonstrating in the street, numbering some four hundred thousand.

At this very moment, Lt. Col. Aldo Rico, who had fought in the Malvinas under the command of Col. Alí Mohammed Seineldín and was the chief of a regiment in the province of Misiones, took over the Infantry School of Campo de Mayo, in the outskirts of Buenos Aires. He had the immediate support of fifty captains who were studying there. Ríos Ereñú cited Rico for rebellion.[94] Earlier Rico had sent a document to his brigade commander complaining about the citation of officers for having fought a just war against Marxist subversion and about the curtailment of military budget, both of which would destroy the armed forces if not stopped; at that time, he favored negotiation directly with Alfonsín.[95] Now he was in open rebellion and his supporters grew to two hundred.

On Good Friday, April 17, Rico issued a statement, announcing that the armed forces had lost all hope. He called for a new resolve: The officers needed to stand up and look for a political solution to a political event that was as pressing as the fight against subversion. He further proclaimed that commands in different provinces shared his beliefs and that those who attempted to repress such dissidence would suffer the consequences. President Alfonsín called Ríos Ereñu and the military commanders that morning to discuss how to stop the rebellion. He verified that the director of military institutes in Campo de Mayo did not have the troops to control Rico, and that the Third Army Corps could not acquire the strength to force Major Barreiro to submit. At noon Barreiro left his garrison for an unknown place. The president ordered the commanders of the Second and Fourth Corps to intervene.

On Saturday, April 18, the commander of the Second Corps, Gen. Ernesto Alais, with great difficulty, gathered troops and went to the place were Rico took refuge. General Alias threatened with cannons; Rico replied that he would throw a mortar into the crowd that had gathered outside. Rico finally flew by helicopter to the army's central building to talk with Ríos Ereñu. When Ríos Ereñu claimed that there could be some solutions to the trials, Rico replied that nobody believed him.[96] The presidential spokesman declared that afternoon that the situation was worrisome and that the cabinet was in permanent session. Ordinary citizens went to the garrison and tried to enter. Sen. Adolfo Gass spoke with Rico and told the people to go leave, since Rico had threatened to repel them with force. Crowds gathered in Plaza de Mayo, and Alfonsín received leaders from different parties and social groups. Ríos Ereñu met with all the generals of Buenos Aires. The General Confederation of Labor announced a general strike in defense of democracy. I spent that long day in the presidential palace (Casa Rosada) and seriously considered asking my family to leave for Uruguay.

Alfonsín slept in his office that night under reinforced guard. Early Easter Sunday, April 19, Alfonsín met with the military chiefs of staff and the minister of defense. Throughout the day I remained in the antechamber of the presidential office, where I saw an incessant parade of people entering and leaving. At noon, General Alais declared that the attack planned for the morning had been suspended to avoid bloodshed, but that the loyal troops still surrounded Campo de Mayo. Political and social leaders signed a compromise in "defense of democracy," which included the need to recognize various "levels of responsibility."[97] At the same time, hundreds of thousands began to fill Plaza de Mayo to protest in defense of democracy. Some youth chants evinced a desire to forcibly confront the military garrison. There had already been some confrontations, mostly verbal, between indignant civilians and those in the rebellious garrisons. Minister Jaunarena left the presidential palace on an unknown mission. Subsequently we learned that he went to meet Rico.

Verbitsky recorded the meeting between Jaunarena and Rico as follows:[98]

Jaunarena said that Ríos Ereñu had already asked to retire, but the government would not discuss the identity of his successor. Likewise, an amnesty was out of the question. Jaunarena also explained that it was already the government's policy to draw distinctions among different levels of responsibility. The government would not let Major Barreiro enter the armed forces again. Rico responded to all this by saying that he himself was prepared to die. Jaunarena answered that, although this was an acceptable personal decision, he was unjust in risking the lives of others. After the conversation, Jaunarena phoned Alfonsín to report that there had been no meeting of the minds.

I distinctly remember Alfonsín's response. After the call, he returned to his office through the antechamber in which I was standing. Through the transparent curtains, we could see him pacing nervously back and forth for about five minutes. We realized that the situation had reached a critical point and that one of the options he was contemplating was asking the mass of people outside his window to go take the military garrison, as they were demanding. All of a sudden, he left the room and went directly to the balcony overlooking the plaza. We followed in something of a trance.

Flanked by leaders of the Peronist Party, Alfonsín addressed the multitude at 2:40 P.M.: "What we are risking is much more than an absurd coup d'état; we are risking the future of our children; we are risking blood spilled among brothers. It is because of this that I have decided to go personally, in a few moments, to Campo de Mayo to ask for the surrender of the rebels. . . . I ask you to wait for me here, and if God wills, in some time I will come with solutions so that each of us can return to our homes and give a kiss to our children, telling them that we have assured their freedom for the time to come." He went to the chapel of the presidential palace and then to the roof to take a helicopter. When the crowd saw his helicopter flying overhead, they spontaneously began singing the national anthem.

All of us who remained in the presidential palace were extremely tense. As I have done on similar occasions, I tried to concentrate on reading a book that I carried with me — which, incidentally, prompted some teasing from the politicians also waiting there. The book was, ironically, appropriate for the occasion — Michael Walzer's *Just and Unjust Wars*.

Alfonsín returned at 6 P.M. and, surrounded by the ministers of the interior and defense, Peronist leaders, and some members of the military, spoke to the populace. The president proclaimed:

> Compatriots . . . compatriots . . . Happy Easter! The rebels have changed their attitude. As it turns out, they will be detained and subjected to justice. They are a group of men, some of them heroes of Malvinas, who took the wrong

path and who reiterated that their intention was not to prompt a coup d'état. But anyway they led the country to this tension . . . through which all of us have lived and in which the Argentine people were the central protagonist. In order to avoid spilling blood, I gave orders to the command of the army not to attack, and now we can thank God. The house is in order and there is no bloodshed in Argentina. I ask the people in Campo de Mayo to leave. And I request all of you: Go to your homes to kiss your children; to celebrate Easter in Argentina in peace.

Of course, the crowd exploded in applause. Alfonsín was considered a hero of democracy. The headline in *La Razón* read: "The Rebels Surrendered to Alfonsín. The People Defended Democracy."

What had happened during the meeting between Alfonsín and Rico? Of course, there were many different accounts. Rico claimed that they negotiated an agreement regarding an amnesty and the removal of the army's chief of staff. The more credible story came from Brig. Héctor Panzardi, a military advisor in the presidential palace who accompanied Alfonsín to the meeting. According to him, Rico and Venturino did not want to force a coup but only wanted to protect the officers who had fought in the Malvinas from the trials. Alfonsín said that although he could not interfere with the independence of the courts, he hoped that the Supreme Court would define the levels of responsibility so as to mitigate their responsibility. Alfonsín then agreed to accept military jurisdiction in dealing with the revolt. Afterwards, he ordered their surrender, which they accepted.

Whatever may have been agreed upon, the indisputable facts are that the rebels were detained and submitted to trial, before a military court, despite Law 23,049. The chief of military staff, Ríos Ereñú, was replaced not by Gen. Isidro Cáceres, the apparent choice of the rebels, but by Gen. José Dante Caridi.[99] Ten chiefs of regiments who had openly sympathized with the rebels were dismissed. A law altering the presumption in the due obedience defense and thus containing the trials was sent to Congress later that spring.

In the immediate wake of the Easter uprising, the government's position began to deteriorate. Several commanders resisted their retirement orders. The following Tuesday, military officials resumed resistance to judicial orders, and the Supreme Court asked all the inferior courts temporarily to turn over all files pertaining to the human rights trials. Many in the military thought that Alfonsín was betraying his pact when the trials continued.[100] On the other hand, the left incessantly repeated phrases from Alfonsín's speech — "The house is in order" and "Happy Easter" — with an ironic twist.

The government's position was made increasingly precarious by two additional factors. First, the economy deteriorated as the initial success of the government's anti-inflationary plans began to wane. Second, the campaign for the September elections began and forced the opposition to distance itself sharply from the government. The government realized that the Supreme Court, which previously had effectively cooperated to reduce the tensions emerging from the trials, would not resolve the due obedience issue. The justices considered that issue a political question that should be addressed by politicians.

This web of problems led several members of the government to look frantically for a solution to the widespread judicial action partially unleashed by the full-stop law. Several alternatives were suggested during a series of meetings between Jaunarena, Minister of Justice Julio Rajneri, and advisors and legislators: an amnesty law, presidential pardons, and a law sharply defining due obedience. The amnesty law was rejected since the military code — which could not be abrogated ex post facto — requires that all those responsible for a crime should equally benefit from the amnesty. In effect, an amnesty would require freeing even those commanders already convicted. The presidential pardons, advocated by the Peronists who wanted all political costs to be assumed by Alfonsín, could not, according to the best constitutional interpretations, benefit people who were under trial but not yet convicted. These individual cases, of course, were exactly the group whom the pardons were supposed to benefit. The law of due obedience, therefore, seemed the only viable alternative.

Incidentally, I had proposed a different solution: to reform the Penal Code through a commission in the Ministry of Justice. The reforms would focus specifically on adopting a system of prosecutorial discretion, allowing prosecutors not to pursue criminal proceedings for a variety of reasons, similar to those in the American and German legal systems. This would allow the attorney general, whether or not following instructions from the president, to choose for prosecution only the most abhorrent crimes. Alfonsín was at first very enthusiastic about this solution. He even embraced me, saying that I had helped him avoid making an awful decision. Subsequently, however, given the resistance of Attorney General Gauna and others — who voiced the opinion, perhaps correct, that such a solution would appear too ad hoc — Alfonsín abandoned the idea.

Therefore, on May 13, 1987, the president sent to Congress a draft of the due obedience law, creating an almost irrefutable defense for middle- and lower-rank officers. In a televised address, he emphasized that he was not pleased with the measure but that it was necessary for the consolidation of democracy. I was deeply upset by this draft law. The president noted my mood and asked if my opposition was based on moral grounds. I said to him that in some sense it was not, since I was not a retributivist in the matter of punishment. But I explained that the relinquishment of punishment would have harmful consequences for society, since it would escalate into a series of new demands. In that case, he replied, the decision was a matter of political "smell." He then asked me affectionately whose nose we should follow, his or mine. I answered, of course, that the people had elected his nose. As I shall suggest later, I believe that his nose and the people who elected it did not err.

The due obedience law was enacted on June 6, thanks to the cooperation of the Peronists, who provided the quorum, even though most of them, including Carlos Menem, criticized it harshly. The law created an irrebuttable presumption that chief officers, subordinate officers, subofficers, and troops in the armed, security, and prison forces had acted under orders and thus were not punishable. The same presumption extended to superior officers, generals, and colonels who had not acted as chiefs of zones and subzones or of armed, security, and prison forces, unless it was judicially decided within thirty days that they had had decision-making authority or had helped formulate orders. This presumption was not applicable to the crimes of rape, kidnapping and concealment of children, and appropriation of real property.

The passage of this law was received with bitter criticism, even indignation, by different sectors of society as well as by the international community, including national and international human rights groups. They thought that Alfonsín's government was betraying his original stance.[101] In my view, the law could be seen as reestablishing, much more concretely and sharply, the limits implicit in the original December 1983 project, which had not been observed because of the action or inaction of other parties. Moreover, there was still much to accomplish. Superior officers who had been chiefs of zones or subzones or of different forces and who had been judicially determined to possess decision-making capacity or to have assisted with the formulation of the orders, as well as the perpetrators of rapes and abductions of children, still faced punishment.

On June 22, 1987, the Supreme Court declared the new due obedience law constitutional. Justices Severo Caballero and Belluscio held that the judiciary should not evaluate the convenience or efficacy of the means adopted by the legislative branch to achieve their purposes, except when they violate basic individual rights or are unreasonable in light of the ends sought. Justice Fayt stated that the court need not decide whether the law limited responsibility or was an amnesty in disguise, since both were within Congress's competence. Justice Petracchi approached the matter differently, arguing that obedience to illegitimate orders cannot justify or excuse behavior. He insisted that the irrebuttable presumption violated the principle of separation of powers by requiring the judges to disregard the objective facts. He also objected to the lack of generality, since it did not establish a similar rule applicable to future deeds. Nonetheless, in view of the circumstances, he concluded that this law should be interpreted as an amnesty authorized by the constitution.

Justice Bacqué dissented and set forth his views in an extremely thorough opinion. He argued that the law was not applicable to the case at hand (involving Police Commissioner Etchecolatz) since that case had already been decided by the lower courts. He also complained that the law was like a judicial decision, deciding facts that are normally reserved for judicial determination. Furthermore, he said, even if it were interpreted as an amnesty, the law was unconstitutional because it lacked the generality required by the constitution. The use of the due obedience defense to exonerate those who complied with any orders, even illegitimate ones, violated elementary principles of civilization that were embodied in the constitution and embraced in international conventions subscribed to by the Argentine state.

Although the Supreme Court upheld the due obedience law, the government fared less well in the political arena. The proposal and enactment of the law, together with social and economic problems, led to the Radical Party's loss of the parliamentary and provincial elections in September 1987. The Peronists gained control of the House of Deputies and the Senate, as well as most of the provincial legislatures, including that of Buenos Aires.

There was tranquility on the military front for a while. On January 15, 1988, however, Aldo Rico, who had been suspended, lost his military grade, and placed under an "attenuated" preventive detention while a military court tried his case, rebelled again in Monte Caseros. This time he protested the decision of the military judge to subject him to more rigorous detention. The government removed several chiefs of command, and four days afterwards the rebellion was put down by the military chief of staff, Gen. José Dante Caridi. Rico and his fellow rebels were put in prison and subjected to a new trial.

In December 1988 there was another rebellion in Villa Martelli, this time led by the person who inspired Rico and other rebels, Col. Mohammed Alí Seineldín. Alfonsín reported to Congress that there would be no further modifications in the course of justice. General Caridi quashed the rebellion for "the dignity of the armed forces," and Seineldín and his coconspirators were detained and tried. These two rebellions provoked much less sympathy within the military, and consequently were easily brought under control.

But the successful suppression of these mutinies did not bring much relief to Alfonsín's government, besieged as it was by other problems. On January 23, 1989, a left-wing terrorist movement, the Movimiento Todos por la Patria, attacked a military garrison in La Tablada, Buenos Aires. Although the attack ultimately failed, twenty-eight members of the group died, eighteen were captured, and eleven defenders of the garrison died. The unforeseen attack weakened the cause for human rights trials, illustrating the perils of left-wing terrorism and the importance of the military. Even more disconcerting was the fact that some attackers were connected with human rights groups. The right-wing press also implied that some members of the group were affiliated with the government, an allegation which, despite its sheer absurdity, had an impact on public opinion, further weakening the government's image.

At the very same time, the economy entered a hyperinflationary spiral. This development was provoked by fear among various economic groups that Carlos Menem, the Peronist candidate for president who was advocating a nationalistic and distributionist message, would win the next election. In fact, Menem did win the election on May 14, 1989. Immediately afterwards, Alfonsín lost complete control of the economy, with hyperinflation mounting to almost 200 percent per month, as fears and expectations regarding the new government percolated through the economy. Menem was scheduled to assume office on December 10, 1989, as the constitution provides. But Alfonsín, amid accusations that he was abandoning a sinking ship, decided to resign and gave the reins to Menem on July 7, 1989.

Initially, there were rumors that Menem, even though he had been detained for five years by the military regime, had negotiated an amnesty or pardons with both the Montoneros and the military. This relief was to extend to both those convicted and those awaiting trial. Menem denied the rumors, emphasizing that he would let justice follow its course. In a meeting with Alfonsín before assuming the presidency, Menem asked his predecessor to issue pardons for all those awaiting trials. Alfonsín expressed his opposition to the request. At most he would agree to pardons signed by both Menem and himself, since he was against issuing pardons and would only do so to facilitate the transition. But Menem refused to cooperate in this plan.

On October 6, 1989, Menem issued three decrees that pardoned almost four hundred people under trial. This was of questionable constitutionality. Article 86 of the Argentine Constitution provides that the president can issue pardons, but only if consistent with article 95, which forbids the president to interfere with pending trials. Those pardoned were divided in three groups: members of the armed and security forces who were accused of state terrorism; members of guerrilla groups accused of committing terrorist acts in the 1970s; and those who had rebelled against the democratic government in 1987 and 1988, including Rico and Seneildín.[102] Only former Gen. Carlos

Suarez Mason, extradited from the United States for human rights abuses, was excluded from these pardons by virtue of the terms of the extradition agreement.

The next year, on December 29, 1990, President Menem signed another set of pardons. This time he pardoned those already convicted for human rights abuses, including Videla, Massera, Agosti, Viola, Lambruschini, Camps, Ricchieri, and Firmenich, as well as Duilio Brunello and Norma Kennedy, both of whom were convicted of crimes committed during the regime of Isabel Perón. The military chiefs convicted for the Malvinas War, including Galtieri, were pardoned as well, even though their original convictions were reversed by a military court. In addition, Menem pardoned Suarez Mason and the former minister of economy, Martínez de Hoz, both of whom were under trial. The public harshly criticized these pardons—nearly 80 percent of those polled opposed Menem's action—but there were no popular demonstrations comparable to those in previous times.

Those pardons that were most acceptable to the populace, due to the lack of popular interest in further trials, were arguably unconstitutional because they freed people who had not yet been convicted. But the Supreme Court, packed by President Menem with political allies, decided otherwise. On the other hand, those pardons that were constitutionally impeccable were not politically necessary, since there was little social pressure to liberate those chiefly responsible for the human rights abuses. Therefore, unlike the laws proposed by Alfonsín, Menem's actions, which clearly damaged the rule of law, were not, in turn, justified by political necessity. To make matters worse, the pardons were not accompanied by any moral condemnation.

In the end, the moral consciousness of society was shaped by the imperfect attempt to achieve retroactive justice through CONADEP and the "big trial." At times following the pardons, those responsible for the human rights abuses acted as if history could be forgotten, but on several occasions the Argentine people spontaneously repudiated and condemned them. This occurred, for instance, when Videla attempted to go to the streets for jogging sessions, when Firmenich appeared on television, and when Massera attended an exercise of the armed forces. Perhaps this shift in moral attitudes will help overcome the corporatism, anomie, and concentration of power that all too long have been hallmarks of Argentine society.

PART **II**

The Normative Dimensions

3

Political Problems of Trials for Human Rights Violations

Retroactive justice in Argentina occurred during a unique democratic transition. Transitions to democracy are generally classified along different axes. This first is *modality* — whether the transition was carried out by *force* or by *consensus*. There is no doubt that the German and the Japanese transitions, and to some extent the Portuguese, were carried out by force. The Spanish and the Brazilian transitions, and to a certain extent the Chilean, were a product of consensus. But the Argentine transition was sui generis, since it was produced neither by force from the groups favoring democratization nor by consensus, but rather by the *collapse* of the authoritarian regime. The Argentine military regime degenerated extensively, creating a vacuum that permitted the democratic forces to prevail. In Argentina, mistake prevented consensus. The members of the military regime were mistaken as to which party would win the election.

Democratic transitions also differ according to *etiology,* the types of factors that ignite the transition processes. Transitions are either *endogenous* or *exogenous,* depending on whether the democratization process is triggered by internal or external factors. The Spanish, Chilean, and Brazilian processes were endogenous, while the German, Japanese, and Italian were exogenous. But there were also some mixed processes. In the case of Portugal, for example internal factors combined with the Angolan war to ignite transition. Likewise, in Greece, the loss of the Cyprus war, combined with the internal problems of the colonels' regime, forced the transition. To a certain extent, the Russian democratization process was also mixed, combining the internal deterioration of the Soviet regime and its increasing inability to keep pace in the arms race with the United States. The Argentine democratization also falls into this mixed category in terms of etiology.

Finally, democratization processes can be classified according to their *continuous* or *rupturous legal status*. In a continuous transition, a new legal system emerges from the old one, adhering to preexisting rules for the creation of new laws. Spain and Chile followed this model. Rupturous transitions are those in which democracy is founded on an entirely new constitution with no link to the old legal system; this occurred in both Germany and Japan. But there is a third category: restoration. The new democracy is founded on an old constitution, once in force but suspended or abrogated by the authoritarian regime. The new democratic legal system is not novel but rather a restoration, not of the authoritarian regime but rather of a former democratic government. Austria and Argentina provide prime examples of this type of transition.

The Politics of Argentina's Human Rights Trials

Categorizing Argentina's transition according to the foregoing criteria — collapse due to a mix of endogenous and exogenous factors, and restorative — helps explain the special difficulties, as well as the special opportunities, entailed in the Argentine experience with retroactive justice. The collapse of the Argentine military regime, triggered both by external and internal factors, created in its wake a certain balance of power which was partially determinative of the course of retroactive justice. The armed forces lost, by 1983, the social status which they had managed to preserve throughout this troubled century. Until 1983 various sectors of society viewed the military as a legitimate alternative for the country's leadership. But in 1983, following the recklessness of the Malvinas War, even these sectors became aware of the risks of military authoritarianism. Furthermore, the sectors traditionally aligned against military rule became stronger and more determined in their opposition because of the lies told by the leaders during that war, the enormity of the human rights abuses, and the corruption and economic mismanagement of the military regime. Even the military emerged in 1983 as profoundly divided among the army, navy, and air force.

Although the armed forces were deeply fragmented and debilitated, they still controlled almost all of the state's coercive power. Throughout the transition, the trials acted as a unifying force. A persistent internal propaganda campaign, with the active participation of the Catholic church, pervaded the military, drawing upon ideals of an organic society and the doctrine of national security. Some members of the military viewed the trials as another episode of the "war against subversion" carried on by former "terrorists" associated with human rights groups, the press, and the democratic parties. These officers were convinced that they had achieved victory in the war against subversion and that victors should not be brought to task for their wartime behavior. The military also had practical reasons for cohesively resisting retroactive justice. The commanders of the "dirty war" deliberately involved as many officers as possible in the crimes. The few officers who resisted participating — the exception rather than the rule — were immediately fired. In reality, the degree of participation among officers differed greatly. However, through internal campaigning by those most involved, the vast majority of the military were convinced that they too would fall prey to the trials. The fact that during all the Alfonsín years no upper-echelon officer who knew how the operations were conducted revealed his knowledge to CONADEP, the courts, or the press (when more than one sensationalist magazine would have compensated dearly for the story) is highly illustrative of the military's cohesiveness.

What were the military's fears, their aspirations, and the threats they could employ to achieve such aspirations?[1] On an individual level, members of the military feared prosecution and possible punishment, and the effects of such action on their honor and material standing. On a collective level, they were moved by the possibility of clashes between sectors of the armed forces and of confrontations between the armed forces and the population. They also feared the dissolution of the armed forces loomed as a potent motivation.

But the armed forces and their individual members did not aspire to reconquer political power. The experience of the previous regime, coupled with the Malvinas War, taught the military that usurpation of civilian responsibilities causes internal divisions, loss of social prestige, and inefficiency in their professional task. They aspired instead to gain recognition, particularly from politicians, for their victory in the "dirty war," to be granted impunity for the price of victory, to remain in control of security matters, and to preserve their privileges. To achieve these aspirations, the military, through control of coercive power, threatened interference with the working of the democratic process, although an all-out coup d'état would have been difficult due to lack of support among the socio-economic establishment and intramilitary schisms. Other less daunting threats, such as resistance to judicial subpoenas and noncompliance with sentences, were more credible.

The political parties, especially the Peronists and the Radical Party, played a major role in the transition process. Also, an emerging conservative third party, the UCEDE of Alvaro Alsogaray, generally aligned with the economic establishment and the military, became loyal to the democratic system during the transition period and added a crucial ingredient of stability. For the first time since 1928, political parties had won an open and clean election and the weaknesses in the armed forces gave unusual strength to the political parties. The parties, however, had weaknesses of their own. There was the traditional hostility between the parties fueled by the warlike logic of presidential systems when combined with disciplined parties and proportional representation.[2] A history of quarrels between Radicals and Peronists, which included accusations of alternatively conspiring with the military to overthrow their respective governments, heightened hostility. In addition, the political parties were internally divided. Alfonsín, for example, transformed the Radical Party, giving it a more principled and progressive stance after the rather conservative image the party had acquired in the decades since the overthrow of President Hípolito Yrigoyen in 1930. Alfonsín brought many new people to the party, including intellectuals and professionals who helped overcome its traditional image. But Alfonsín also had to placate and incorporate the party's vanguard to establish a continuity with the past, calm society, and control the party's internal apparatus.

With regard to retroactive justice, the Radical Party, under Alfonsín's leadership, believed that full investigation and some degree of punishment were crucial steps in overcoming the dynamics that had long plagued and divided Argentine society — concentration, anomie, corporatism, and ideological dualism (see Chapter 2). Alfonsín's vision, therefore, was moved by forward-looking considerations. But these considerations were, of course, two-sided: Even though Alfonsín believed that punishment of the worst abuses were essential for the long-term consolidation of democracy, he was also fully aware that a miscalculation could jeopardize democracy. Alfonsín understood that massive violations of human rights are possible only outside a democratic system, as illustrated by the considerable differences between the abuses committed during Isabel Perón's government and those committed after the coup. Therefore, if he threatened democracy through trials and weighty sentences to discourage human rights violations, he might in fact be risking future violations.

In trying to chart this delicate course, President Alfonsín confronted difficulties within his party. Traditional Radical Party members, some of whom occupied important governmental positions, were more inclined to be forgiving of the military and pressed for some type of amnesty. But some of the newer members, many of whom held influential positions in Congress and in the universities, advocated a more aggressive stance.

The opposition parties were also a source of difficulty. In public, the Peronists took an intransigent stand in favor of retroactive justice, but they pressed for concessions in private. They virtually controlled the Senate, held a formidable minority in the House of Deputies, controlled political power in the provinces, and forged strong relationships with trade unions and with many promilitary groups. After the UCEDE's support for nullification of the self-amnesty law, this party reverted to justifying the "dirty war" and undermining the legitimacy of the trials.

What were the correlative fears, aspirations, and threats of the political parties? Of course, everyone feared the loss of political power. The government feared that if it was seen as too lenient with the military, that would impair its social ascendancy and ultimately its electoral chances. Indeed, that is what happened in 1987. Opposition parties, on the other hand, feared that if the government was too successful in its quest for retroactive justice, the Radical Party would be unbeatable.

The parties were united, however, in the fear that if they gave too many concessions to the military, it would be impossible to consolidate democracy, finding themselves in situations similar to those of Frondizi and Illia, where the government was subjected to suffered permanent demands from the military. All the political parties also feared loss of prestige on the part of Argentina, mainly in the international sphere. A very real fear that all parties shared was a resurgence in military coercion. Although a direct coup was most improbable, there was a risk of what must be considered indirect coups. Once violence escalated, society might demand an authoritarian government to restore order. Alternatively, resistance to judicial orders might produce a power vacuum and the consequent diminution of the government's legitimacy; people might believe that only a coalition that included the military could fill such a vacuum.

The aspirations of the political parties, primarily those of the Radical Party, were quite clear. The government should expose human rights abuses and should punish those in control of the repressive apparatus, perpetrators should recognize the destructiveness of their acts, the public should join to foreclose similar episodes in the future, the human rights groups should moderate their claims and also condemn subversive terrorism. All of this should be accomplished within the confines of the democratic process. The government and other political parties could use legislative power to achieve such aspirations. While mobilizing social groups remained an option, the government was fully aware that this remedy entailed substantial risks of violence.

In addition to the military and the political parties, human rights organizations played a key role in the transition and might be seen as the third collective agent influencing the course of retroactive justice. They emerged from the military dictatorship with enormous, well-earned prestige for their courageous opposition to repression. This gave them considerable influence, which they used through their connections with members of the various parties. But perhaps the greatest source of their power was their international ascendancy, because the government's own prestige depended on Alfonsín's positive international image as a human rights crusader and as somebody who would once and for all overcome the traditional Argentine penchant toward authoritarianism.

The human rights groups' stance toward retroactive justice was intransigently retributive. They sought to punish each and every person responsible for the abuses, regardless of their degree of involvement. They held a Kantian view of punishment; even if society were at the verge of dissolution, it had the duty to punish the last offender. Peculiarly, the human rights organizations would not admit that those who disappeared had in fact died. The founding faction of the Madres de Plaza de Mayo took this position to an extreme, even trying physically to impede judicial proceedings which would order the opening of mass graves. Similarly, human rights groups opposed civil compensation because it would implicitly acknowledge the finality of the disappearances. Indeed, human rights groups pressed for the codification of a new crime — making people disappear — to avoid prosecuting perpetrators for murder. There were important differences among the various human rights groups, though the most radical ones had a leading edge. None were happy when left-wing guerrilla movements began to reappear.

The human rights organizations maintained a critical counterweight to the government's action on retroactive justice, pressing for a bicameral commission and for civil jurisdiction and refusing officially to join CONADEP. These groups practically broke relations with the government after its attempt to circumscribe the trials. In fact, some of these groups made a serious attempt to expel Alfonsín from the Asamblea de los Derechos Humanos, over which he had copresided during the military regime. The influence of these organizations on public opinion faded with time, but in the early stages they were powerful.

The worst fear of these human rights groups was, of course, that the government would grant complete impunity to those responsible for state terrorism and that the structural forces that made such human rights abuses possible would remain uncorrected and, therefore, capable of regenerating abuses in the future. As such, they aspired to penalize all who were remotely responsible for the deeds and to remove them from any position of power. The most radical of the human rights organizations hoped for structural changes in society and in its armed forces. To achieve these ends, the human rights organizations threatened to agitate public opinion, both domestic and international, as well as to exert pressure on both legislators and judges.

To meet the demands for retroactive justice without jeopardizing the long-term viability of Argentina's fledgling democracy, President Alfonsín developed a strategy founded on the following objectives:

1. unrestrained search for truth;
2. symmetrical justice for terrorism, whether from the left or from the military government;
3. limited retroactive justice for those involved in state terrorism both by (a) delimiting categories of responsibility and (b) circumscribing the duration of the trials;
4. recognition by the leaders of the military regime that state terrorism is wrong.

The implementation of this strategy was extremely difficult because formidable legal obstacles emerged from the government's status as restaurateur of the old Constitution of 1853, with its limits on ex post facto laws and due process guarantees, and because of the conflicting pressures generated by threats from the military and the demands of the human rights organizations. Given these legal and political obstacles, Alfonsín attempted to achieve his objectives by the following means:

1. forward-looking legislative protection of human rights;
2. a presidential commission, CONADEP, to investigate past abuses;
3. trials, with a summary procedure and under the initial jurisdiction of military courts;
4. executive decrees ordering the prosecution of those most responsible for terrorism;
5. a norm of due obedience that would cover most acts except those committed by officers with decision-making capacity and others which were so abhorrent that a judge could say that the officer knew or should have known that the order was illegitimate;
6. rapid intervention on appeal by the civilian courts.

The events that ensued in Alfonsín's effort to achieve retroactive justice could be seen as a clash between ends and means. For example, the precariousness of democracy forced Alfonsín to give the military courts primary jurisdiction over the trials, as well as to approve a relatively broad interpretation of the due obedience laws. Yet these two tactical policies thwarted achievement of one primary goal — obtaining recognition on the part of the military of the evils of state terrorism. His inability to pursue all the tactical means also jeopardized his goals, specifically, his desire to limit the trials in terms of both duration and categories of responsibility, though the 1987 due obedience law more nearly accorded with his intentions.

With hindsight, one might conclude that it would have been better if Congress had enacted the project that Alfonsín asked his advisors to draft in 1984. It forced the Supreme Council to act within three to six months; defined "decision-making capacity," as mentioned in Law 23,049, on the basis of military rank and responsibility; precisely defined "abhorrent and atrocious acts," rejecting the presumption of mistake about the legitimacy of orders commanding such acts; and permitted members of the military to await trial outside of preventive detention as long as superiors took responsibility for their appearance. The approach embodied in this draft probably would not have had the boomerang effects of the instructions and the full-stop law, and would have made the due obedience law unnecessary, since it would have achieved the same effect in a much cleaner way. It might have isolated the people involved in the most atrocious acts and thus curtailed the prosecutions.

Events beyond the government's control thwarted Alfonsín's basic strategy, however: The Senate initially decided to include, as an explicit exception to the due obedience law, abhorrent and atrocious acts, which could conceivably cover every act of repression. The Supreme Council refused to go forward with the trials, and many judges, especially in the interior of the country, were reluctant to take up these cases. Of course, after the original strategy failed, the government substituted new alternatives, but even these were thwarted. The Federal Court of Buenos Aires reacted against the instructions given to prosecutors. The Supreme Court refused to define sharply due obedience. Following enactment of the full stop law, judges, especially in the interior, almost frenetically took up the task of indictment.

What is interesting about the events that thwarted Alfonsín's strategy is that they were performed by agents whose autonomy is essential for democracy and the rule of law — Congress and the courts, both military and civilian. Therefore, these events poignantly illustrate the depth to which Alfonsín's government consolidated democracy, and the concomitant costs involved in that consolidation. The human rights groups also heavily influenced Congress and the courts. In the case of Congress, human rights groups pressed for modifications of the executive's 1984 draft concerning due obedience. While human rights groups did not directly influence the Federal Court of Buenos Aires' rejection of the instructions to the prosecutor and the Supreme Court's decision not to circumscribe the scope of due obedience, it is clear that these groups resisted limiting responsibility and their demands may have had an effect. Indeed, they were directly responsible for the interior courts' alacrity following the full-stop law. On the other side, the military insisted that the Supreme Council not go forward with the trials (whether or not its members received the famous white feathers) and, according to rumors, made the interior courts, mainly that of Córdoba, reluctant to take over the trials dropped by the military court.

If, fantastically, both the military and human rights groups had accepted Alfonsín's basic strategy, the government might have succeeded. Even with the military's and human rights organizations' fundamental disagreement over the government's strategy, one wonders whether there was an equilibrium that was Pareto-superior for all the groups involved and whether the government's position, if permitted to succeed, was indeed that Pareto-optimal solution. The human rights groups would have secured the unprecedented investigation of CONADEP and the punishment of those who bore primary responsibility for state terrorism and torture without the military uprisings and Menem's pardons. The military would have avoided the internal confrontations among ranks and loss of social prestige and, instead, would have achieved some degree of recognition. The democratic parties and the administration would have achieved their long-term objective of reinvigorating the rule of law.

A number of obstacles prevented achievement of that equilibrium. One was the distrust of the goals of Alfonsín's government. The military thought the government intended to launch hundreds of trials and weaken the armed forces. The human rights groups, on the other hand, believed the government was moving toward some sort of amnesty. It was difficult to secure government assurances on either front because there was no external means of implementing those assurances. It would have been necessary to negotiate with legislators and judges, yet such negotiation was difficult given traditional Argentine distrust of political negotiations, often seen as dirty and spurious. Skepticism toward political negotiation was fueled by the dynamics of the presidential system coupled with disciplined parties. Peronists, for example, would not have agreed to a strategy which, if successful, would have added credibility to the incumbent government and, if unsuccessful, would also have tainted the opposition. Judicial independence, while a legitimate concern, also might have interfered with negotiations but perhaps should not have precluded negotiation altogether. Perhaps the same result could have been reached through control of prosecutorial discretion.

Furthermore, the demands of the military and the human rights groups, instead of counteracting each other, worked somewhat synergistically to debilitate the government's strategy. Notwithstanding their antagonism, the military and the human rights groups shared the same retributive view of punishment (with the obvious difference that the military thought they were not to be blamed for the "dirty war," while the human rights groups thought quite the opposite), whereas the government endorsed a preventionist view of punishment. The military and human rights organizations also converged on many tactical courses of action. For instance, both believed that every act performed during the repression could be deemed atrocious or abhorrent; the human rights groups believed that justified widespread prosecution, while the military saw it as a basis for an amnesty. Both the human rights groups and the military preferred intervention of civil courts over military courts, the former because they distrusted the military courts and the latter because they preferred that the military courts not condemn the methodology of the "dirty war."

A similar convergence occurred when the human rights groups criticized the government and helped formulate national and international opinion that tarnished the government's social and international standing. The military welcomed this since it ultimately undermined the government's credibility. Military intelligence therefore helped human rights groups spread rumors that Alfonsín had negotiated with Rico on Easter Sunday. Also, the attempt of the human rights organizations to influence courts and legislators served the interest of the military, for it constrained or limited the administration's agility.[3]

Once it became obvious that an equilibrium would not be achieved, a prisoner's-dilemma-type scenario ensued among the government, military, and human rights groups, and of course it worked to the detriment of all. Each group escalated its demands to neutralize the radical demands of other groups and to compel the government to meet its stated aspirations. In the end, the objective of self-recognition of culpability remained unfulfilled. But the due obedience law, combined with the full stop law, replaced, in a coarse way, Alfonsín's original strategy. The due obedience law satisfied the government's main goal of identifying those deeply involved in the repression and thus limiting the trials for state terrorism, but it had its problems, both practical and moral. It excused atrocious crimes. To some extent, this problem was lessened by the fact that the law covered only past acts and would not be applied prospectively, but the blow to the administration's credibility and to the human rights cause was great.[4]

By the end of the Alfonsín administration, the government had produced the CONADEP investigation and the *Nunca Más* report, the "big trial" which attracted enormous national and international attention, convictions for fifteen persons responsible for state terrorism and trials of forty more, including members of the right and the left. The government had therefore satisfied most of its general strategic objectives, although through different tactical means from those envisaged at its inception.

This qualified success in the domain of retroactive justice, in part based on innovation and luck, did not necessarily satisfy the more future-oriented needs to consolidate democracy and prevent human rights abuses in the future. In order to achieve these ends, collective consciousness must (1) understand the risks of authoritarianism, (2) reject the use of means to achieve beneficial ends if those means are, in and of themselves, detrimental to intrinsic values, and (3) perceive that those who employ such detrimental methods are not above the law but risk punishment. While Argentine popular consciousness seems to have satisfied the first two requirements, thanks to the impact of the Malvinas War, CONADEP, and the "big trial," the same cannot be said of the third. I think that the clumsiness in the communicative capacity of Alfonsín's government and the harsh criticism by various national and international groups succeeded in convincing people that the whole retroactive justice policy had failed after the full stop and due obedience laws and that impunity instead had won. People, therefore, did not realize how exceptional this attempt at retroactive justice was and what the population itself, through popular pressure, had achieved. Menem's pardons therefore went down easily, since most people thought that the whole project had already been spoiled by Alfonsín's due obedience law. But even those pardons, which, as I said in the previous chapter, were either politically unnecessary or unconstitutional, could not detract from the fact that, for the first time in Latin America, justice acted against state terrorism and the weight of the law was felt for some time by the most responsible people. This experience in retroactive justice created a social awareness of the risks of authoritarianism and and inclination to reject the very model of organic society that led to the violation of human rights in the first place. It minimized the possibility that a social consensus will ever come to favor military intervention in the future.

In fact, a disincentive may have been created for future military revolts. As Carlos Acuña and Catalina Smulovitz state, "In this way and as a result of the crisis that the armed forces began to suffer from their own government as well as from the political and legal components of the political struggle associated with human rights, it is possible to foresee that, in the long term, the military actor will be left without the capacity to question constitutional power and finally will be subordinated to it."[5] This conclusion must be juxtaposed against Samuel Huntington's extremely negative evaluation: "In contrast to Greece, the efforts to prosecute and punish in Argentina served neither justice nor democracy and instead produced a moral and political shambles."[6] The relationship between retroactive justice and democracy, which Huntington so acerbically highlighted in this quote, will be the focus of the remainder of this chapter.

The Explanatory Variables

Human rights abuses have rarely been redressed during transitions to democracy, and, when they have been, such attempts have generally been quite modest in comparison to the magnitude of the abuses. In the context of the experiences discussed in Chapter 1, however, the Argentine attempt to investigate and punish massive abuses of human rights appears rather weak compared to those carried out after World War II, especially in Germany, Japan, Italy, France, and Belgium. Although justice in these countries was grotesquely disproportionate to the magnitude of the crimes, hundreds, even thousands were punished as a result of their involvement in massive human rights abuses. This stands in stark contrast to the Argentine experience, with a mere fifteen people ultimately punished for state terrorism. On the other hand, compared to Europe after World War I, southern Europe during the 1970s, Latin America during the 1980s, and Eastern Europe in the 1990s — and compared to the United States after the Vietnam War, and Asia and Africa after the fall of their dictatorial regimes — the Argentine attempt at retroactive justice appears quite imposing, even intrepid. The Greek attempt at retroactive justice, so celebrated by Huntington, is perhaps most similar to the Argentine, with the notable difference that Greece convicted more perpetrators and subsequent Greek governments did not issue pardons.

What explains all these differences? One key variable might be the type of transition in which the government was involved. At the beginning of this chapter, I described the Argentine transition as prompted by a collapse of the military government. In this sense, it was similar to the Greek transition, in which the military regime collapsed and democratic forces filled the vacuum. The Portuguese transition was a mixture of collapse and force, in which the troubles in Africa, coupled with domestic hardships, led to a sharp deterioration in the regime. The downfall of the Marcos regime in the Philippines was largely prompted by collapse, as were the Eastern European transitions between 1989 and 1991.

When the transition is more coercive, a new balance of power contributes positively to the prospects of retroactive justice. The force required to displace the authoritarian regime may also be useful in bringing its agents to task for human rights abuses, depending, of course, on whether the new government holds a monopoly on the country's coercive apparatus. The cohesiveness of the groups which support retroactive justice, as compared with those which resist it, will also determine its effectiveness. In the cases of Germany, Japan, France, Italy, and Belgium, the force effecting the democratic transition was overwhelming, although there were differences among countries depending on whether indigenous groups participated in the transition.

When the democratization instead is effected through negotiations aimed at building consensus, effective retroactive justice is less likely to ensue. Of course, there may be negotiations that do not encompass retroactive justice. But this is seldom the case, since the stakes are too high to avoid being left out of the bargain between members of the old and new regimes. Naturally enough, during the Spanish transition, the government of Adolfo Suarez obtained concessions from those opposed to the old regime by bargaining over issues of retroactive justice. One of the most important concessions gained was an amnesty for individuals tried for political crimes and sometimes convicted under Francoist legislation.[7] In the case of Uruguay, the amnesty question was not explicitly included in the Naval Club pact between the military and their civilian successors,[8] but there were rumors of negotiations to that effect. The retention of Gen. Hugo Medina as head of the army served as an implicit pact that eventually led to the amnesty law enacted by President Sanguinetti. In Chile, all the agreements that guided the transition process, including plebiscites and reforms to Pinochet's constitution, rested on an implied assumption: The amnesty law enacted by the military would be respected.

When the transition to democracy is prompted by the collapse of the previous regime, retroactive justice is more difficult than when the transition is effected by force but easier than when effected through consensus. In Argentina, the transition was much less coercive than the European transitions after World War II, thus explaining the relative difficulty and modesty of retroactive justice. Alfonsín's access to coercive power was even scarcer than that of Karamanlis in Greece, since, despite the fact that the events of August 11, 1974, appeared similar to the events of Easter Week in 1987, Karamanlis enjoyed the support of some of the army not involved in the colonels' human rights abuses. In the Philippines, the domestic coercive power available to Corazon Aquino to carry out retroactive justice was close to nil, since it depended mostly on the good will of Gens. Fidel Ramos and Juan Enrile, who were themselves responsible for some human rights violations. She did, however, enjoy some direct coercive support from the United States military forces based near Manila, made visible by a show of force during the seventh attempted coup.

Coercion is not necessarily a decisive factor in the retroactive justice equation. In Argentina and Greece, retroactive justice progressed quite far despite the fact that coercive power remained in the hands of the military, many of whom were strongly associated with the previous regime. In Germany and Japan, attempts at retroactive justice were more restrained than in Italy, France, or Belgium, even though the Allies harnessed more of their coercive power to effect the democratization. While the modality of the transition has some predictive value concerning retroactive justice, it is far from decisive in explaining its course, as illustrated by the modesty of retroactive justice in Eastern Europe, paradigmatic of collapse, and the boldness of retroactive justice in Greece. Therefore, it is important to examine other features of the transition process.

As we saw, democratization processes may also be classified according to their legal status — whether continuous, rupturous, or restorative. This variable appears relevant to the success of retroactive justice. When the new democratic regime is legally continuous with the old authoritarian one and the human rights violations to be tried were legally protected at the time of their commission or afterwards (say, by an amnesty law), the principles against ex post facto reversal of that legal protection create formidable obstacles to retroactive justice. This occurred in Eastern Europe, Spain, and Chile. This obstacle is not entirely unsurmountable, however. In the case of Chile, for instance, the Commission of Truth and Reconciliation investigated the patterns of human rights abuses, and its findings greatly influenced public opinion. Moreover, in Chile some believed that the amnesty law did not preclude judicial investigation of the human rights violations. Also, resort to other means of retroactive justice, such as civil compensation, remains a real possibility. Nevertheless, legal continuity makes retroactive justice an uphill battle.

When there is complete legal breakdown or rupture, as in postwar Germany and Japan, the path of retroactive justice is the smoothest. From the legal vantage point, there can be criminalization of deeds that were lawful under the former legal system; norms against ex post facto changes in criminal definitions, procedures, and statutes of limitations are not applicable. Amnesty laws of the previous regime can simply be ignored.

When the transition to democracy involves a process of legal restoration, as happened in Austria, Greece, Uruguay, and Argentina, retroactive justice acquires an intermediate degree of difficulty. While legal constraints erected by the previous authoritarian legal system may be overcome, new constraints may arise from the restoration of the earlier, democratic constitution. In Argentina, for example, article 18 of the Constitution of 1853, prohibiting ex post facto criminal legislation, combined with article 2 of the Penal Code, which establishes that the defendant receive the benefit of the law most favorable to his cause, made the validity of the self-amnesty law difficult to challenge. Alfonsín's response was to question the legitimacy of the military regime and, by implication, the laws emanating therefrom. In other words, Alfonsín highlighted that his new democratic system was discontinuous with the military regime and thereby avoided a major legal obstacle to his retroactive justice program — the self-amnesty law. Yet the prohibition against ex post facto criminal legislation still applied to laws enacted during previous democratic periods and thus precluded changes in law enacted during those periods, such as those establishing the jurisdiction of the military courts and the defense of due obedience.

Once again, legal status only partially explains the success or failure of retroactive justice. In some processes of legal restoration, retroactive justice progressed quite far, as in Austria and, to a lesser extent, Greece, while in others, such as Uruguay, retroactive justice was quite truncated. On the other hand, some countries that inaugurated new legal regimes, such as Cambodia and the Philippines, did not progress too far with retroactive justice, while Chile, the prototypical case of legal continuity, made important headway in its quest. Therefore, we must turn our attention to the very human rights violations that are the subject of retroactive justice and see how they might explain the differences in the experiences of various countries.

The more heinous the human rights abuses, the more likely that the attempt to punish them will succeed. The crimes committed by the Nazis occupy the first rank in the horror list of atrocities, and logically they correspond with the most extensive attempt at retroactive justice undertaken so far, even though this attempt has generated disappointment due to the disproportion between crimes and the punishment that resulted. The case of Greece, as compared to Portugal, also demonstrates the correlation between human rights abuses and retroactive justice, since some of the atrocities committed by the colonels had no parallel under Oliveira Salazar's regime. In Latin America, while the Argentine experience with kidnapping, clandestine detention, torture, and executions had parallels in Uruguay and Chile, the horror of the violations in Argentina was much greater. According to David Pion-Berlin, most of the clandestine detentions in Argentina, as opposed to Uruguay, resulted in the death of the prisoner.[9]

These correlations between atrocity of the deeds and effectiveness of retroactive justice, however, fail if we take into account that the Soviet Union probably approximates most closely the Nazi regime, and no serious punishment has yet been attempted or even contemplated. The Spanish Civil War and the first years of the Franco regime were quite savage; the human rights violations in Cambodia are almost without comparison; and the differences among the seriousness of abuses in Chile, Uruguay, and Brazil were not so clear as to explain their different experiences with retroactive justice.

The obvious factor that needs consideration is quantity. Should we take into account numbers, in both absolute and relative terms? If so, the Soviet massacre of dissidents is startling but pales in comparison to the Nazi atrocities. The human rights violations in Argentina were quantitatively more extensive than in Uruguay and Chile. On a per capita basis, however, Uruguay has the highest number of violations, Chile is second, and Argentina is third, which, of course, is negatively correlated to their attempts at retroactive justice. However, the case of Brazil, as we saw in Chapter 1, supports the correlation since human rights abuses were far more sparse than in their Southern Cone neighbors, a fact that perhaps explains Brazil's passivity toward retroactive justice.

The time period from when the human rights violations occur to when retroactive justice is attempted also helps explain its relative success. The more time that passes, the more difficult it will be for retroactive justice to succeed. The clearest example is Spain; the worst abuses were committed three or four decades before they could be tried. Similarly, in the Soviet Union, the worst atrocities of Stalin's regime were committed more than forty years prior to the collapse of the Soviet system. In most post-communist countries in Eastern Europe, with the exception of Romania, the worst atrocities — the Slansky trials in Czechoslovakia in 1952, the Soviet repression of the Berlin uprising in 1953, the Soviet invasion of Hungary in 1956, and the repression of the Prague Spring in 1968 — occurred many years before the collapse of the communist regimes. In all of these examples, retroactive justice was quite limited in scope and effectiveness.

In the Southern Cone of Latin America, there is also a clear correlation between the lapse of time and the success of that retroactive justice. In Chile, the worst abuses occurred between 1973 and 1976, and democratization occurred in 1989; more than thirteen years would have passed before investigation and the proposed trials took place. In Brazil the greatest terror occurred between 1969 and 1974; the democratization took place in 1989 with the direct election of Collor de Mello. In Uruguay, most of the abuses occurred before 1973, and democratization was completed nine years later. But in Argentina, the military carried out serious abuses until 1979, and democratization took place only four years later. The relative success of retroactive justice in Argentina, as opposed to Chile, Brazil, and Uruguay, may be partially explained in terms of the time lapse. However, this correlation is far from absolute. For example, Chile's attempt at retroactive justice would seem more improbable than Uruguay's, even though more time would have passed between Chile's worst abuses and the democratization process. Yet the facts indicate otherwise.

The relevance of time and the correlation between tardiness of retroactive justice and its success come from a variety of factors, including survival of perpetrators, preservation of evidence, and strength of retributive feelings among the public. In Spain and the Soviet Union, and, to a large degree, Eastern Europe, limited survival of perpetrators and preservation of evidence could explain the relatively unenthusiastic approach toward retroactive justice. But in Brazil, Chile, Uruguay, and Argentina, the death of perpetrators or disappearance of evidence was not an issue. Not enough time has passed. Therefore, only through its effect on the retributive feelings of the victims and the general public would the time factor be linked to retroactive justice in those cases.

Retributive feelings among society at large may differ from those of the victims. The victims, in fact, are often unconnected from the society conducting the trials in terms of space, time, nationality, race, and religion. When this is so, as it is most pronouncedly when the violations occur in the course of colonial or semicolonial wars, little effort will be made at retroactive justice. This obviously happened in the Vietnam War: The retributive feelings of the American people were relatively low due to the distance of the Vietnamese people, their race, and their "alien" customs.[10] Even when the victims and victimizers share the same national identity, retributive feelings may be low if social identification with the victims is weak. Here the example is post-Nazi Germany, when attempts to punish genocide against Jews and other minorities were relatively unsuccessful given the magnitude of the crimes. In fact, when speaking with some Germans in 1982 about the atrocities committed by the Argentine military, some told me that the Argentine atrocities were worse than those in Nazi Germany because the Argentines committed crimes against their own nationals! In South American countries, also, many people contained their retributive feelings toward the perpetrators by distinguishing themselves from the other—they described the victims as left-wingers or terrorists. I imagine that a similar phenomenon is occurring in Eastern Europe to repress retributive feelings. Most likely, people perceive the victims of the worst repression as belonging to the most radical sectors.

Retributive feelings also depend on whether society identifies with the perpetrators. Perhaps the case of Austria suggests that this correlation is not perfect, since retroactive justice there was applied in rather broad strokes, making it difficult to circumscribe the group of perpetrators. But, speaking more generally, when those who violate human rights are viewed as an isolated group, especially when it is an alien one, retributive feelings tend to be high. This probably explains the differences between the relative success of retroactive justice in countries like Japan and Germany, on the one hand, and Italy, France, and Belgium, on the other. In Germany and Japan, the criminals could not be distinguished from the rest of society. Even though Italy had a domestic dictatorship, the worst abuses were attributed to the Nazis and a small, fairly well identified circle of collaborators. French and Belgian offenders similarly could be circumscribed and separated from the rest of society. Obviously, in the criminal trial in Israel against Eichmann, retributive feelings ran high because of the close association to the victims and the absolute dissociation from the perpetrators. In South America, the disassociation between society and perpetrators was facilitated by concentrating blame on uniformed men, which they sometimes rightly resented.

The more readily society propagates a justificatory story for the atrocities, the more identified society will be with the perpetrators, and retroactive justice will be correspondingly difficult to carry out. Of course, many German citizens during the Nazi regime justified genocide by arguing that the Jews jeopardized German values and interests. In the case of Argentina, important sectors of the population thought that repression was legitimate in the face of the very real danger of subversive terrorism. This sort of identification with the perpetrators was much more attenuated in the case of Greece, and it is one of the most important factors explaining the much smoother course of retroactive justice there.

The degree to which responsibility is widely distributed through society also affects the success of retroactive justice. Václav Havel, in his opposition to trials in Czechoslovakia, argued that the diffusion of responsibility through society created important moral and legal dilemmas for human rights trials.[11] It is also a factor of political relevance. In general, the more diffused the responsibility, the less retributive society at large will be, since more sectors of society will have been involved in the atrocities by action or omission, by complicity or concealment. Therefore, identification with offenders is stronger. In Nazi Germany, Soviet Russia, and in most of Eastern Europe, responsibility was very diffuse, contributing to the limited nature of retroactive justice in those countries. In the South American cases, responsibility was shared by the press, the church, economic groups, and professional and cultural associations, as well as the military. With rather diffuse responsibility, it is no wonder that some South American countries had great difficulty with retroactive justice, as opposed to, say, Greece, where the colonels isolated themselves from economic groups, conservative parties, and the monarchy. During the Argentine trials, in fact, defense attorneys tried to expand responsibility for the crimes throughout society, while the human rights groups tried to concentrate blame on the military.

The success of retroactive justice also seems to depend on the very manner in which the trials are conducted. Above, I discussed the relevance of the time that lapses between the atrocities and the commencement of retroactive justice. But the duration of the investigation and trials is also important. Long proceedings tend to undermine the success of the trials, since public support, so vital for the success of the enterprise, may fade with the passing of time, as happened in Argentina after 1986. Publicity is important for promoting social enthusiasm, but too much publicity may incite reactions among the affected sectors. In Argentina, Alfonsín's government was quite conscious of this problem and for that reason allowed films of the trials to be shown on newsreels but without sound. The government was very reluctant to permit CONADEP to develop a television program and ultimately agreed to do so only on condition that the minister of the interior give the opening speech.

The impartiality of the trial court and its procedure is not only a prerequisite for justice but also adds credibility to any attempt at retroactive justice. From the beginning, therefore, the Argentine government intended to prosecute both the military and the left-wing terrorists. Likewise, the Commission of Truth and Reconciliation in Chile was charged with investigating not only state terrorism but also subversive terrorism. The availability of evidence also contributes to the relative success of retroactive justice, as illustrated by the Eastern European controversies with the secret police files. The Argentine trials also underscore how important it is that responsibility be clearly circumscribed. Unnecessary expansion of responsibility, and concomitant expansion of the eligible defendant base, make the trials quite unwieldy. All in all, the trials must be "sharp" to accomplish their goals.

The personal variable — the decision of certain leaders to proceed with retroactive justice in light of strategic considerations and moral evaluations — is also highly probative. When comparing Argentina, Chile, and Uruguay, Pion-Berlin noted that it is difficult to explain completely the differences without taking into account the personal differences among Alfonsín, Aylwin, and Sanguinetti (I would include Sarney and Menem on this list). I believe that there were crucial moments in the Argentine case when, if President Alfonsín had decided to stop the retroactive justice process shortly after the "big trial," he could have done so with relatively few real obstacles. The leadership of Karamanlis seems also to have been decisive in the Greek successes in retroactive justice.

As part of the leadership factor, some account must be taken of the cohesion among the democratic actors, especially the political parties, on the issue of retroactive justice. In Argentina, cohesion among the various democratic players was less than in Greece, for instance. Right-wing parties opposed the investigation and trials, supporting only the invalidation of the amnesty law. The Peronist Party supported many of the crucial laws and generally followed President Alfonsín's lead when democracy seemed most at risk. But the Peronists did not support CONADEP; nor did they support the laws which limited responsibility, although they lent indirect support by providing the necessary quorum.

The comparison between Greece and Argentina is one of richest sources for extracting conclusions about the political dimensions of retroactive justice. As

Huntington states, "The conditions that confronted the Alfonsín and Karamanlis governments were quite similar. The results the two governments achieved were very different. . . . How can the difference in the Argentine and Greek outcomes be explained?"[12] I disagree with Huntington's unequivocally negative evaluation of the Argentine experience. Yet the fact remains that the Greek process was smoother than the Argentine, and thus his question must be addressed. The answer, which is not strikingly different from Huntington's, lies in the factors I have just isolated. Although Greece did not suffer nearly the number of human rights violations as Argentina — which, contrary to fact, should have made Argentina's attempt easier — all the other factors mentioned in this chapter favored the Greek attempt: the balance of power was different in Greece since, as Huntington remarks, some senior officers were supportive of the trials against the colonels, while in Argentina almost no active military person supported trials there;[13] the armed forces in Greece were weakened by their simultaneous engagement in the Cyprus conflict (if that engagement had been successful, this would have had an opposite effect); society's identification with victims was greater in Greece because many Argentines still distinguished the victims as left-wingers and even terrorists; the identification of society with the perpetrator was greater in Argentina, since the threat of subversive terrorism had been quite serious, leading several powerful sectors to justify the military's actions; the diffusion of responsibility in Argentine society was greater because, once cooperation and concealment are included, many people were implicated in the military's conduct; political cohesion among the democratic forces, even among those rather politically distant from the military, was much weaker in Argentina; the judicial system in Greece apparently sharpened the trials as compared with those in Argentina; and the time lag between the deeds and the commencement of the trials, as Huntington remarks, was much longer in Argentina than in Greece.

The following list of the main positive and negative factors affecting retroactive justice is offered more as a summary than as a precise and predictive formula:

POSITIVE FACTORS

- coercive nature of the process of transition (Cr)
- legal discontinuities (Ld)
- heinousness of the abuses (H)
- absolute and relative quantity of the abuses (Q)
- social identification with the victims of the abuses (Iv)
- sharpness of the trials (Sh)
- leadership (L)

NEGATIVE FACTORS

- consensual nature of the transition (Cn)
- time span between deeds and trials (T)
- social identification with perpetrators of abuses (Ia)
- diffusion of responsibility (D)
- cohesion of the perpetrators (Cp)

Thus, the following formula approximates the probability of retroactive justice successfully progressing during a democratization process:

$$\text{Prob. (RJ)} = \frac{p\,(Cr, Ld, H, Q, Iv, Sh, L)}{n\,(Cn, T, Ia, D, Cp)}$$

where p is a function of the positive factors, n a function of the negative factors, and it is assumed that p takes on values between 0 and 1, while n takes on values greater than or equal to 1.

Should Democrats Punish or Pardon?

What, if any, general lessons can be gleaned about the strategic advisability of human rights trials in periods of democratic consolidation? Will these trials hurt democracy or help it? Initially, it may seem that the most general lesson is that there is no general lesson. Much depends on the specific nature of the transition. But the Argentine case study, set against the context of similar experiences with retroactive justice in other countries, suggests that we may be able to draw additional generalizations.

Samuel Huntington lists four arguments in favor of prosecutions:

1. Democracy is based on law, and no group, including public officials and members of the armed forces, should be above the law.
2. Trials underscore the viability of the democratic system, for if the military is powerful enough to preclude trials, democracy will be too fledgling and weak to survive.
3. Trials are necessary to assert the supremacy of democratic values and to garner society's support for them.
4. As a means to uncovering the truth, trials necessarily fortify accountability and ensure that state agents bear a strong sense of individual responsibility.

Huntington then offers two arguments in opposition to human rights trials:

1. Democracy is based on reconciliation and leaving past divisions behind.
2. Amnesties create solid bases for democracy, in that they neutralize incentives for powerful groups like the military to interrupt the democratic process as a way of freeing themselves from criminal prosecution.

Huntington believes that experiments with retroactive justice have been "shaped, almost exclusively, by politics, by the nature of the democratization process and by the distribution of political power during and after the transition."[14] I disagree with this conclusion, since many of the factors that effect retroactive justice have a strong moral component, such as identification with victims and offenders and diffusion of responsibility, and a legal component that must of course be taken into account when crafting strategies. Nevertheless, the strategic arguments set forth by Huntington for and against prosecutions are important and deserve to be weighed against one another.

Huntington's own conclusions, after reviewing different experiences, including Argentina's, is that when the democratic transition is accomplished through transformation of the previous regime, prosecutions should be avoided, since the political costs far outweigh the moral gains. When democratization occurs by replacing the old regime, trials for the *leaders* of past authoritarian regimes may be effective if the population considers them morally and politically desirable and if they are commenced and completed within one year. Huntington alternatively recommends a public and dispassionate accounting of how and why the crimes were committed. In the end, the least problematic course of action may be described by the injunction "Do not prosecute, do not punish, do not forgive, and, above all, do not forget."[15]

A radical variant of Huntington's theses can be found in Bruce Ackerman's highly provocative book *The Future of Liberal Revolution.*[16] Ackerman warns against the "mirage of corrective justice," arguing that liberal revolutionaries forging a new democratic system usually possess high moral capital and low organizational capital. Becoming entangled in retroactive justice risks loss of the moral capital due to scarcity of the organizational capital. Ackerman believes that the moral and legal difficulties inherent in ascribing responsibility to both high- and low-level officials, the fear and resentment that retroactive justice would engender, and the creation of deep divisions among various sectors of society inevitably exacerbate the difficulties inherent in achieving retroactive justice. Ackerman uses the Argentine experience as the illustrative example, pointing to Alfonsín's having "only a handful" of convictions as evidence of failure. He believes that the debacle of Alfonsín's unsystematic retroactive justice program paved the way for Menem's subsequent condemnation of "the entire campaign." Ackerman concludes that Alfonsín instead should have used his moral capital to effect "the speedy discharge of the worst offenders in the officer corps and taken advantage of his early popular support to call for a new constitution that placed a stringent set of institutional limitations on the military in general and on arbitrary arrest and punishment in particular."[17] .

I think that Ackerman, like Huntington, is incorrect in his assessment of the

Argentine experience. Leaving aside the fact that more than "a handful" had been convicted when Alfonsín left office, I believe that the progress of the retroactive justice program coincided roughly with Alfonsín's original program. After the due obedience law, the controversy surrounding retroactive justice quieted and the judiciary dealt with its tasks in an orderly fashion until Menem's pardons. Nonetheless, the most troubling aspect of Ackerman's argument is not his mistaken description of what actually happened, but his counterfactual assumption: He fails to recognize that the whole legitimacy of Alfonsín's government, his moral capital, rested not on his charismatic or revolutionary appeal but on his strict compliance with the Constitution of 1853. If at the very beginning of his term Alfonsín had called for an early constitutional reform, major political, economic, and social groups in the establishment would have suspiciously interpreted such action as a highly self-serving maneuver to change the government political and economic rules. This would have been more risky politically than the trials. Moreover, I believe that the existing constitution protected liberal values and subordinated the military to civilians, in some senses even better than its American counterpart. Admittedly, its perversities led to hyperpresidentialism; these, and only these, aspects of the constitution required reform, but I believe that waiting for "quieter" times was crucial to the success of such reform.

Returning to Huntington, note that his strongest political argument against trials is that prosecutions may undermine or destroy the necessary basis for democracy. In the end, the validity of that assessment depends on the positive impact the investigation, trials, and punishment of past human rights abuses has on the interests of those sectors of society most crucial to the consolidation of democracy.

Retroactive justice, of course, negatively affects the interests of those who would be punished, and that may lead them to overthrow the democracy. But they risk a further punishment for rebellion, unless the coup is successful, which of course depends on how powerful the rebels are and whether they are able to win the support of other groups in society, such as the economic elite. On the other hand, the positive effects of the prosecutions on democracy look quite dim. Those victimized by human rights violations who may "benefit" from the punishment of the perpetrators are not likely to turn to an authoritarian system if their interest is not satisfied, since they would again risk being victimized once democracy breaks down. The most obvious positive effect of punishment is to discourage potential perpetrators from overthrowing democracy and instituting an authoritarian regime. Strictly speaking, however, the punishment is not for rebellion against democratic institutions but for human rights violations. Although the two are often intermingled in practice, they are not necessarily so. At best, trials for human rights violations have an indirect deterrent effect on future rebellions, though even that is far from clear. All one can say is that those facing the threat of trials may calculate that if they rebelled against democratic institutions and failed, they would be less likely to receive pardons and amnesties and more likely to suffer harsh penalties. But even this effect depends on their failing in their coup.

Therefore, if we take into account only political considerations, narrowly understood to mean self-interest, those opposed to trials clearly win, and there we would lack a strong reason to undertake retroactive justice during a transition process. Some who broaden the picture and take into account values and concerns about the legitimacy of the regime are of a similar mind. A notable example is Juan Linz:

> The new rulers [of transitional democratic regimes] also have a tendency, probably based on their feeling of moral superiority, to waste energy in what might be called *ressentiment* politics against persons and institutions identified with the old order. This would consist in petty attacks on their dignity and their sentiments. . . .
>
> Bitterness over symbolic changes and the emotional costs of *ressentiment* politics are not easily forgotten. . . . Faced with problems of equal dimensions, a regime with a high commitment to its legitimacy has a higher probability of survival than a regime without such commitment. Legitimation, therefore, becomes the primary task of democratic leadership. Establishing the initial agenda in the period of consolidation, the negative consequences of *ressentiment* politics or foreign policy liabilities, and the difficulties of incorporating potentially loyal forces not in the regime-building coalition are all clearly relevant to this problem. . . . Democracies build their legitimacy on the basis of loyalty to the state or the nation. In fact, certain sectors of society, particularly army officers, civil servants, and sometimes intellectual leaders, feel a stronger identification with the state or the nation than with a particular regime and reject in principle the partisan identification of the state. . . .
>
> One solution that can be successful is a purge of those unwilling to make a clear and public commitment to the new political order. . . . However, to do so in modern societies that recognize acquired rights, and in liberal democracies that guarantee freedom of opinion, is far from easy. It is likely to result in ambivalent and contradictory policies that, instead of achieving the desired result, arouse the indignation of those affected.[18]

Recalling Huntington and Ackerman, Linz argues that the value judgments of those subject to the purges, trials, or condemnations will be negatively affected by retroactive justice. When those human rights violations, as in the case of Argentina, are seen by many as justified given the real risk posed by subversive terrorism, the negative effects in people's valuation of what Linz labels *ressentiment* politics may be even greater. They may see the new regime as revengeful and perhaps even dominated by those very subversive elements. They may view the trials as political manipulations and hence illegitimate. They may regard the sentences as unjust, tainting the legitimacy of the new regime. This sense of injustice may stem from their belief that the human rights violations were a necessary and unavoidable means of establishing democracy. They may resent the fact that constitutional and legal strictures are not followed in the trials and may find this hypocritical given the proclaimed moral superiority of democracy. Moreover, if the trials are intended to demarcate a legal discontinuity with the previous order, they may alienate those sectors who were affiliated with the previous regime.

I believe that these negative effects on value judgments are quite real and require careful consideration. Yet account must also be taken of the fact that trials for human rights violations committed in the past are great occasions for social deliberation and for collective examination of the moral values underlying public institutions. There are few occasions of this sort in the life of a society. Contrary to Ackerman's assumption, the enactment of a new constitution does not always constitute such an occasion, especially in Latin America, since it is viewed by many people as either too technical or the result of politicians' rather corrupt self-interests. Instead, the drama of a trial, with the victims and perpetrators under the public light, with accusations and defenses, with witnesses from all social sectors, and with the terrifying prospect of punishment, inevitably attracts great public attention and may even provoke "dummy" trials in the streets or around dinner tables. In this sense, trials for human rights violations may be much closer to what Ackerman labels "constitutional moments" than many attempts at formal or informal constitutional reforms.[19] But why do we need such discussion, and what is its relationship to the consolidation of democracy?

As I stated in the last chapter, authoritarianism is the product of certain social trends that cannot be overcome merely because the interests of some powerful people happen to favor democratic resolution of conflicts. In Argentina, these underlying trends are an organic conception of society resulting in an unsolved dualism; corporatism, which allows groups such as the military and trade unions to enjoy special privileges and protections through control from the top down; anomie and unlawfulness, which means that certain groups are considered to be above all normative restraints and that certain ends are achieved through any means; and concentration of institutional, economic, and social power.

It is obvious how these trends undermine the democratic ideal in favor of authoritarianism and simultaneously undergird the massive human rights violations. An organic society may be compatible, to a certain extent, with a populist conception of democracy but not with a liberal one based on equality and the possibility of questioning traditions. Corporatism is a direct affront to democracy, although it may not be so under a pluralist conception, because political power is assigned by virtue of membership in a group rather than by political strength, and privileges are never challenged in the political system.[20] Anomie implies that many social issues are not, in the end, solved through democratic rule making but rather by the will of the strongest.[21] Concentration of power obviously implies the absence of the checks and balances, and thereby a paucity of democratic mechanisms.

These four endemic trends are also strongly related to massive human rights violations. The organic conception of society is a holistic one which sacrifices individuals for the collective nation or state when it is deemed in danger. Corporatism implies that certain groups have a special status and are not accountable to the rest of society for heinous acts, such as the sacrifice of human beings seen as enemies of the status quo. Corporatism, for example, justifies special jurisdictional rights and due obedience laws, since people of lower rank cannot take into account interests other than those of the leaders of the corporate entity in question. Anomie frees the privileged groups from accountability and legal constraints, removing moral limits to the use of means to further the ends of the holistic entity. Concentration of power is at its height when the possibility of investigating and judging various means, including human rights violations, is prevented.

Still, there is another quite direct and strong relationship between massive human violations and authoritarianism. When those who are convinced of the moral rightness of what they are doing—which was apparently the case in Argentina both among members of the state apparatus and among many left-wing terrorists—we have a situation that might be labeled *epistemic moral elitism*.[22] Those within selected groups believe that they can resolve deep moral questions affecting society and decide what is in the interest of all, including those who did not participate in such moral discussion. In the case of Argentina, and in most of the other situations discussed in Chapter 1, perpetrators of human rights violations convinced themselves in a quite secluded setting that they were acting justly. If one defends, as I do, an epistemic view of democracy, the fact that these decisions attain goals through massive violations of human rights, without full and open discussion among all the affected people, is almost a natural consequence of the moral blindness that was exhibited.

When massive human rights abuses are investigated and tried, provoking public deliberation, the social dynamics responsible for such violations become the object of public discussion and collective criticism. What is being discussed is the value of democracy itself. Democracy is thereby strengthened by both the content and the process of collective debate. In fact, this type of value-searching deliberation was evident in the debates surrounding the trials in Argentina. The accusations, the defenses, judicial decisions, and arguments taking place among the various sectors of society were precisely about the role of the military and other groups in a democratic society, the moral limits for the achievement of certain goals (the accusers of the military often pointed to the lawful manner in which terrorism was fought in European countries), the rule of law (the most common conciliatory argument was that the military could have achieved the same ends through summary trials and open death sentences under appropriate laws that sanctioned such actions), and the advantages of a division of power to protect human rights (it was often said that, even in the degraded democracy of Isabel Perón, there were fewer violations of human rights than under the military). Therefore, when authors like Acuña and Smulovitz argue that the military, as a corporation contesting political power, was weakened by the trials, public deliberation about the military's role — deliberation that is provoked and enriched by the trials — should be seen as an important mechanism responsible for such a weakening.

Of course, the educative effect of the trials may be felt among different sectors of society — by society at large, which discovered that it was turning a blind eye while the human rights abuses were occurring around them; by the groups that actively supported the perpetrators, who, through trials, were forced to admit the magnitude of the atrocities and to rehearse their possible justifications; and by those who precipitated the human rights violations. The result is a process of collective deliberation that is especially conducive to overcoming the tendency toward the type of moral elitism that endorses the undemocratic decision making that underlies such massive violations. Through the process of deliberation, these people may come to shed their previously held moral convictions and, at the same time, realize that elitist moral knowledge is highly unreliable. Admittedly, this deliberative process may be highly emotional, embittering many sectors and destroying civic friendship. This is the danger that Huntington and Linz emphasize and caution against. But there is also the possibility that deliberation, despite all the tensions and bitterness, will facilitate a convergence around certain basic values or create, in Ronald Dworkin's terms, "a community of principles," so vital for a democracy.[23]

If the factors weighing against retroactive justice, based primarily on self-interested dispositions, are decisive, some of the advantages of deliberation can be achieved by less intrusive mechanisms, including investigatory commissions, such CONADEP in Argentina or the Commission of Truth and Reconciliation in Chile. Some of the drama of the trials will be absent, but a great deal of positive public controversy can nonetheless be generated. Even a referendum whose result would maintain an amnesty law may be beneficial if it provokes, as it did in Uruguay, a deep public debate about the central values of democracy and human rights.

I must emphasize that all depends on what makes democracy self-sustainable. If one believes that self-interested motivations are enough, then the balance works heavily against retroactive justice. On the other hand, if one believes that impartial value judgments contribute to the consolidation of democracy, there is a compelling political case for retroactive justice.

Ultimately, the political argument for some sort of retroactive justice is based on moral valuations. In fact, the argument depends not on the validity of moral valuations but on the connection between the attitudes based on these valuations and the sustainability of democracy. Still, it is important to examine the validity of the moral valuations to determine whether there are independent moral arguments for and against retroactive justice. Not only are the moral considerations importantly intermingled with political considerations thereby shaping the kind of democracy to be consolidated, but they may provide a further reason for the trials. While there may be circumstances in which the trials and investigation of human rights abuses undermine the stability of democracy, it may also be true that the stability achieved by forgoing retroactive justice may undermine the moral values underlying democracy.

4

The Morality of Punishing and
Investigating Human Rights Violations

Is it morally permissible, or even obligatory, for a society, through representative state officials, to disclose, acknowledge, prosecute, and eventually punish state-sponsored human rights violations? To answer this question we must examine the moral status of both the human rights violations and the means to redress such violations. In beginning this examination, I would like to consider a position best exemplified by Hannah Arendt. In *The Human Condition,* she argues that it is impossible, even immoral, to punish radical evil.

> It is therefore quite significant, a structural element in the realm of human affairs, that men are unable to forgive what they cannot punish and that they are unable to punish what has turned out to be unforgivable. This is the true hallmark of those offenses which, since Kant, we call "radical evil" and about whose nature so little is known, even to us who have been exposed to one of their rare outbursts on the public scene. All we know is that we can neither punish nor forgive such offenses and that they therefore transcend the realm of human affairs and the potentialities of human power . . . . Here, where the deed itself dispossesses us of all power, we can indeed only repeat with Jesus: "It were better for him that a millstone were hanged about his neck, and he cast into the sea."[1]

Some may look to the feeling of powerlessness that Arendt describes to explain why retroactive justice is so rarely practiced when confronting massive state-sponsored human rights violations. A more nuanced explanation may be that the goals that justify punishment rarely can be achieved in such circumstances.

Retribution is a goal that clearly justifies retroactive justice: The evil caused by the violations of human rights should be met by the closest possible equivalent. As I stated in my analysis of the Argentine case, the victims of repression, the human rights groups that allied themselves with the victims, and those who represented the perpetrators adopted a retributive view of punishment, although with quite opposite conclusions. The victims and the human rights groups invoked Kant, asking for the punishment of every last individual responsible for the atrocities, even if society were at the brink of dissolution. The perpetrators thought that they should be praised since their acts were morally justified, indeed obligatory. Both sides looked to the past rather than to the future in measuring the evil and assessing the blameworthiness of those responsible for it. They rejected the notion of punishment as a mere means for obtaining a broader social good.

In *The Ethics of Human Rights,* I developed a number of principles that might be used to lend support to the retributivist. One, the principle of personal autonomy, establishes the value of the individual freely adopting ideals of human excellence and of life plans based on then. Another, the principle of inviolability of the person, proscribes infringements on the autonomy of an individual for the sole reason that the autonomy of others would thus be enhanced. A third, the principle of dignity of the person, holds that individuals should be treated according to their decisions, intentions, and expressions of consent, and that these may be taken as antecedents of obligations, liabilities, and any loss of rights. Otherwise stated, the principle of personal autonomy determines the goods which are the content of rights; the principle of inviolability of the person establishes barriers to protect individual interests against group or collective interests; and the principle of dignity allows individual consent to limit rights that might otherwise emanate from the previous two principles.

These three principles may be invoked to support a retributive view of punishment. Retribution respects autonomy because it allows life plans of various individuals to be free of interference provided these plans do not interfere with other people's plans. Retribution is also respectful of people's inviolability by not using them as mere means for social ends. Finally, retribution is highly respectful of the value of human dignity, since punishment would be based entirely on their own actions. Nevertheless, I believe that retributivism raises serious philosophical problems.

On a broad theoretical level, retributivism conceives of punishment as a response to unlawful acts and presumes that the punishment is an adequate response. Of course, it is necessary to clarify the meaning of "adequate." Some authors believe that adequacy is wholly determined by the legal system — that the penalty is adequate if it is established by the legal system. But this view is grossly mistaken, for it presupposes a positivist theory of law, according to which any legal determination, regardless of substance, is binding. With such positivist presuppositions, retributivism could no longer serve as a theory for evaluating or even interpreting the legal system — for instance, for choosing those acts which are unlawful among the wider class of acts which could be penalized by criminal laws. To serve that purpose, "adequate response" must be understood to mean "just response," and the relationship between crime and punishment must be determined by morality, not by positive law.

Retributivism also presupposes that it is sometimes appropriate to redress one evil with another evil. However, when I add the evil of the crime to the evil of the punishment without taking into account other factors, my moral arithmetic leads me consistently to believe that we have "two evils" rather than "one good." The key may be in the concept of blameworthiness, which is often used by retributivists to avoid the many unwelcome implications of preventionist theories of punishment: the punishment of an innocent; the placing of murder, manslaughter, and accidental killing on equal footing; and the general disregard of excuses. However, because retributive punishment is predicated on blame, the subjective attitudes of the alleged perpetrator will become essential for determining the negative value of this person's actions, and hence for determining their punishability.

Blame depends on intention. Consider the excuses which effectively counteract blame for some act. By denying a certain intention, perhaps not directly but through denial of the requisite knowledge, a perpetrator is frequently exonerated or relieved of blame. For instance, the excuse of mistake implies that the agent did not want to act as she or he did but rather was mistaken about a relevant fact. The same holds with the excuse of compulsion, or with excuses that undermine the basic voluntariness of the act. More generally, it could be said that all excuses raise questions regarding the agent's relevant desires or intentions, since they are the only thing that the agent controls. Donald Davidson has said that "we never do more than move our bodies; the rest is left to nature,"[2] but that seems wrong. According to retributivism, the agent merely intends to do something, and the rest, including the movement of his body, is left to nature.[3]

The dependence of retributivism on blame, and thus on intention, leads us to the abyss of pure subjectivism. We can not take into account the external results of a particular act — for instance, the difference between a completed and an attempted murder — nor are we allowed to consider whether somebody's life was really in danger, or even whether the agent performed certain bodily movements. A firm decision to kill should suffice. Admittedly, we might still require some external manifestation for evidentiary reasons and for avoiding excessive speculation into people's state of mind, but these considerations are merely instrumental and secondary. Given strong and uncontroverted evidence of people's intention to commit some evil deed — a spontaneous confession, for example — we should proceed with the punishment under retributivism. Under such views, Hitler would deserve the same punishment as those anti-Semites before and after him who endorsed some type of "final solution."

The subjectivism of retributivism is in part predicated on the view that the individual's state of mind (intentions, decisions, and choices) is the only matter in the control of the individual. For a determinist, however, even intentions, decisions, and choices are the unavoidable result of factors that individuals do not control, such as cultural socialization, economic structures, neurochemical processes, and psychological traumas. I assume that this descriptive determinist hypothesis may be correct. If it is, we need to explain why we keep blaming people for what they do, and this explanation must avoid the assumption that we blame people only for what they control. Elsewhere I have tried to provide that explanation by distinguishing three different dimensions of blame and trying to show that all of them are compatible with descriptive determinism.[4]

In an extremely succinct summary of that analysis, let me suggest that, in the first place, blame may have a manipulative, pragmatic dimension insofar as its expression may deter others from committing similar acts in the future because they may wish to avoid the pain and discomfort that blame normally involves. Obviously, this dimension of blame does not presuppose the falsity of descriptive determinism; it merely posits a causal relation between blaming somebody and that person's motivation to act. Second, blame may have a reactive dimension, since its expression may constitute an emotional response to certain acts. To blame somebody for an evil deed is to express a reactive attitude of the sort analyzed by Peter Strawson.[5] This reactive dimension of blame does not require the falsity of determinism, since, as Strawson argues, blame is not suspended just because the intention which is the object of blame is caused by certain factors.

Third, blame has a descriptive aspect which focuses on the connection between the person and his or her act. It is this descriptive dimension of blame which interests the retributive theorist. Unlike someone who justifies punishment on preventionist grounds, the retributivist is not interested in the manipulative dimension of the blame.[6] Nor will she rely on the reactive aspect of blame associated with punishment. The retributivist will insist that the difference between punishment and, say, revenge arises from the fact that punishment is not a mere emotional reaction. The retributivist must concentrate her attention on the descriptive dimension of blame because this is the only remaining aspect that makes punishment meaningful in retributive terms.

Blame describes the relationship between certain conduct and an individual's intention, decision, or choice. It need not assume that the intention, decision, or choice is not determined — in the descriptive sense — by factors other than further intentions, decisions, or choice. Why couldn't blame just acknowledge that an act was the product of the agent's intentions, decisions, or choices, regardless of their ulterior causes? As Robert Audi writes, "Our normal wants and beliefs are not alien determinants of action which we must control in order to control it; they are that by virtue of which our actions express our reasons and, in some sense, our nature."[7] For this reason, blame is fully compatible with determinism.

But if one could blame someone for things not necessarily within their realm of control, why should the descriptive aspect of blame hinge on the agent's decisions, intentions, and choices? Why do intentions, decisions, and choices, as opposed to the agent's bodily movements, have a privileged status as object of blame if they are not necessarily under the agent's control? In response, Jonathan Glover argues that, for the purposes of blame, the agent is synonymous with his intentions.[8] But this does not seem to be correct: The intentions of the person are too superficial and fleeting to constitute the agent. Other theorists try to justify the subjectivism of retributivism by introducing the notion of character. Here the premise is that we blame people for the character they have — we blame someone for what sort of person she or he is — and that an individual's character manifests itself in certain intentions, decisions, and choices, all of which may result in overt action.[9] Sometimes this theory is taken to imply that one should be punished for his character, irrespective of the acts he performs, and conversely that one should not be punished for chosen acts which are "out of character."[10]

The great appeal of the character theory lies in the domain of excuses, such as duress, necessity, and mental disorder. None of these denies the agent the desires and beliefs that constitute his intention. In the case of duress, the agent voluntarily and intentionally committed certain wrong actions, but an ensuing threat made it unreasonable to expect him to act otherwise. In the case of necessity, the threat is instead presented by some objective danger of a harm which is not necessarily greater than the harm caused by the agent. In the case of mental disorder, the agent is under certain constraints that make it unreasonable to expect him to act according to legal prescriptions. Standards of reasonableness and normalcy are presupposed in all of these cases, and these standards are not about specific acts but serve to evaluate inclinations, dispositions, and general capabilities. In other words, they are standards which allow us to separate certain acts and intentions from evil character traits.

Therefore, as I argued long ago,[11] there is an essential connection between the retributive view of punishment and the evaluation of people's character. Indeed, the institution of blaming presupposes such a connection. George Fletcher is completely right when he asserts that "an inference from the wrongful act to the actor's character is essential to a retributive theory of punishment. A fuller statement of the argument would go like this: (1) punishing wrongful conduct is just only if punishment is measured by the desert of an offender, (2) the desert of the offender is gauged by his character—i.e., the kind of person he is, (3) and therefore, a judgment about character is essential to the just distribution of punishment."[12]

The character theory may give a more satisfactory account of retributivism, but it does not avoid the subjectivism of retributivism. It merely broadens the inquiry. The evaluation of the agent's moral character is an evaluation of dispositions, inclinations, and capacities, which manifest themselves through desires, beliefs, and emotions and eventually materialize into intentions, decisions, and action. Those who look to intention as the arbiter of blame, correctly identify the psychological event which is the product of different character traits. But they are shortsighted in failing to perceive that this combination of character traits significantly underlies the assessment of blame on the basis of intentions. Instead, agents' choices should be evaluated in the wider context of character traits.

Because of this subjectivism, character theory does not avoid the problem common to all faces of retribution—the irrelevance of the victim. The object of punishment is character. What follows the choice, intention, or decision of the individual—that is, his bodily movements or lack thereof—is not relevant at all for blame (except as evidence of the intention of the agent). Whether these bodily movements occur or not, once the firm intention to act congeals, is a matter of pure chance and is alien to the agent's character. As a variant of retributivism, character theory inevitably equates completed crimes with possible and impossible attempts, rejects any justification which does not embody the good will of the agent, and punishes expressions of bad will which do not lead to external harm.

Speaking more generally, rehabilitated by character theory, retributivism will involve the state in perfectionism and thus, contrary to the initial assumption, violate the principle of personal autonomy. If blaming somebody necessitates the evaluation of moral character, blame necessarily involves ideals of personal virtue or excellence. To blame is to assert that somebody's moral character, as evinced by certain actions and subjective attitudes, falls short of that ideal of excellence. The action that is the object of blame may degrade the agent's character and the quality of her life. A liberal state—that is, a state committed to the principle of personal autonomy—should not therefore act on the basis of praise or blame. In assessing blame, the state does not merely *discuss* moral ideals with people, or at least it does not do so from a position of equality, as the underlying rules of moral discussion require. Directly or indirectly, the state coerces when it assesses blame, and in doing so it impinges on personal autonomy by endorsing some ideals of personal excellence over others.

I believe that this link between punishment, retribution, and moral blame—not the sense of powerlessness—underlies Hannah Arendt's view about the impossibility of both pardoning and punishing radical evil. Operating under a retributivist theory, she feels the need to blame and yet finds it impossible to blame, and thus to punish, the worst offenders of humanity. Reactive feelings such as blame presuppose a framework of human interactions and exchanges, and it is difficult to imagine that offenders of humanity, who viewed their own victims as subhuman objects, had bought into such a framework.[13] No dialogue, actual or hypothetical, could go on between victims of Treblinka or of the Argentine military repression and their persecutors, since dialogue itself presupposes participants fit for dialogue. Indeed, it was precisely this kind of exchange that the perpetrators denied their victims, although there may have been isolated instances when perpetrators engaged in dialogue with their victims.[14] Therefore, the proper response to the worst perpetrators is to suspend reactive attitudes, similar to what we do with insane people, in this instance not because they are insane but rather because they have gone beyond the pale of humanity by rejecting the framework of interactions that blame presupposes.

Arendt also questions the viability of punishing and pardoning radical evil because, under a retributive theory, blame and retributive punishment must be proportional to the magnitude of the evil committed. But how can this be done? Our vocabulary for moral blame soon runs out when we want to condemn the genocide of six million persons or the torture of children. To say that these acts were wrong sounds like a kind of irony. Our level of emotion may be raised, but our terms for describing moral heinousness have a limit. If retributive punishment must also be proportional or in some sense adequate to the evil, how can the punishment of these deeds be distinguished from those of an ordinary murder? If we normally condemn capital punishment, should we make an exception for these cases (as the government of Alberto Fujimori in Peru apparently tried to do retroactively for the leader of the leftist guerrilla movement known as the Shining Path, Abimael Guzmán)? Should we also make an exception to our abhorrence of prisoner mistreatment, imitating what we condemn the prisoners for doing?

Finally, Arendt questions the viability of evaluating the character of someone like Eichmann — an evaluation required by retributivism, since retributivism rests on blame which, in turn, calls for character evaluation. Arendt tried to evaluate Eichmann's character, and she became extremely perplexed. Eichmann had no special hatred toward his victims. He was extremely respectful of the established order, and of the laws and regulations in force. He was even aware of the Kantian categorical imperative and knew that he was living outside its bounds. His overwhelming objective in organizing the technical aspects of mass murder was to further his own career, not to cause harm to others, which he saw as a necessary consequence rather than a means in itself. Arendt was baffled and concluded that his attitude epitomized "the banality of evil" (the famous subtitle of her book). Of course, banal evil is still evil. But are we prepared to blame a character which we evaluate as banal rather than full of burning hatred, sadistic inclinations, and cruelty? Even if retributive punishment were justified in general, despite the objections I have voiced so far, it may be unsuitable for radical evil.

A preventionist theory of punishment, which has traditionally been the foil to retributivism, may fare better.[15] Preventionism looks to the principle of prudential protection of society. It rests on a principle that punishment is legitimate if it is carried out in an effective and economical way that prevents a greater evil to society than that involved in the punishment itself. This principle — the so-called principle of the prudential protection of society — involves many conditions, including efficacy (punishment must successfully avoid evils), economy (the punishment chosen imposes the least evil), balance (evils entailed in punishment are less than those prevented), and inclusion (evils suffered by those receiving punishment must be counted in the balance).

When we combine the principle of prudential protection of society with the principle of personal autonomy, still another condition of preventionism emerges: The evils relevant to the balancing discussed above are those which frustrate people's personal autonomy. In other words, we should count as evil only the frustration of people's interests or life plans chosen according to their personal ideals. This conclusion leads to an objective stance regarding what types of behavior the law should seek to prevent through punishment. Because people's inclinations, dispositions, intentions, beliefs, and desires cannot directly harm anybody's interests except their own, they should not figure in the descriptions of things the law should seek to prevent by means of punishment. For instance, the law should seek to prevent "someone's death" or perhaps "the death of somebody as the result of someone else's action," not "the wish of somebody to kill some other," or even "the death of somebody by some other who wanted the former to die" or "the intentional killing of somebody by some other." The aims of a liberal system of criminal law are satisfied when individuals are not actually harmed by each other, even if society has degenerated to such an extent that individuals generally have a debased moral character and the worst of feelings and wishes toward each other.

Some have criticized the preventionist theory of punishment — even with the limitations I have just described — on the ground that it implies a holistic vision of society and ignores the issue of distributing burdens and benefits through its policy. That is, the Kantian critique of the purely utilitarian justification of punishment — punishment of men is a mere means to benefit others — is completely justified. The remedy, however, should not be a return to retributivism, which in any event involves a type of perfectionism that is inconsistent with liberal or Kantian political philosophy, but a further refinement of preventionism.

Elsewhere I have put forward such a theory, predicated on the idea of consent. It rests on the notion that the distributions of burdens and benefits, even inequitable ones, are justified in the cases of contracts, marriages, torts, and political representation provided that the person suffering the burden consents to the suffering.[16] Here consent has certain objective dimensions and does not depend on, for example, the agent's subjective attitude toward the law. In the case of a contract, the agent need not *accept* the law which binds him to a certain obligation or liability, though the law in question must be just and legitimate. Nor is it necessary in completing the contract that the agent explicitly state, "I consent to such and such." Many contracts are satisfied with tacit consent, only demanding that the agent perform a certain type of act (for instance, getting into a bus or a taxi, asking for food in a restaurant, raising a hand in an auction, taking something from a supermarket shelf), cognizant of the fact that the act is an antecedent to the imposition or assumption of a certain obligation or liability. Crucially, consent in the case of contracts, marriages, or analogous institutions does not require that the agent affirmatively wish that the normative consequence be enforced against her; it is sufficient that the agent *know* that the normative consequence, reflected in the obligation or liability, is a result of her action.

An analogous theory can be applied to the criminal law provided certain constraints are satisfied, specifically, that the law creating the offense must be just. This means that the principle of prudential protection of society must be satisfied, the law must respect basic human rights, and it must be enacted through legitimate mechanisms.[17] Once these conditions are met, the distributive problems that have traditionally plagued protectionism are overcome by the fact that the agent consented to assume criminal liability by voluntarily committing a crime, knowing that the crime carries certain necessary consequences, regardless of the agent's attitude toward the actual enforcement of that liability.

This approach entails a blend of subjective and objective elements. To be susceptible to punishment, agents must have acted voluntarily and must have known the characteristics of their acts which are relevant to the criminal law. Furthermore, they must know that the law makes their acts the antecedent to certain penalties.[18] On the other hand, my approach avoids the pitfalls of retributivism and its unavoidable inquiry into character in order to determine if someone is blameworthy. In that respect, it is similar to civil law: When an agent consents to pay a debt, we need not analyze her character in order to decide whether she is blameworthy. In sum, my view of punishment avoids the problems of the more traditional forms of preventionism (not being able to justify the distribution of punishment and thereby treating people as a mere means to an end) without relying on a retributive theory that degenerates into perfectionism, a position that violates one of the fundamental principles of liberalism — personal autonomy.

How does radical evil fare under a theory of punishment that combines prevention with consent? To approach this question, let us examine first the element of the prudential protection of society: What are the evils that punishment prevents and how it does it prevent them? Obviously, punishment for state-sponsored human rights violations aims to dissuade similar violations in the future. But this does not seem a likely outcome of the Argentine trials and penalties. As Jaime Malamud Goti writes:

> Authors who believe in the deterrent effect of punishment will find that convicting state criminals hardly supports their theoretical claim. Punishment may deter officers from staging a coup d'état. Being exposed as criminals at home and before the international community is a bitter experience, as some Latin American dictators have discovered. Few would like to share Pinochet's or Videla's reputation. Following the court's convictions, not many officers would have liked to be in the shoes of the Argentine commanders. Then again, should they take over the government in the future, the deterrent effect of punishment would discourage them from surrendering their power to a democratic successor.
>
> But such dissuasive consequences would be applicable only to the generals at the top. For the rest of the officers, the deterrent impact of convic-

tions would be neutralized by immediate benefits that violating others' rights would bring about: within the armed forces, praise by their comrades and superiors. Hypothetical remote punishment was counterbalanced by immediate rewards from the transgressor's immediate circle.[19]

In Malamud's eyes, the main goal of preventionism—dissuading similar acts—is not likely to be realized. Radical evil requires an evil political and legal framework in which to flourish. Without that framework, it is unlikely that massive, state-sponsored human rights violations will ensue regardless of whether punishment for previous violations takes place. With that framework in place and given certain antecedent circumstances, however, violations are highly likely even with previous convictions and punishment for human rights violations.

As Malamud acknowledges, the trials for human rights violations may dissuade would-be leaders of a military coup from carrying it out. This alone would be an enormous contribution and, in effect, an indirect way of preventing massive human rights violations. But it is not clear that this rationale would justify punishment in most settings. First, it may be possible to achieve the same ends by prosecuting past acts of rebellion rather than deterring coups indirectly by prosecuting conduct—human rights violations—that frequently emerges from the rebellion. In addition, since those who carry out the coup d'état are not necessarily those who violate human rights, the former group would not always be discouraged by punishment of the latter. Second, the stability of a democracy is linked to many complex factors, only a few of which are affected by the content of the criminal law. For example, the stability of democracy is insured by powerful allies who are not affected by penalties for individuals. Third, trials and punishment for human rights violations may trigger the breakdown of democracy in an effort to avoid the results of the trials themselves. Or democracy may not be reestablished if significant sectors fear the result of the trials.[20] Consequently, punishment of radical evil is not justified on preventionist grounds if we focus on certain specific acts, like threats to the viability of the democratic system.

A fuller analysis of the the consequential value of trials for radical evil requires further delving into the cause of such evil. As I stated in Chapter 2, radical evil in Argentina emerged from several trends endemic to that society: ideological dualism, an organic conception of society that favors corporatist groups, the systematic depreciation of the rule of law, and the concentration of power. Behind the phenomenon of radical evil lie insidious cultural patterns which must be countered if that phenomenon is ever to be prevented, and herein lies the key to justifying the trials on moral grounds. In the end, I believe that trials for massive human rights violations can be justified on preventionist grounds provided the trials will counter those cultural patterns and the social trends that provide fertile ground for radical evil.

Judith Shklar reaches a similar conclusion in her analysis of political trials.[21] She distinguishes legalism as an ideology from legalism as a social policy. As an ideology, law is completely isolated from politics, in which case most political trials, including Nuremberg, would remain unjustified. As a social policy, however, legalism looks at law as a political phenomenon and celebrates events like Nuremberg as triumphs because they awaken "the dormant legal consciousness." To achieve these effects, human rights trials, such as the "big trial" in Buenos Aires and Nuremberg, function in three different ways.

First, they highlight the scope and nature of the atrocities. This function is extremely important because authoritarianism thrives by misleading and confusing the public not only about values but also about empirical facts. No wonder the recent upsurge of nazism in Germany began with a historical revisionism that denies the reality of the Holocaust. Thomas Nagel has emphasized the need for a public acknowledgment of deeds as a way of overcoming the grasp of radical evil.[22] Similarly, films such as *The Official Story* depict how deeply the need to know was felt in Argentina following the military regime.

Of course, the truth — an important byproduct of the trials — may also be attained through other means, such as an official truth commission, like the CONADEP in Argentina, the Commission of Truth and Reconciliation in Chile, and the commission established in Germany to investigate Communist abuses. If a truth commission replaces the criminal justice system, however, it will be a second-best solution because the public inquiry into the truth is much more precise and much more dramatic when done through a trial, with the accused contributing to the development of the story. In fact, the quality of narration in an adversarial trial cannot be fully replicated by other means. Even when pardons are issued at the end of a trial, they do not counteract the initial effect of such emphatic public disclosure.

Second, Shklar notes that trials further the rule of law because of how they are conducted. When trials take place before impartial courts, with ample opportunity for the accused to be heard, thorough consideration of defenses, and adherence to the procedures governing evidence and the imposition of punishment, the benefits of the rule of law are showcased. In a trial setting, the value of the rule of law is further highlighted when the meticulous procedures of the court are juxtaposed — as the prosecutors repeatedly did in Argentina — with the lawless conduct of the defendants.

Third, the trials may lessen the impulse toward private vengeance. Shklar points out that a traditional goal of the criminal justice system is to substitute institutional justice for private revenge. It contains the vengeance among victims and relatives and thus avoids a possible blood bath. The need to avoid vengeance is no less present in the radical evil context, as shown by the cases of France and Italy, where private vengeance was rampant after the fall of the fascist regimes in World War II. In Argentina, the prospect of private revenge, which could have ignited bloody confrontations typical of the 1970s, loomed in the minds of those advocating some degree of retroactive justice.

There is a fourth goal which is connected with the previous one and which is emphasized by Malamud. The trials enable the victims of human rights abuses to recover their self-respect as holders of legal rights. I do not think that this should be interpreted as a specialized form of retributivism since the evil they suffered is not neutralized by the evil suffered by the perpetrators. What contributes to reestablishing their self-respect is the fact that their suffering is listened to in the trials with respect and sympathy. The atrocities are publicly and openly discussed, and their perpetrators' acts are officially condemned. The true story receives official sanction. This process not only assuages the desire for revenge but reconstitutes the self-respect of the victim.

To this list, I would add a further benefit of retroactive justice in the context of radical evil: The trials promote *public deliberation* in a unique manner. Public deliberation counteracts the authoritarian tendencies which led, and continue to lead, to a weakening of the democratic system and massive human rights violations. All public deliberation has this effect, but especially when the subject of the public discussion is those very authoritarian tendencies. The disclosure of the truth through the trials feeds public discussion and generates a collective consciousness and process of self-examination. Questions like "Where were you, Dad, when these things were going on?" become part of daily discourse. The contrast between the legality of the trials and the way the defendants acted is prominently noticed in public discussion and further contributes to the collective appreciation of the rule of law. Public discussion also serves as an escape valve for the victims' emotions and promotes public solidarity, which in turn contributes to the victims recovering their self-respect.

With the aforementioned advantages of retroactive justice come the obvious disadvantages, and they too must be taken into account under the preventionist view of punishment. Trials may pose serious risks to the stability of the democratic system; they may provoke further human rights violations; and, as emphasized by Huntington and Linz, they may foster social hostility and acrimony, undermining the fraternity necessary to support the democratic system. The trials themselves may offend some principles inherent in the rule of law, such as the prohibition of punishment without previous criminal legislation or the rule against special courts. Therefore, the spirit of legality which emanates from the fair way in which the trials are conducted and from public exposure of the atrocities may be overcome if the legality of the trials themselves is seriously questioned.

Another countervailing consideration, inherent in any punishment under the principle of prudential protection of society, is the harm to the defendants themselves. In some cases this harm is insignificant compared to the harm caused, but in some other cases the harm may be relatively significant, especially when we factor in the suffering of the relatives of the accused and also the suffering of colleagues who may receive blame by association.

The process of public deliberation is the optimal way to forge a balance between the advantages and disadvantages of trials for human rights violations, as well as between the rights which are promoted or preserved by the trials and those which are endangered by them. Through public deliberation, we avoid the epistemic moral elitism that is perhaps the one legitimate concern of relativists. Yet this must always be done against a background which views punishment as a prudential means to protect society against greater evils and imposed only on the basis of consent. Otherwise, it would be vulnerable to the Kantian edict against using human beings as mere means.

Consent to criminal responsibility is implied when one acts voluntarily, with knowledge that punishment for that act is a necessary normative consequence of its performance. To assure the requisite knowledge, that normative consequence must be established by the laws in force when the act is committed. This precondition to a just punishment is a formidable obstacle when trying to justify this type of retroactive justice. The human rights violations we have examined were state-sponsored and, in most cases, the state adapted its laws so that such acts were not illegal at the time they were committed. Even when they were technically illegal, there are, as the case of Argentina highlights, additional obstacles to prosecution arising from intervening amnesty laws and statutes of limitations.

We are left, therefore, with a question regarding the moral justification of trials and ensuing punishment. We cannot fully address these doubts without taking law into consideration, since the morality of the trials in part depends on their legality. I will take up the law in the next chapter, and will also consider defenses such as necessity, lawful defense, state of war, obedience to superior orders and statute of limitations. This inquiry may modify our moral evaluation of the trials.

5

Legal Problems of Trials for
Human Rights Violations

Retroactive justice raises two legal questions. The first, the question of legality, asks how the presence or absence of certain legal norms affects the viability and legitimacy of the trials. A second inquires into the defenses — lack of agency, necessity, lawful defense, state of war, due obedience to orders, or the statute of limitations — that the accused have typically used in these trials.

Legality

Problems of legality arise from discrepancies between the law existing at the time of the violations and the laws that are deemed a necessary basis for punishment. Some problems can arise when there are too many laws, others when there are too few laws. Too many laws may obstruct retroactive justice. Similarly, when there are too few laws, a legal system may lack the legal framework necessary to sustain retroactive justice. To understand why these variants constitute obstacles to retroactive justice requires exploration of the impact of law on practical reasoning. This, in turn, requires that we delve into the ancient controversy between natural law and legal positivism.

WHEN THERE ARE TOO MANY LAWS

Because the massive human rights violations we are considering are state-sponsored, they are usually performed under color of law or, alternatively, the state assured impunity after the violations were committed by passing amnesties, pardons, or retroactive permissive legislation. Obviously, it would be absurd for the government simultaneously to promote these violations and their prosecution and punishment. When it does, there must have been an internal power struggle within the regime.

In the typical case, therefore, those who want to prosecute these deeds must ignore the fact that the very acts which are the subject of the prosecution were fully lawful according to the legal system in force at the time of their commission. Judith Shklar takes up this problem in her treatment of legalism as a social policy, arguing that we must weigh the breach of legality required by human rights prosecutions against the benefits these trials provide by awakening the legal consciousness. But Shklar's consequentialist position, followed by many others, raises its own set of objections and requires that we analyze the value of legality. Is it subject to a cost-benefit calculation?

To answer this question, we must probe the notion of law and take up the traditional controversy between natural law and legal positivism. This controversy surfaced during the Tokyo war crimes trials, in which the American prosecutor, Joseph Keenan, as well as some of the judges appealed to the idea of natural law, while Justice Radhabinad Pal of India rejected it. To demonstrate how this issue could be introduced in the Tokyo trial or other human rights trials like the Buenos Aires one, I shall set forth a fictional judicial debate over this issue.[1] I imagine we are in the city of Nusquam today and the date is November 25, 1948. The Allied Forces' Military Tribunal for the Far East meets to deliver its judgment against the twenty-eight people accused of crimes against the peace and crimes against humanity. After hearing the arguments of the prosecution and the defense and having received the evidence offered by both parties, the members of the court issue the following opinions:

> *Justice Sempronius.* Distinguished colleagues: We are gathered here to deliver judgment about deeds that were part of what was doubtless the most abhorrent event in the history of humanity. The men sitting here were among those contributing to the suffering of millions of people. Moved by a messianic world view, they conspired to wage an unjust war and committed egregious abuses during that war. They violated fundamental principles of human dignity by causing deaths, inflicting torture, and persecuting people without cause under a totalitarian system of government. Defense counsel does not deny the deeds but questions the legal characterization which make the deeds punishable. Defense counsel maintains that these people have committed acts which, whatever their moral value, were perfectly legitimate according to the law in force at the time and place in which they were committed. The defendants, according to this thesis, were public officials who acted in observance

of legal norms enacted and enforced by the proper bodies of the Japanese empire. The defendants were not only authorized to do what they did but in some cases were obliged to act in that manner. Defense counsel reminds us of an elementary principle of justice which the civilization that we represent has long accepted and which was ignored by the regime for which the defendant worked—*nullum crimen, nulla poena sine lege praevia,* proscribing imposition of a penalty for an act which was not prohibited at the time when the act was performed but was, on the contrary, lawful. We would be contradicting our own philosophy and adopting the one we say we are combating if we ignored this principle and punished the defendants.

These are the arguments of defense counsel. But I believe that one of the greatest services that this court may lend to humanity is to debunk once and for all the absurd and atrocious doctrine enclosed in the thesis of the defense counsel. According to him, a legal system is established each time a human group succeeds in imposing a set of rules on a certain society and gathers enough power to enforce its rules, regardless of the moral content of those rules or the moral legitimacy for enacting them. This has been encapsulated in the obscene slogan "The law is the law," which has served to justify the most abhorrent oppressions. Since ancient times, however, lucid thinkers have demonstrated the fallacy of this proposition with compelling arguments.

They have shown that above the rules enacted by men there is a system of immutable and universal moral principles—sometimes called "natural law"—which establish patterns of justice and rights that belong to men simply because they are men. The positive rules enacted by men are only law insofar as they do not contradict those principles. When we confront rules like the ones which authorized the acts we are judging, calling them "law" denaturalizes this sacred name. What is the difference between these rules and those of a criminal organization except that the former have been more stable because they have ignored in a more radical way elementary principles of justice and morality? Defense counsel's position implies that judges should submit themselves to the internal order of the criminal organization they are judging.

Since the rules of the regime to which the defendants belonged do not constitute a true legal system, they are incapable of legitimizing the acts which were taken in their name. To ignore the rules of the regime, and to apply directly the moral principles blatantly violated by those acts in order to punish the acts in question, does not, thus, violate the principle of legality. . . . I vote, consequently, for the conviction of the defendants.

Justice Caius. I share the moral sentiments that my distinguished friend Sempronius has made of the acts we are here to judge. In formulating and expressing them, however, I am acting not as a judge but as a human being and as a citizen of a civilized nation, and I do not believe we are allowed as judges to rely on those moral judgments to arrive at a decision in this trial.

Moral judgments are subjective and relative. Historians and anthropologists have shown how they have varied with time and space. What a people at a certain time considers to be morally abominable, another people at another time considers to be perfectly reasonable and legitimate. Can we deny that an authoritarian regime such as the one we are confronting generated a moral conception which was honestly endorsed by most of the society of this country? The idea that an immutable and universal "natural law," which is accessible to human reason, exists is, in the best of cases, an illusion that emerges from projecting our own feelings onto external reality. In the worst case, it is a manifestation of cultural imperialism which may be enforced only by virtue of military victory.

One of the noblest ideals of humanity is that social conflicts should be solved not according to the capricious moral feelings of those who happen to be in power, but according to settled legal rules: This is the ideal of the rule of law. The legal system of a community is a system of rules the content and scope of which may be objectively verified through empirical means, independently of our subjective valuations. Each time we encounter established institutions like courts of justice and a set of norms which are enacted and enforced by a human group that has the monopoly of means of coercion in a defined territory and which exercises force in a stable way, we face a legal system which can perfectly well be identified as such, regardless of our moral assessment of the value of its rules. Moreover, those rules can provide solutions for most if not all conceivable cases, especially if we accept that there is an implicit rule of closure in any legal system that permits those acts which are not explicitly prohibited. There is no doubt that there are relationships between law and morals — law is influenced by moral ideals — and that from the moral point of view the law should reflect the moral values that we happen to endorse. But this is not essential to the identification of law as such. And once we identify a legal system, we must recognize the binding quality of its rules and the legitimacy of the acts done in accordance with them.

The implications of this approach to this case are crystal-clear: We are confronting acts which were authorized by a genuine legal system, which was recognized as such by our own countries before the declaration of war. It is true that we are not judges of that system and thus obliged to apply its norms. But the rules of our own legal system contain the principle of legality and, thus, direct us to take into account what was legal at the time and place of the commission of these acts. Distinguished colleagues: Let us oppose the barbarism of this regime with our deep respect for the rule of law. Consequently, I vote for acquitting the defendants.

Justice Ticius. The opinions of my learned colleagues have perplexed me. I am conscious of our historical responsibility to advance clear and compelling principles which express the response of the civilized world to barbaric deeds such as those judged here. However, I cannot find in the previous opinions elements that allow us to infer those principles. My friend Sempronius has said that there are principles of morality and justice which are universal and accessible to human reason. On the contrary, my friend Caius denies that these principles exist and has asserted that moral principles are subjective and relative. Both positions seem unsatisfactory to me.

The first does not tell us how we know those principles and how we avoid the charge that we are imposing our feelings on others whom we consider, in an elitist way, more ignorant or morally inferior to us, when perhaps they are only weaker. The position of Caius also raises serious doubts: Is it really true that when we morally condemn acts like those we are confronting here, we are only expressing our emotional states or voicing the prejudices of our society? From the fact that societies and men differ in their moral evaluations, can one infer that all of them are equally reasonable and just? Is it reasonable to assume that we cannot judge people according to the principles we deem valid but only according to those they themselves assume, whatever they are? Is it possible to make moral judgments and to assume at the same time that opposite moral judgments may be also valid?

I confess that the two previous opinions leave me in an uncomfortable position. I am not convinced by the arguments so far given to justify principles of justice, yet I am not prepared to accept that they are subjective and relative. But we can leave this difficult matter to the philosophers, since in the end it is not relevant for our task. Even if we adopted a skeptical position about the foundation of ethical judgments, we cannot but formulate them, and if we do so, we are committed to act in accordance with them. We are not here to justify our ultimate ethical principles. What we need to decide is whether, as judges, we must apply those principles in order to decide this case or whether we must exclusively apply the legal norms which in fact authorized the acts committed by the defendants. For Sempronius this disjunctive does not arise, since for him identifying legal norms requires that they pass through the filter of moral principles. I cannot accept this stance and I agree with Caius's rejection of it. The law must be identified on the basis of factual and empirical features. This is the way in which we should proceed in order to adopt a scientific approach to the legal system and prevent mixing law and morality, which only serves to confuse the content of both. When we go to an unknown community and want to know what its legal rules provide, it is absurd that we answer the members of that community by resorting to our moral judgments. Not all who speak of the "imperial law" adhere morally to its content, and Sempronius sometimes has to resort to cumbersome circumlocutions in order to speak of that system without calling it "law."

I am uneasy with my colleague Caius's position. He tells us that the rules of a legal system are binding at the time and place in which they are in force. But what does this mean? If this only implies that these rules prescribe certain behavior, this is true, but the same is true of the orders of a robber. If, instead, Caius means that there is a different obligation to observe the legal rules—one which does not apply to the orders of the robbers—the question is, from where does that obligation emerge? The answer cannot be that it emerges from another legal rule, since this would invite the question of whether we are obliged to obey that legal rule, and at some point we would run out of legal rules. The only response is that the obligation emerges from another set of norms which is intrinsically obligatory and whose bindingness does not need to be supported by other norms. But the only norms that are supposed to have these properties are norms which, if they exist, do not exist on the basis of some enactment and therefore do not provoke the question of how "ought" could be derived from "is." These are norms of an ideal system of morality.

Consequently, for all his moral skepticism, when Caius speaks to us of the bindingness of the legal norms that he recognizes on the basis of pure facts, he is resorting implicitly to a moral principle. He is being inconsistent when he claims that we, as justices, must leave aside our moral convictions, since he is relying on some legal principle. Moreover, the moral principle upon which my friend Caius relies seems dubious. There are some reasons of security, order, and peace which may establish some duty to observe the existing legal order, even when its content is objectionable. But it is entirely implausible to assume this principle is absolute and not to acknowledge that it is overridden when weightier moral values, such as the preservation and promotion of fundamental rights, are at stake. If a judge of the time in which these deeds were committed had ignored the legal system in force in defense of human dignity, we would not have condemned him but would have praised him highly. Could we proceed otherwise with regard to this very court and our own behavior? Certainly not!

Both the principle of effectiveness of international law and the principle *nullum crimen, nulla poena sine lege praevia* of the civilized municipal systems are important principles to be scrupulously observed in normal circumstances, since they express moral ideals of national sovereignty, personal security, and social peace. But no moral value is absolute, and there is an urgent need for the court to affirm the value of human dignity and inviolability of the person. Therefore, the laws permitting these acts should be completely disregarded. I vote for the conviction of the defendants.

Who is correct—the natural lawyer or the legal positivist? The positions articulated above define the traditional controversy about whether or not there is an intrinsic relationship between law and morality. I believe, however, that the way in which this debate is structured is misguided. The controversy presupposes *conceptual essentialism*—itself a metaphysical thesis which holds that there are true or false concepts reflecting a supposed reality which transcends the empirical properties presented by the objects that the various concepts embrace. However, such a thesis seems doubtful. It is one thing to maintain that there is a reality in the books in front of me — with their properties of having paper sheets printed in ink and bound together in a special way — and quite a different thing to say that the *notion* of a book also belongs in that reality.

Since the beginning of this century, *conventionalism* has displaced conceptual essentialism as the dominant legal philosophy, and it acknowledges that conventions may vary according to human needs. More recent positions — like those of Saul Kripke and Hilary Putnam, which are in some sense essentialist — have emerged,[2] but such positions have little to do with the traditional essentialism that underlies the controversy between natural lawyers and legal positivists. Natural law theorists do not presuppose that concepts are determined by supra-empirical aspects of reality but resort instead to empirical evidence or conceptual schemes. Legal positivists believe that there are concepts that we cannot do without, but such nonconventionalist stances are not applicable to all concepts but only to the most basic or to those that denote natural classes.

Starting from a conventionalist premise, I believe that there are several notions of law, depending on the needs of diverse kinds of legal discourse. *Purely descriptive* notions of law may be useful in sociological, historical, and strategic discourse. In fact, it would be extremely inconvenient, as Ticius asserts, if a sociologist, concerned with describing a certain law, had to determine the values supporting the law. Various descriptive legal concepts may be useful for different purposes. For instance, one may refer to the accepted rules for those who have access to the state's coercive apparatus, primarily the judges, to justify their decisions. Another conception may refer to the previous rules plus all those which follow logically from them. Still another descriptive notion of law may refer only to the norms which are accepted by judges as justification for their decisions.

But, contrary to what Ticius assumes, there may be also various *normative* concepts of law which require that law serve justice and social morality. There may be reasons why these valuative and normative concepts of law, like that defended by Sempronius, are especially useful in the discourse of lawyers and judges. One of those concepts may guide the standards that judges *ought* to apply when justifying their decisions. A narrower version of this normative concept may refer to the standards which judges ought to apply by virtue of their being empowered by certain authorities.[3]

If this claim were accepted, as I believe it should be, the famous controversy between natural law and legal positivism would be erased from the agenda of legal philosophy and be replaced by more substantive discussions. The normative concepts of law advocated by natural lawyers would then be perfectly compatible with the descriptive concepts defended by positivists, insofar as they are deployed in different contexts of discourse.[4]

In fact, this controversy, as we saw in the positions of Sempronius and Ticius, has no practical implications if the advocates of each position abide by their conceptual stances. The ideological version of positivism defended by people like Caius does have practical implications but is rarely openly defended by scholars. It holds that all power justifies itself and that the prescriptions enacted by those who enjoy the monopoly of force in a society are in and of themselves reasons for justifying action. But, as I have shown elsewhere, law does not in and of itself justify actions or decisions.[5] Legal norms do not by themselves constitute operative reasons that justify actions and decisions, like those of judges, unless they are conceived as deriving from moral judgments — normative propositions which are to be accepted autonomously from an impartial point of view. If law is reduced to some facts, such as the fact that some people who monopolize power issue prescriptions and that those prescriptions are obeyed by most of the population, the law cannot justify actions and decisions without committing the naturalistic fallacy.[6] In my view, law can only produce those reasons if it is backed by moral principles. In order to infer law from a descriptive proposition like "Legislator L prescribed, 'Those who commit murder should be punished with life imprisonment,'" normative propositions such as "Those who commit murder should be punished with life imprisonment" as well as "Legislator L ought to be obeyed" are necessary. Legal reasoning must rest ultimately on normative propositions of this sort, which are of moral and not legal character. If the normative proposition which grants authority to the legislator is a legal one, it is derived from another pair of propositions, one of which describes the prescription of authority, while the other states that the authority should be obeyed.

The force of this view can be seen by considering the problem of the so-called de facto laws, which was central to the debate in Argentina over whether retroactive justice could be carried out given the existence of the amnesty law. As I said in Chapter 2, the Argentine Supreme Court, starting with a decision in 1865, reinforced in 1933 in *Malmonge Nobreda,* and expanded by the *Ziella* and *Arlandini* decisions of 1947, recognized the validity of the laws enacted by the military regime. This doctrine was abandoned in 1984 in decisions like *Aramayo* and *Dufourq,* only to be readopted in 1990 in the *Godoy* case by a court that President Menem had expanded.[7] The Supreme Court upheld the validity of these laws because military regimes were in possession of the coercive apparatus in society and could assure peace and order. In *Godoy,* the court asserted that the contrary conclusion would result in a state of serious uncertainty and insecurity; therefore, one must recognize the validity of laws enacted by the military regime despite, so the court said, "our affective or ideological valuations in favor of democracy."

It is clear from this reasoning that it is not the mere fact that certain laws are efficacious which underlies the decision to observe them. To pretend to jump from such a conclusion to a unique judicial decision is to commit, as I said, the famous naturalistic fallacy. The jump is sometimes concealed, as Genaro Carrió has observed, by an equivocation in the use of the word "power" which allows us to jump inadvertently from factual power to normative power.[8] But in the *Godoy* case the reference to moral values — in this instance, certainty and serenity — is explicit. Of course, certainty and security are real values, but they must compete with others which sometimes, as when basic human rights are involved, may take precedence. The Supreme Court in *Godoy* assumed that security and certainty are objective values and that democracy is an "affective or ideological" value, but no reason was given for that distinction. As we shall see in the following section, democracy may involve a sort of meta-value which may help us determine other values, and for that reason democratically enacted laws that are uniquely relevant for practical reasoning. For the moment, however, it suffices to say that the flaws of ideological positivism emerge when we look at the problem of too many laws as an obstacle to retroactive justice.[9]

The rejection of ideological positivism removes the obstacle to retroactive justice presented by laws enacted by authoritarian regimes which either authorized the human rights abuses, sanctioned an amnesty, or otherwise let the acts pass with impunity. Justices Sempronius and Ticius realize that the decision to embrace certain norms to justify more specific decisions must be based on certain values and moral principles which, in the case of radical evil, heavily weigh against the validity of those very norms. This is why the amnesty law enacted by the Argentine military was not, as we saw in Chapter 2, merely abrogated (which would not avoid its being applied to the generals under the principle that required the application of the law most beneficial to the accused) but rather nullified.

The debates surrounding the trials in Nuremberg and Tokyo, like some in Eastern Europe, are highly muddled by the remnants of ideological positivism. These remnants prevent us from realizing that what is really at stake is not the option of either law or morality but the confrontation between different moral values. However, freeing ourselves from ideological positivism does not clear all the obstacles from our pursuit of retroactive justice. While we can remove some laws, such as the amnesty, that stand in the way of retroactive justice, there are moral reasons which require that retroactive justice be based on the positive presence of other laws which in fact may be absent. This will be the topic of the next section.

WHEN THERE ARE TOO FEW LAWS

When we disavow the validity of laws enacted by authoritarian regimes, we may create a legal vacuum. There simply may not be any law left to guide punishment for the atrocities. Given the justification of punishment developed in the previous chapter, this lack of law seems to be a problem. Perhaps, however, the reliance on law is an illusion. I argued in the previous section that law is irrelevant to practical reasoning, since it must rely ultimately on moral principles and values.

This leads to the paradox that I have described as the "superfluousness of the government and its laws."[10] If, for a legal norm or law to justify an action or decision, we must unavoidably show that it derives from moral principles, why not look for the justification of such an action and decision directly in those moral principles? Do we need government and its laws?[11] If the government acts in a morally correct way and enacts the laws required by the moral principles which justify them, those laws are superfluous. If the government acts to the contrary, because of malice or mistake, its laws should not be taken into account except, of course, for prudential reasons. The only laws which might have some significance are those which solve coordination problems and yield morally indifferent or equivalent solutions; an example is a law that establishes the direction of traffic. Therefore, it seems illusory to require the presence of legal norms for punishment in general and for retroactive justice in particular. Moral values must suffice.

I have demonstrated elsewhere that the paradox of the superfluousness of law may be overcome in different ways. Specifically, the epistemic justification of democracy justifies some laws and prevents them from being completely absorbed by morality. Although legal rules do not in and of themselves justify actions and decisions if they are not supported by moral principles, those rules are not necessarily superfluous. When laws have a democratic origin they provide reasons to believe that the moral principles endorsed by them justify action. Because of its inherent tendency toward impartiality, the democratic system of collective discussion and majoritarian decision making is more reliable than any other procedure for making collective decisions and reaching morally correct solutions, and as a result the laws that result from that procedure have a presumption of moral validity. Of course, this conclusion is fallible. But if the preconditions which support the democratic tendency toward impartiality are satisfied, the conclusion will hold more often than with laws enacted by, for example, an authoritarian process. We may strongly believe that a majoritarian decision is wrong, but if those preconditions are satisfied we have a substantive moral reason to observe it. Otherwise we would undermine the effectiveness of the democratic process, which is generally more reliable than individual reflection.

This epistemic value of democracy is only relevant for those decisions that call for impartiality. Decisions that depend on the adoption of an ideal of personal excellence, on the other hand, are not favored by the epistemic value of democracy because these self-oriented ideals evaluate actions by their impact on the quality of life for that actor and not on the interests of other people. Impartiality is not required and democratically enacted laws have no special authority. In this domain, the principle of personal autonomy controls and society is precluded from interfering with individual choices. Also, in philosophical, scientific, or purely factual questions, the majority has no more title to knowledge than any isolated individual.

However, when the democratic enactments refer to intersubjective moral issues, like those involved in retroactive justice for massive human rights violations, the collective consciousness is relevant to our practical reasoning, for it provides epistemic reasons for determining the substantive moral principles on which that practical reasoning must be based. The absence of democratic laws to regulate the trials and punishment for human rights violations therefore constitutes an obstacle to carrying them out. This absence was not felt in Argentina because the democratic nullification of the amnesty law allowed Alfonsín to reestablish the former democratically enacted penal laws. But this vacuum was clearly felt in the Nuremberg and Tokyo trials and is currently an issue in Eastern Europe.

Resort to natural law is frequently espoused as a solution to this legal vacuum. But this traditional recourse to natural law involves an elitist moral epistemology, for it implies that individual reflection will result in the optimal balance between different moral values. This epistemic elitism was correctly mocked by Justice Pal of India in the original Tokyo trial, who emphasized how recourse to natural law could lead to different conclusions. As we saw in the last chapter, this variety of moral epistemics is what can be rescued from the generally unacceptable moral relativism that was defended at the World Conference on Human Rights held in Vienna in 1993.

At Nuremberg there was an attempt to fill this vacuum by resorting to international law. But, as we saw in Chapter 1, jurists were skeptical about using this approach with war crimes because a treaty like the Hague Convention was not a criminal code. Telford Taylor had some doubts about this ex post facto resort to international law for crimes against peace,[12] and Judith Shklar has only contempt for "concealing" the lack of legal support for the trials.[13] International conventions are now much more specific with regard to crimes such as torture and genocide, but they are a far cry from criminal statutes that satisfy the principle *nullum crimen, nulla poena sine lege praevia*.

We can bifurcate the problems that emerge when there is a paucity of law. First, there is the need for a democratic enactment which would settle, with epistemic authority, the value questions involved in the trials. The second problem is the need for prior notice. The first problem may be rectified by an ex post facto law: The balancing of different values and rights, which can only be effected with epistemic authority through collective discussion and majoritarian decision making, may be done after the wrongdoings and before the trial. From the point of view of epistemic reliability, if the process of discussion, and ultimately lawmaking, occurs close to the time that the trials take place, it will be all the more reliable. The problem of prior notice is more difficult to solve. A retroactive piece of legislation does not fulfill the condition of prior notice, encapsulated in the principle *nullum crimen, nulla poena sine lege praevia*. To determine whether this requirement can be fulfilled in situations like the Nuremberg trials, we must explore the rationale behind notice.

Punishment must be based on consent, thus avoiding the charge that those punished are being used as a means to benefit others. Consent does not require that individuals wish for the penalty in question, nor that they approve of the criminal law in question. Consent merely implies that the individual performed a voluntary action with knowledge that a necessary normative consequence is punishment. While it is not enough to foresee as probable the normative consequences, consent exists when one knows that there is a norm that imposes an obligation or liability if certain acts are performed. It is not necessary that one know that the enforcement of these norms is a necessary factual consequence of an act. When one describes consent in this way, it appears that consent can only be given when (a) there is a rule establishing the punishability of the act and (b) the defendant knows that such a rule exists. Mistake of law is therefore a valid excuse. Consent is the best way, in my opinion, to provide a firm ground for the principle of legality, which requires that there be a previous written law proscribing the conduct in question.

The usual question that arises, however, is whether the requirement that there be a prior law can be modified without obliterating the consent necessary to sustain punishment. One proposal, applicable in cases like Nuremberg, is to rely on moral norms rather than legal norms. If we are dealing with moral justifications for punishment, it is the consent to be subject to a normative moral consequence that should be relevant. When there is a prior law authorizing punishment, the consent to be subject to a normative legal consequence involves acceptance of a moral normative consequence. But why could not that consent to accept a normative moral consequence entail acceptance of the moral normative consequence itself? This question may appear circular, but it is not. One may consent that if one consents and if the punishment is socially useful, one may lose the moral immunity against punishment that individuals normally enjoy.

Does this moral norm legitimating punishment belong to positive morality or to critical morality? Positive morality requires the existence of a social practice that in effect legitimates punishment for the particular acts in question and collective decision making that has epistemic authority. If the agent acts with knowledge that this practice of social morality exists, he consents to undertake the normative moral consequence ensuing from it. Whether this is enough to justify punishment is a point of contention. Positive moral norms are not the result of democratic enactments and thus may be the result of ancestral traditions and prejudices and not of the process of deliberation and collective decision that has epistemic authority. But a democratic enactment may be ex post facto while converging with a moral practice which precedes the act. The ex post facto law therefore may be the basis for the consent of the agent. The democratic enactment retroactively legitimizes the moral practice, showing that it strikes the right balance of rights and values. Admittedly, moral practice may not fulfill the further requirement that punishment be socially useful. But this is not an obstacle as long as the punishment — as opposed to the moral norm — is socially useful. It does not matter why people justify punishment endorsed by moral practice provided it objectively prevents more harm than it causes.

Although there is much to recommend this way of looking at the matter, it presents some problems. First, one may question the notion of a social morality that legitimates certain penalties without the existence of an actual practice of imposing those penalties. Of course, the practice of punishment will not exist at the time the deeds take place because the perpetrators control power, and thus for the most part it consists of attitudes rather than actions: "So and so should be punished." But this is vague, and it does not permit us to recognize a neat positive morality that would justify punishment on grounds that the agents consented to the liability. Even when dealing with crimes that are not state-sponsored, punishment in the absence of legal norms would amount to private revenge, and it would be questionable to ground punishment on such individualized emotion, even if retroactively endorsed by a democratic enactment. Private revenge would be condemned by others, undermining the very notion of a clear positive morality. Second, in many situations positive moral norms favoring punishment do not exist. In Nazi Germany, for example, Nazi ideology legitimized many of the atrocities and did not in any way endorse punishment of those actions. I would not claim that there was a unanimous endorsement of Nazi ideology; many Germans opposed it passively or ignored the deeds. But the actions and attitudes of Germans did not converge so as to form a moral practice that condemned the atrocities or legitimized punishment — a precondition for the consent necessary to support punishment.

Another approach is to rely on the norms of a critical or ideal morality, the existence of which is established not by social practices but by their intrinsic validity as supported by reason. The agent would consent to punishment when we assume that a theory of punishment, such as the one defended here, is valid and he acts knowing that validity. This implies that the agent knows that certain conditions — prevention of greater harms and consent — which validate punishment ensue from his action. Obviously, this involves a certain moral elitism, perhaps the worst imaginable — one must assume that my theory of punishment is valid! But putting that to one side, the distinction between coincidence and convergence may seem to support this solution to the problem of fair notice. There must be a democratic enactment that coincides with the ideal moral norm, but this does not mean that the democratic enactment must precede the act or that the agent acknowledges the ideal moral norm because of the democratic enactment. There is no need for convergence. All that is required is that the agent know when he acts that his act morally allows society to impose a punishment on him of a certain kind, namely, to prevent greater harm, and the subsequent democratic enactment must confirm that judgment.

This alternative, however, poses a number of problems. One is that punishment is justified only when the offender is conscious of the immorality of his deed and of the morality of his punishment, but not when he is morally callous or when he disagrees about the moral justification of the punishment (perhaps because he does not think that the punishment would be preventive). Another problem is that this alternative legitimizes punishment only of members of the majority which later on endorses that punishment and not of the members of the minority who voted differently. Of course, the vote of the minority may be designed to protect themselves from punishment; they may, in fact, have endorsed mentally the same position as the majority. But this only shows that the facts needed to make this alternative viable are indeed elusive.

In the end, then, except in the rare cases when there is a clear international law or clear positive moral norm under which the agent consents, there is no way of doing without a positive legal norm prior to the act. This legal norm does not necessarily need to result from democratic processes as long as it is later confirmed by a democratic enactment. Only when the agent acts knowing that there is a legal enactment that makes his act a crime punishable in a certain way, can one fairly say that he consented to punishment which in turn justifies the imposition of such punishment when it is a prudential means of protecting society.

At first blush, this conclusion seems to condemn definitively the trials and punishments at Nuremberg and elsewhere in which the human rights abuses were not crimes at the time of their commission. But this is not the case. As soon as the validity of the laws authorizing these acts, like the anti-Semitic Nuremberg laws of the Nazi regime, are dismissed because they are not the product of a democratic process, the atrocities are clearly crimes according to the previous layer of valid laws. At this point, the problem of too few laws collapses into the previous problem of too many laws and suggests the same solution — to dismiss the undemocratic laws endorsing the human rights abuses and to rely on the earlier laws declaring them punishable. Many of the earlier laws were perfectly democratic, such as those of the Weimar Republic. Others were not, but in that case, drawing once again on the distinction between convergence and coincidence, the laws could have been endorsed by ex post facto democratic enactments. The offenders might argue that they did not know that there were laws that made their acts punishable when they committed them. But in that case they should be charged with the consequences of epistemic moral elitism — the wrong and arrogant belief that the individual and isolated reflection of some, leading to dictatorial norms, is more reliable than what was democratically enacted.

In sum, when trying crimes such as those committed by the Nazis, there is a clear solution to the problem of legality. These deeds should have been judged according to the crisp rules of the criminal code — which was enacted in 1871 in the case of Germany — that was in force before being modified by the totalitarian regime which legitimized the human rights violations. The deeds should be tried, to the extent possible, under the substantive and procedural laws, and by the judges provided by them, that would have been in place at the time of the deeds if it were not for the totalitarian enactments endorsing the abuses. This approach was followed for the most part in Greece and Argentina and could be applied in the former communist countries in Eastern Europe. They all had at some earlier point perfectly appropriate criminal laws, sometimes enacted by democratic regimes, which declared the abuses punishable. The laws authorizing the abuses should be held void ex nihilo, for their undemocratic origin allows an examination of the obnoxiousness of their content. The more difficult case is Uruguay, where a democratic enactment — a referendum after the transition — granted amnesty to human rights violators. When the democratic process results in a balance of rights and interests which points toward forgiveness, it is presumed, though dissent is always possible, that this course of action is the correct one. This follows from a justification of punishment which relies not on retribution but on prudential social protection, and from the rejection of an elitist epistemic stance about when the preconditions for right punishment are satisfied.

The Defenses
GENERAL REMARKS ON JUSTIFICATIONS AND EXCUSES

In most human rights trials, defendants advance legal defenses: lack of agency, necessity, lawful defense, the existence of a state of war, due obedience to orders, statute of limitations, and the unjust selectivity of prosecutions. It is important to analyze the rationale behind these defenses and their scope to determine their applicability to these types of crimes.[14]

In the ordinary criminal process legal defenses are classified as either *justifications* or *excuses*. Justifications for criminal acts are associated with the requirement that punishment be socially useful. Excuses are associated with consent. When an agent of unlawful criminal conduct does not consent to assume the liability of punishment, he may be excused for his behavior. He may not be mentally fit to consent, either because of immaturity or because of insanity. Likewise, he may be acting under serious duress or the mistaken belief about the factual underpinnings of his act. Or he may not know that the law imposes punishment for that act.

Some argue that consent is excluded when behavior is causally determined — a rather far-reaching conclusion, since all behavior is causally determined. In my view, however, that behavior is excusable when it has been affected by causal factors which have had an unequal impact on the agent when compared to the rest of the relevant social group.[15] If all of its members were minors, or insane, or under duress, or under the same mistake, it would be irrational to excuse their criminal behavior. The idea of freedom which is behind the validity of consent is intimately linked to that of equality. In other words, the principle of dignity of the person should be interpreted in accordance with the principle of inviolability of the person.

What are the legal and factual circumstances that an agent must be aware of in order to consent to punishment? The first response which comes to mind is "all circumstances which serve as conditions for punishment." If the agent is mistaken about any condition, he is not aware that criminal liability will be a necessary consequence of his act and therefore does not consent to punishment. But this unqualified response seems inadequate. The agent may believe wrongly that he will not be put in jail because all the prisons in town have been destroyed by an earthquake, and this mistake about a condition of his liability to punishment does not seem to undermine his consent. What accounts for this intuition? We must distinguish between factual and normative conditions for punishment. Consent requires knowledge of the normative conditions for punishment — but not of the factual conditions — because liability must be a normative consequence of his action.

There are some normative conditions of punishment that seem to be irrelevant for consent. Suppose that the law exempts diplomats from punishment to facilitate smooth and cordial international relationships. Imagine somebody wrongly believing that he is a diplomat when he commits a crime. Should he be exempted from punishment? No, for the reason for the immunity is not present, because international relations would not be harmed by punishing him. But can he legitimately claim that punishment is unfair, since he relied on the immunity and thus did not voluntarily assume the liability for punishment? Is his case similar to somebody who thinks he is killing a bear when he is killing a man or to someone who has sex with an individual younger than fifteen and intentionally ignores the legal proscription against having sex with minors? There is a fundamental difference between the diplomat's case and the second set of cases. One who kills a man believing that the victim is a bear or who has sex with somebody younger than fifteen ignoring that this is legally prohibited does not consent to do what the law seeks to prevent; on the other hand, one who wrongly believes that he is covered by diplomatic immunity does consent to do what the law is directed to prevent. He knows that he is working against the law since he is doing something that the law devalues, although he believes that he is luckily exempted from punishment for reasons independent of the action itself.

This distinction may not be fully persuasive, since punishment requires that the agent consent to punishment, not merely that he consent to perform an unlawful act. What is needed is a rule which makes one legally liable to punishment for committing an unlawful act. The person who consents to commit an unlawful act consents to undertake liability to punishment — he consents to commit an act which the law seeks to prevent by threatening punishment for its commission. Once liability to punishment is made dependent on the unlawfulness of the act, the person who consents to perform an unlawful act consents to liability to punishment.

Normative reasons may preclude punishment, but these reasons are excluded from consideration when formulating criminal laws or determining what is lawful or unlawful. The paradigmatic case is diplomatic immunity.

Laws granting immunity are internal rules of government, addressing the convenience of imposing certain penalties. They are not secret rules, but citizens should not rely on them. They are not addressed to citizens. A similar point can be made about other laws. For instance, the German criminal code authorizes the prosecutor to abandon a case if it involves some danger to the security of the state. This, however, is not relevant to the unlawfulness of the act and should not be taken into account by the agent. An example can be found in Argentina, where the punishment is modified when the victim of a theft is a relative of the perpetrator.

Another problem arises when the agent wrongly believes that excuses apply, either because he ignores the law or because he is mistaken about factual circumstances that would excuse him (for instance, he wrongly thinks that he is a kleptomaniac, or that he is under duress). The solution to this problem seems clear. Excuses, unlike justifications, do not affect the unlawfulness of the act since they do not have an impact on what the law seeks to prevent. Therefore, the person who believes wrongly that her behavior is excusable knows that she is committing an unlawful act.

LACK OF AGENCY

In trials for human rights violations, it is frequently alleged that the defendants charged did not kill or torture another: "I did not do it." This defense, if successful, would undercut the legitimacy of punishment since the attribution of the action described in the criminal statute is a precursor to deeming it unlawful or to claiming that the agent has consented to criminal liability necessary for its performance.

There are specific ways in which agency is denied in trials for human rights violations. One raises the question of "many hands." As more people participate in a criminal act, we tend to hold each one of them less responsible. Robert Nozick describes this defense in the following terms: Responsibility is contained in something like a bucket, and as more people share what is in the bucket, less is attributable to each person.[16] Nozick rejects this defense and asserts that the fact that many agents are responsible for a deed should not necessarily diminish the responsibility each one bears. This is correct, but it is also true that in some cases the intervention of many people may imply an attenuation of responsibility.

As Mark Osiel claims, it is puzzling that some philosophers agree with Nozick, while others think that the presence of "many hands" should lead to a diminution of responsibility. We can explain this divergence in views if instead of looking at responsibility for evil deeds we look at credit for good deeds. If I do something to save the life of a person, my credit is not diminished if somebody else has done something which is also enough to save that life. On the other hand, if I only do part of what is necessary to save a life and the intervention of others was necessary to save that life, I get less credit than had my efforts alone sufficed. If I send twenty dollars to a fund that will enable someone to have a vital operation, I do not receive the same credit as if I had paid the whole cost of the operation. It is nonetheless to my credit to have chosen to participate in a collective action which, because of the contribution of numerous others, will be successful in its altruistic goal.

The same is true of contributions to evil deeds. The participation of many does not by itself diminish moral blameworthiness if any of them separately would have produced the final result. Responsibility is attenuated if each participant only contributed partially to the end result, which would not have occurred but for the contribution of the others. Responsibility may be increased if one has chosen to join an especially dangerous enterprise because of the number of participants. In sum, numbers by themselves do not alter responsibility. These conclusions are affirmed by the preventive theory of punishment. It does not matter whether others contribute to the end result if punishment prevents acts which by themselves produce harmful results. Also, there is less need to prevent acts which merely contribute to harmful results. And the preventive need increases when one's contribution to an extremely harmful way of acting is magnified because of the numbers of people participating in such acts.

As we saw in Chapter 3, the diffusion of responsibility among many people is one of the factors that affect the feasibility of trials for human rights violations. But I do not think that this difficulty arises because of possible attenuation of responsibility when many people intervene. It arises, rather, from identification of many sectors of the population with the perpetrators. Furthermore, when there are many perpetrators, an inevitable feeling of injustice surfaces because of the necessary selection of only a few people to prosecute.

There is another problem of agency which is somewhat related to the issue of "many hands": How is it possible to hold those who have not killed or tortured anybody with their own hands responsible for murder? Is it possible that Videla, Eichmann, or Göring were killing or torturing people while they were sitting in comfortable offices? Would that attribution of responsibility be possible while at the same time we declined to hold responsible those who actually shot victims or put on them electric prods or opened the valves of the gas chambers?

This problem was tackled in the decision convicting some of the Argentine junta members. The decision held each of the commanders responsible for the deeds of his subordinates without limiting or undermining the responsibility of the latter. The Federal Court of Buenos Aires used the theory of the "control of the act," developed by the German scholar Hans Welzel, to determine who perpetrates a crime. This theory holds that the perpetrator is the person who controlled the course of events which led to the act; he is the master of the crime. This theory, according to the court, can be extended to "indirect perpetrators," where the person who controls the course of events is not the same as he who carries out the act described by the criminal statute. Normally, the notion of indirect perpetration is applicable when the person who controls the course of action uses another person as a mere instrument. But the court extended it to a situation in which the immediate agent was responsible for the planning and commission of the crime, while another — the indirect perpetrator — used the whole apparatus of power, of which the immediate agent is merely a small piece, as his instrument. In such cases — sometimes called "criminals behind desks" — the indirect perpetrator preserves full control of the commission of the crime notwithstanding the responsibility of the immediate agent, since the indirect perpetrator used a whole anonymous machinery for committing the crime and the identity of its members did not matter to him; if some of them refuse to cooperate, they will immediately be replaced by others. The immediate agents need not be found guilty, but they must be completely interchangeable with others in the eyes of those who enjoy complete control of the power apparatus. According to the court, each of the junta members had full control over the men, orders, places, arms, vehicles, and so forth that were necessary to carry out the disappearances.

The majority of the Supreme Court dissented from this view of agency, preferring instead to convict the commanders as instigators of the subordinates who committed the crimes. Whether the Argentine commanders were punished as perpetrators or as instigators was largely inconsequential, in the sense that the penalty was the same; the Argentine penal code equates instigators and perpetrators. Yet I am doubtful about the correctness of the Supreme Court's approach. Instigators, like accomplices, are accessories to the principal and their culpability requires individualized proof of the principal's act, something that was not done in the Argentine trial.

To some extent, the agency problem arises from the language of the statue — the description of the proscribed actions may be inapplicable. Was Göring killing while sitting at his desk sipping coffee if a person was dying because of action initiated by him? Is it is a little too wild to suppose that he could be raping a woman while reading a novel? The difficulty could be avoided if statutes, instead of using language like "the individual who rapes another," read "the individual who contributes to the event of a person being raped." This wording would also allow us to adjust the amount of punishment to meet the contribution to the crime without having to fit each actor's contribution within a rigid category. (Sometimes, the one who commits the action described by the statute contributes less to the crime than the one who is deemed an accomplice.)

Yet the agency problem may have a deeper and more normative source. It is suggested by the intuition that a person who commits x cannot be held responsible when action y intercedes in the causal chain between act x and result r. In that case, r cannot be causally ascribed to x but only to y.[17] Such a result seems to be implied by the principle of dignity of the person explained in the previous chapter. The principle of dignity of the person implies that voluntary actions should not be treated as mere accidents or natural events, and that it is impossible to skip over voluntary acts in order to ascribe responsibility. Instead, a person must absorb responsibility for events caused by their actions.

However, I believe that the principle of dignity of the person cannot be applied to cases in which the harm is produced by collective action. A producer of a play does not merely contribute to its exhibition before the actors actually perform; she also contributes to their acting and to their success in performing the play. The same occurred with the rape case I posed, or more pointedly with the commanders in Argentina. As the Court of Appeals rightly said, the lower-ranking officers who kidnapped or killed people or who tortured them were provided by their commanders with a blueprint which affected action before, while, and after the deeds were performed. Therefore, I believe that the Court of Appeals was wrong when it resorted to Welzel's extremely vague theory of "control of the act," and doubly wrong when it resorted to the concept of indirect perpetrators. The commanders were not indirect perpetrators, nor were they instigators, as the Supreme Court later stated. They were simply perpetrators, together with the people who physically abducted people, killed them, or raped them. There is no interruption in the causal chain by a subsequent voluntary act. The theory of coagency would have been sufficient.

Some responsibility for human rights abuses may be due to omissions, but even so, I believe criminal responsibilitiy can be ascribed to high-ranking officers. There are two kinds of criminal omissions: In the case of the "simple omission," A has omitted x (i) when A is capable of doing x; (ii) when A has the duty to do x or is expected to do x; and (iii) when the description of omitted action x requires the performance of specific bodily movements or bodily movements which cause a certain specific result, and (iv) A did not perform those bodily movements. The second kind of omission is called "improper omission" or "commission by omission" and requires the following conditions: (i) that the result x, the occurrence of which is relevant for the application of the description of action x, has in fact taken place; (ii) that the agent omitted the action y; and (iii) that the performance of y would have prevented the occurrence of the result x.[18]

The first sort of omission rarely leads to human rights abuses but rather to minor offenses like failing to help an injured person. The second kind of omission has often been the cause of serious crimes, like those used to impute responsibility to Gen. Tomoyuki Yamashita of Japan for the behavior of his troops in the Philippines, or to Capt. Ernest Medina in the My Lai massacre during the Vietnam War. To use such a theory to prosecute high-level perpetrators, there must be a duty to act positively in order to prevent the result, which in most cases is grounded on on the perpetrator's role and position of command. I believe, however, that the need to postulate such a duty in order to ascribe responsibility for omissions diminishes once one views the responsibility in terms of originating and maintaining collective action, for such is necessarily comprised of omissions as well as affirmative actions.

NECESSITY

Quite often the defendants in trials for human rights violations plead the defense of necessity. This defense can be taken either as a justification or as an excuse, depending on whether the court holds that the action was correct, since it avoided a greater evil, or that the agent is excusable, since although the action generated a greater evil than it avoided, the threat of this evil exerted an insufferable pressure on the defendant. I shall only refer in this section to necessity as a justification. Necessity as an excuse is a form of duress which does not usually occur in these situations.

In Argentina, the commanders initially invoked the defense of necessity; they were to save the country from left-wing or subversive terrorism. Indeed, the actions of the terrorists were extremely serious, and their terrorism could not be covered by the defense of necessity, since the foreseeable consequences of such terrorism were far worse than the evils it sought to eradicate — repression and social injustice. Left-wing terrorism was the product of an epistemic elitism regarding facts and morality, since it was not based on deliberation with the people the terrorists allegedly protected. If that deliberation had ever taken place, it most likely would have been seen that terrorist activity would only cause more repression and social injustice. Thus, it is clear that subversive terrorism caused significant social harm and that there was a prima facie case for the necessity of action aimed at containing or suppressing it.

The Court of Appeals rejected the commanders' defense of necessity. The court reasoned that if the action of the military was aimed at preventing the killings and kidnapping by terrorists, the military's action did not cause lesser evils but rather evils of at least the same degree.[19] The decision stated further that if, alternatively, the evil to be prevented was not the commission of those crimes but the perhaps greater evil of implanting a totalitarian regime, the defense of necessity also would not apply since that particular evil — a left-wing totalitarian regime — was not imminent, as required by the defense of necessity. According to the court, the subversive terrorists were never close to gaining power, nor had they occupied any territory. Given the lack of imminence from this terrorist threat, the military could have used less-offensive means to prevent it, such as enacting more severe criminal legislation.

I think that the court was right in its treatment of necessity, and that its decision is quite instructive for similar trials. The defense of necessity requires three conditions: (i) balance: that the evil prevented be greater than the evil caused; (ii) efficacy: that the necessary action effectively prevent the expected evil; and (iii) economy: that there be no other means less harmful for preventing the expected evil in an at least equally efficacious way. The Court of Appeals of Buenos Aires concluded that there was no balance or economy. Probably, for some agents, balance was achieved because they believed that the good of a national being was supreme and because they refused to factor in the harms caused to the alleged terrorists or even persons labeled "dissidents" because they saw all these persons as less than fully human.

But should necessity ever be admitted as a justification? Necessity seems to derive directly from a utilitarian way of thinking which aggregates benefits and harms accruing from an action. Authors such as Michael Walzer believe that political leaders have no choice but to think in utilitarian terms and admit necessity in extreme cases, though in doing so they dirty their hands and bear the burden of guilt and responsibility.[20] Thomas Nagel, on the other hand, believes that this issue reveals a clash between absolutist and utilitarian moral thinking, both of which have a moral pull.[21] According to Nagel, the absolutist limitations on what can be done to a person for the sake of valuable aims have to do with what we can justify to him or her. While we can conceivably say to a person we are abandoning, "You understand, I have to leave you to save the others," we could not say to a person we are torturing, "You understand, I have to pull your fingernails out because it is absolutely essential that we have the names of your confederates." Nagel's test seems to depend on something quite irrelevant — the fact that we cannot simultaneously appeal to somebody's understanding and try to force that person to cooperate by torture. He overlooks the possibility of retroactive justifications of torture, which were quite common in Argentina. In passing, however, Nagel states something quite significant about the absolutist view — it conceives of each person as a small entity interacting with others in a large world[22] — and it may be revealing about the limits of the necessity defense.

To have rights implies that autonomy cannot be curtailed each time the autonomy of others, even when they are more numerous, is at stake, as the necessity defense presupposes. This is the requirement of the principle of the inviolability of the person. But since the rights of a person may be violated not just by action but also by omission, we are brought back to a utilitarian way of thinking. This is so because, since we are infringing on the principle of inviolability of the person either by action or by omission, we have no alternative but to prescind it and directly apply the principle of autonomy of the person, which has an aggregative character. But the principle of inviolability of the person still has some capacity for guiding action even in these cases. If the rights which are in conflict protect goods of different importance for autonomy, we are obliged to preserve the good of greater importance, regardless of the numbers of persons who enjoy one or the other good. When we sacrifice a good of lesser importance to achieve a greater measure of autonomy, we are infringing less the principle of inviolability. However, there are situations when the goods at stake are of the same significance to many people's autonomy. In this case it is true that we must turn attention from the principle of inviolability of the persons and apply the aggregative principle of autonomy.

Nevertheless, the principle of dignity of the person can come to our rescue, preventing us from admitting the justification of necessity under a fully utilitarian view. The principle of dignity of the person implies that we are not causing, by action or omission, harm when the harm produced by the voluntary actions of others intervenes more proximately than our action or omission. The causal chain is interrupted when the voluntary action of another person intervenes between our action or omission and the harm. This claim rests on the notion that decisions and voluntary actions should not be taken as natural phenomena even when they are causally determined, and it has strong implications once we recall the assumption that, according to Nagel, underlies the absolutist view — namely, that we are small persons interacting with others in a large world. We should not absorb the causal results of other people's actions as if they were the results of our own actions just because we contributed to that result (except when we are coagents in the way explained in the last section). This means that an agent, even a governmental official, cannot plead necessity based on the need to avoid the harms that will be caused by the voluntary actions of other people. There is no need for the official to take that action, since the harm threatened by others will be their responsibility.

When, in Bernard Williams's famous example,[23] the sergeant offers the foreign explorer the opportunity of killing one Indian in order to spare the lives of many others, the explorer may refuse the offer on the basis that he would not be killing the other Indians, even by omission; the sergeant would be doing the killing. If a terrorist group threatens to kill a kidnapped person if the government does not inflict a lesser harm to some other person, the government may refuse on grounds that the killing would be performed by the terrorists and not by the government. Observe that this view is not based on the distinction between action and omission, nor is it based on a mysterious idea of agency. The person in these cases is not an agent because he does not cause the result. And he does not cause the result because the principle of dignity of the person prevents us from discounting voluntary actions causing results, ascribing them to previous voluntary actions. This does not mean that one has no duty to try to prevent others from causing harm, but this duty is of a lesser weight than the duty not to cause harm oneself either by action or by omission.

Translating this discussion to Argentina, it is doubtful that the commanders could have pled necessity even if the evils to be avoided had been imminent and greater than the evil caused. Those evils would not have been caused by them but by third parties, the subversive terrorists, and therefore the commanders would have had a less weighty duty to prevent them. The evils caused by subversive terrorism would have to have been much greater and much more numerous than the evils caused by repression itself for the justification of necessity to have succeeded in this case. In other words, because the evils to be prevented would be caused not by the commanders but by others, we must discount the weight of those evils in the balance underlying the justification of necessity.

LAWFUL DEFENSE OR SELF-DEFENSE

When those causing evil are the aggressors, it is permissible to cause a *greater* evil than that involved in their potential actions in order to prevent the results of such action. English speakers generally call this "self-defense." But the "self" in that expression is misleading, since the defensive action may benefit not the agent but third parties. If somebody is going to be robbed, I can cause some greater injury to the robber in order to defend his would-be victim. Hence the term "lawful defense."

In the trial of the military in Argentina, the defendants argued that subversive terrorism was an aggressive force and the actions committed in the context of the "dirty war" were designed to repel that unlawful aggression. The Court of Appeals of Buenos Aires rejected this defense.[24] It said that article 34(6) and (7) of the Argentine Penal Code requires the following conditions for the lawful defense of oneself or others: (a) illegitimate aggression; (b) a rational need for the means employed to stop the aggression; and (c) a lack of provocation on the part of the person defending himself or another person. The court acknowledged that neither society nor the military government provoked these aggressions. In the case of some acts — such as repelling an armed attack to a military garrison with gunfire — the means employed were even rational. It held, nonetheless, that in the disappearances, where "subversives" were kidnapped, tortured, and killed after their aggression had ceased, the aggression was no longer present and the means were not rational, thereby precluding the defense.

I am not entirely satisfied with the way in which the Court of Appeals dealt with this defense. I would be inclined instead to admit that until mid-1979 there was an ongoing aggressive guerrilla movement. I do not believe that the aggression necessarily ceased once the aggressors had been disarmed and subdued. Rather, I would emphasize that the means employed to repel the aggression were irrational and disproportionate. The military regime went far beyond what was needed to neutralize the aggressors and used unreliable ways of determining who were aggressors and who were not. There is little doubt that the means chosen to fight subversive terrorism were way out of proportion to the evils caused by the terrorism. More people were abducted, tortured, and killed, and in the process the dictatorship also destroyed the rule of law and legal certainty. In the end, the legitimate means for a society to use against terrorism can be found in the criminal law, provided it follows the substantive preconditions set forth previously.

At any rate, the justification for lawful defense is quite enigmatic.[25] The mystery lies in the requirement that the person who defends himself, or another, may cause the aggressor a somewhat greater harm than threatened by the aggressor's action. Some cases of defense are also cases of necessity. In the face of unlawful and willful aggression, the means used to repel it may involve lesser evils than those prevented (with all the previously discussed qualifications that necessity requires). These cases could be called cases of "necessary defense" and could be completely subsumed into the defense of necessity.

In other cases of lawful defense, any evil, even a greater one, may be caused in order to prevent the evil embodied in the aggression. German legal doctrine holds that all cases of lawful defense are of this kind. For instance, Johannes Wessel states, "Given that there is no reason why the law must cede in the face of injustice, and he who acts in lawful defense acts, at the same time, in favor of the code of integrity of the legal system, Article 32 of the Penal Code . . . does not presuppose a proportionality of goods. Consequently, it may be permissible for an aggressor to be killed, in a way which is adequate to the intensity of the attack, not only to protect life and body, but also to defend property."[26] This view does not seem tenable as a general thesis. Rather unpersuasively Wessel argues that he who kills in order to defend his property, for instance, is defending the integrity of the legal system rather than attacking it.

If this argument is dismissed, what other argument could be put forward to justify the pure case of lawful defense? One conceives of the aggressor as putting himself outside of society. The harms inflicted on the aggressor are not to be balanced against the evils prevented because by virtue of his attack he places himself outside the universe of people whose interests matter. This thesis was defended by thinkers such as Rousseau: "Furthermore, the evil-doer who attacks the fabric of social rights becomes, by reason of his crime, a rebel and a traitor to his country. By violating its laws he ceases to be a member of it and may almost be said to have made war on it."[27] Of course, this view helped justify the repression in Argentina by the military, since it could be said that terrorists placed themselves outside of society and lost the human features that were the source of moral personality. On this account, the evils the military inflicted on them should not be considered in determining the balance between evils caused and evils prevented. But if Rousseau's theory were true, even the commission of a slight crime would justify not only the most brutal reaction of the victim but the harshest penalties, and this seems absurd. We cannot degrade completely the value of a human being just because he or she violated the law.

While it may be impossible to justify lawful defense as a general matter, a more limited version of the defense may be plausible. Here I am thinking of cases in which the good threatened by the aggressor's action is so basic that society has no right to force the would-be victim to suffer it. Suppose a person is attacked by a gang of ten people and will save his life only if he kills all ten. Should he let himself be killed to prevent a far greater evil, from an impersonal point of view? Certainly not. In these cases labeled "extreme self-defense", we are compelled to combine the impersonal point of view with what Thomas Nagel calls the "personal perspective."[28] This version of lawful defense does not, however, extend to the defense of others, except perhaps close relatives, since in defending others one must, in fact, be impartial.

This reformulation of lawful defense is not wholly adequate, for it applies to necessity situations in which there is no aggression, and yet there is an important difference between extreme necessity and extreme self-defense. In the case of necessity, the permissibility of extreme actions may be reciprocal. In the classic case of the *tabula uniux capax,* two people may legitimately try to throw each other overboard. In the case of extreme self-defense, on the other hand, the permissibility of extreme action is one-sided. The would-be victim may lawfully resort to extreme means for preserving his own life, but the aggressor cannot. What accounts for the difference?

To answer this question, we must focus on the lawful-defense cases that lie between "necessary defense" and "extreme self-defense." In this middle category, the evil caused to the aggressor is greater than that prevented, and the evil prevented is not extreme. It may at times seem paradoxical to justify an imbalance between the harm prevented and the harm caused. I believe, however, that consent is the key. Similar to my beliefs on the legitimacy of punishment, when lawful defense is allowed by the law, the person who willfully attacks another knowing that the law permits this defense consents to waive the immunity against harmful actions that persons normally enjoy. This does not relieve him of the requirement — as found in the theory of punishment — that the law imposing the normative consequence must be justified independently. In other words, I believe that a law allowing a defense is justified if, when the benefits are aggregated, it is a net social benefit. This appears to get us back to the requirement that the evil caused to the offender is not greater than the evil threatened by him. But because the aggressor has consented to forgo his immunity, we can take into account the preventive benefits that society as a whole receives because of the defensive actions. In effect, many crimes are not committed because the would-be perpetrators fear the defensive action. This social benefit should be added to the benefit that the would-be victim receives from preventing the crime, and this somewhat explains why the evil inflicted on the criminal can be greater that the evil he was going to cause. Hence the concept of "punitive defense." The imbalance, however, is not limitless, but rather is bounded by the additional social benefit of defensive actions. This limited imbalance is made possible only by the consent of the attacker. Otherwise, he would be a mere means for obtaining a social benefit. Lawful defense, therefore, is very much like official punishment.

Once we introduce consent, we can return to the extreme lawful defense and distinguish it from extreme necessity. Extreme necessity may be reciprocal among participants, and extreme defense cannot be reciprocal — there is no lawful defense against lawful defense. In extreme defense there is an asymmetry between the aggressor and his victim: The former has consented to waive his immunity against harmful defensive actions, while the victim has not. Therefore, the extreme defensive action of the attacker is not in its turn justified (thus the requirement in the Argentine penal code that the defender should not have provoked the aggression).

In the end, then, we are left with three types of lawful defense: necessary defense, extreme self-defense, and punitive defense. In cases of massive human rights violations, perpetrators may allege all three. But, as the Court of Appeals rightly found, the requisite conditions of lawful defense could not be met in the case of the military in Argentina. Necessary defense requires that the harm avoided be much greater than the harm caused, and this was far from being the case in Argentina; extreme self-defense is only operative when one defends oneself or people close to one against radical and irreversible evils, and again this is not normally the case in situations where repressive regimes quash opposition; and punitive defense requires that the benefit of the defensive action (the value to society and the would-be victim) outweigh the evil caused by that action, and that rarely occurs outside the realm of official punishment.

STATE OF WAR

The defendants in human rights trials sometimes do not rely just on necessity or self-defense but rather claim a state of war. They assume that the alleged human rights violations were committed in a war context where normal moral and legal rules should not hold. In other words, a state of war has its own rules and it thus legitimizes the alleged human rights abuses.

In Argentina, the commanders claimed that they had the duty to fight the impending terrorist threat. They argued that they had won the war and that winners of wars should not to be tried. They maintained further that the war they fought was not a conventional war, but a dirty one, against an enemy without fatherland or flag, which did not identify itself or follow any rule of warfare. War led these commanders, so it was argued, to adopt extraordinary measures, but these were the only ones which could lead them to victory.

The Federal Court of Appeals was prepared to see the terrorists as waging a war. Argentina was in the grips of a revolutionary war with a relatively small and ruthless group of people fighting to gain control of certain territory. The court stated that evidence revealed that the guerrilla groups controlled some territory but not enough to establish territorial dominance, which was seen as a preliminary step to installing a revolutionary government. The court, however, rejected the defendants' argument that a state of war means that there is no law, either domestic, international, or natural. According to the court, the Argentine legal system is a closed system which embraces every action, whether lawful or unlawful — no action is outside of the law.[29] The domestic legal system, beginning with the national constitution, created mechanisms for dealing with emergency situations, and the government must adhere to it. The constitution, for example, provided for a state of siege which imposed strict limits on the measures that could be taken in emergency situations. Even international law — for example, the Geneva Convention on the law of war — establishes some restraints.

I, however, do not believe that law is a closed system. I agree with Carlos Alchourrón and Eugenio Bulygin that the principle that says everything that is not prohibited is permitted — needed to make the law a closed system — is a necessary truth only if "permitted" is arbitrarily defined to mean "not prohibited."[30] If, instead, "permitted" is understood to include "positively authorized," then the principle becomes a contingent one and may or may not be true. This means that the legality of an act is not a question of logic but rather depends on evaluative questions which the courts can hardly avoid.

There are three main views about the moral and legal status of war. The most extreme is the Machiavellian one — war does not know law, moral or legal. A second view is that war is an extremely special human situation which requires specific moral and legal norms. The third view is that the same moral and legal principles that apply to other circumstances of human life apply to war.

To determine which of these views is more plausible, one must distinguish between the *jus ad bellum* and the *jus in bello*. We must distinguish between the rules which might control the decision to wage a war and the rules that control behavior during war. In some human rights trials, such as Nuremberg, both types of rules were invoked and applied to condemn a variety of acts. In Argentina *jus in bello* was the relevant category. According to Michael Walzer, the two types of rules are independent; complaints about how one is conducting a war cannot be redressed by claiming one did not initiate the war. He adds, "War is distinguishable from murder and massacre only when restrictions are established on the reach of battle." He calls the set of norms, customs, professional codes, and legal precepts establishing those restraints the "war convention." Walzer believes that war convention is subject to a process of revision and criticism, though it remains an extremely imperfect artifact, especially in modern war.[31]

I do not believe that there is anything inherent in moral principles which makes them inapplicable in a state of war. On the contrary, war is a recurrent human condition in which there is urgent need to apply principles of autonomy, inviolability, and dignity of the person in order to ground and interpret the applicable legal rules. Even the justifications of necessity and self-defense should not be displaced when there is a state of war.

It is important, however, to distinguish collective from individual action during war. Collective actions, as we saw when we discussed agency, are those organized by governments and military leaders, creating a system of behavior, incentives, and disincentives. Necessity and lawful defense may be applicable to collective action, as they are to individual action, but nevertheless the requirements of these defenses must be established. As we just saw, collective action in Argentina could not be justified in terms of either necessity or lawful defense.

Collective action initiating or conducting a war may not be justified, while individual action that takes place during that war may be. Likewise, individual action may not be justified within a collective war effort that is fully justified. If conscripted, a soldier may not be doing anything wrong in fighting in a war, even when his country is on the wrong side. Even in an unjust war, a soldier may be justified in repelling an attack on his life in self-defense. Or a person may have joined a just war as a mercenary and thus act wrongfully, or he may act wrongfully in the context of a just war if he mistreats prisoners or the civilian population. If we distinguish between collective and individual actions during wartime, the normal justifications and excuses should be applied. The war conventions try to codify basic moral principles in the context of war. For instance, we protect civilians because they do not display threatening behavior and they have not waived their immunity against defensive actions.

DUE OBEDIENCE

Individual actions performed during war are linked to collective action inherent in war. War is conducted by armies, and armies necessarily follow a special type of discipline which requires absolute obedience to the military commanders on the part of subordinates. Accordingly, article 514 of the Argentine military code establishes the principle of due obedience, along with article 34(4) of the penal code. These legal provisions provide that when a soldier commits a crime when following the orders of a superior, the only person responsible for the crime is the superior, unless the subordinate exceeds the scope of the order and therefore becomes an accomplice. The defense is available only to those who mistakenly believed the order legitimate even though in fact it was illegitimate.

Due obedience was an absolutely crucial issue during the Argentine human rights trials. One of the elements of the Alfonsín government's strategy was an interpretive law of article 514 of the military code that created a rebuttable presumption for those who had no decision-making authority that they erred about the legitimacy of their orders. They would have believed the orders legitimate. However, this initial strategy was seriously thwarted when the Senate introduced an exception to the presumption, making the presumption unavailable for those who committed abhorrent or atrocious acts. This opened the gates to wider prosecutions. Military unrest grew, and the attempts to contain the trials, through instructions to the military prosecutors and the "full stop" law, failed. The administration then proposed, and the Congress passed, a modification to the due obedience law: The notion of decision-making capacity was sharply defined and confined to high military ranks; the presumption about the beliefs of lower officers concerning the legitimacy of orders they received made unrebuttable; and the exception for atrocious and abhorrent acts was dropped. This law divided the military, making it easier to suppress further rebellions, and accounted for the fact that when Alfonsín left office, his administration had convicted fifteen people for human rights abuses, while forty were awaiting trial.

The ebbs and flows of the Alfonsín government centered on due obedience, although it was not discussed much at the trial. I believe that the Argentine due obedience law had serious negative side effects. First, it set a precedent — obedience to orders can excuse illegal behavior. Second, as Argentine Supreme Court Justice Jorge Bacqué stated in his dissent, the legislature in enacting the law encroached upon judicial terrain by identifying particular factual back-drops under which the due obedience clause would serve as a viable excuse.

Is it possible for due obedience to justify criminal behavior? At first glance, such a justification would seem to be a priori precluded by logic. It is anomalous that the performance of an illegal act can be justified merely because a commander ordered the illegal act. However, when viewing justifications in light of the preventive objectives of the criminal law, such a justification seems more plausible. The law may seek to prevent orders to commit certain acts but may not seek to prevent such acts when performed pursuant to orders. The law may give priority to military discipline rather than to the harm caused when one acts under that discipline. The law could prevent such harm instead by punishing those who issue the order.

But to punish those who give orders is generally not sufficient to prevent serious human rights abuses. As we saw in Chapter 1, it is often difficult to subject those in high positions to criminal prosecution for radical evil. Further-more, punishing only those who issue orders converts moral persons from autonomous, inviolable, and dignified human beings to machines who will abuse fellow human beings without regard to their own moral and legal re-sponsibility. There is no fact of legal and political organization which should override the moral responsibility of agents who inflict terrible harm and suffer-ing on fellow beings. Moral persons may defer to a certain epistemic authority without relinquishing autonomy, but deference may not convert such persons into moral automatons. Even in terms of military efficiency, automatons are not valuable: One who is capable of committing atrocious deeds because he has been ordered to do so is not capable of the fine judgment needed in a complex activity such as modern warfare. On the other hand, it is infeasible to allow subordinates complete latitude in deciding whether to follow the orders they receive. This would force subordinates into a permanent state of delibera-tion, destroy armies as hierarchical organizations, and impede their efficacy. It is possible, however, to create guidelines to prevent situations from reaching either extreme.

The democratic legitimacy of the commander should be a prerequisite to obeying his orders, for only with such legitimacy can a presumption that orders are morally admissible exist. In the Argentine context, the commanders had usurped democratic power and therefore destroyed a possible source of epistemic moral ascendancy. The overall justness of the war should also be a prerequisite, especially when the subordinate has joined it voluntarily. These prerequisites, however, are insufficient to justify obeying an illegitimate order. General respect for human dignity should serve as a permanent barrier to obeying such orders. Even when there is a general tendency to follow orders, it is common to observe resistance when the orders offend basic human values.[32] Walzer mentions the example of a German soldier who was shot by his comrades for stepping out of an execution squad.[33] Likewise, some American officers refused to follow Lieutenant Calley's orders in the My Lai massacre. In Argentina, a few officers asked for early retirement to avoid participating in the repression. In sum, a soldier may defer to the decisions of his superior on moral matters when the superior enjoys democratic legitimacy, when the war is just, and when orders do not offend basic principles of human dignity.

Under the account just given, obedience to orders might be a justification, but this is so in a narrow category of cases and should never apply to cases of radical evil. What might have a broader reach is obedience to orders as an excuse, that is, as a factor that excludes consent. Can a due obedience defense excuse rather than justify a particular action? The receipt of an order does not, in and of itself, undermine the voluntariness of one's act and therefore one's consent to punishment. However, an order may occur in a context so coercive as to constitute duress or may lead to a mistaken confidence in the subordinate.

In Argentina, duress and mistake were prevalent among the lower ranks of the military, who endured a pervasive atmosphere of pressure and propaganda, sometimes amounting to brainwashing. While the pressures alone did not amount to duress, the propaganda generated an aura of legitimacy surrounding the military's action. According to Mark Osiel, the Catholic church, whose priests reassured the predominantly Catholic officers of the holiness of the war in moments of hesitation, contributed significantly to the legitimacy of the war.[34]

In contrast, the excuse of mistake can only be used in limited circumstances, depending on notions of moral consciousness and responsibility. That is why, in Argentina, in the first interpretive law, the presumption that subordinates were mistaken about the legitimacy of their orders was rebuttable. The judge could have inferred from the very nature of the act that the accused knew that the order to commit the act must be illegitimate or based his action on extremely unreliable sources of moral knowledge. On either theory, the accused should be held accountable for his actions.

Insofar as due obedience is a derivative excuse based on duress or mistake, it can be regulated retroactively without affecting the principle against retro-activity of the criminal law. Because excuses are irrelevant to the lawfulness of an act, previous knowledge of such excuses should not be a prerequisite to their applicability vis-à-vis those acts. In Argentina, even if the law that inter-preted the military code's due obedience law was deemed to have modified it, this modification would not offend the prohibition against retroactive crimi-nal legislation and would not be unconstitutional.

In the end, we are left with two conclusions: due obedience is a justification of criminal conduct only in very rare circumstances; and due obedience should serve as an excuse only in cases where there is either duress or a mistake about the legitimacy of the orders. In Argentina, due obedience was not available as a justification. Many subordinates could invoke due obedience as an excuse, either because they acted under duress or because they were mistaken about the legitimacy of the orders. Those who carried out the most abhorrent deeds, however, could not benefit from this excuse.

STATUTE OF LIMITATIONS

Defendants on trial for massive human rights violations frequently al-lege that the statute of limitations has expired, thereby precluding punish-ment. After World War II, many countries extended, or even abolished, the statute of limitations to facilitate prosecution of Nazi war criminals. In other cases, the running of the statute of limitations was suspended during the pe-riod in which it was impossible for prosecutions to ensue. In the early 1990s, the Hungarian Parliament, for example, approved a law extending the statute of limitations of some crimes committed under communism, although the Constitutional Court declared that law unconstitutional.

The moral grounding of the statute of limitations defense is unclear. I am inclined to accept a theory advanced by Derek Parfit: A statute of limitations involves a conception of personal identity which is not an all-or-nothing prop-erty but rather tends to fade with time, insofar as the continuity of valuations, memories, and attitudes becomes weaker.[35] I believe that many people have the impression regarding Nazi criminals who face trial almost a half-century after the atrocities that they are not the same people who committed the crimes and that their punishment is therefore less just than it would have been at the time. There are other secondary reasons for the existence of a statute of limitations: difficulties in gathering evidence for events which occurred long ago and the social disruptiveness of reopening old resentments and fears.

These arguments in favor of a statute of limitations are weighty, but those who have committed criminal acts should not be allowed to profit from the fact that they, or the regime to which they belong, impede justice. Therefore, legal rules that suspend the statute of limitations when prosecutions are impossible also appear attractive. This may be accomplished by retroactively extending the statute or declaring it to have been suspended during the dictatorship. Initially, this seems to clash with the principle which prohibits the retroactivity of criminal legislation, and this would be illegitimate under a liberal system of criminal law. This appearance, however, is deceptive. The prohibition of retroactive criminal laws is linked to the requirement that one must consent to assume the liability of punishment. When a new crime is created and/or modified, or the accompanying punishment is enhanced, it undermines the requisite consent. But consent is tied only to knowledge of those circumstances which are relevant to the unlawfulness of the act — the fact that this is one of the acts that the law seeks to prevent by way of punishment — and not to knowledge of other factual or normative conditions for actually imposing punishment.

The statute of limitations is not relevant to the legality of the act. Prevention by way of punishment is in no way qualified by the delineation of a term during which the state's claim to punishment would expire. Even if we justify a statute of limitations on grounds that individuals change over time, this justification has nothing to do with the underlying reasons that law seeks to prevent these types of acts. People should decide whether or not to commit an act according to norms of unlawfulness and consequently run the risk of relying on factors which are irrelevant to such norms. If somebody commits a crime because he hopes that before he is caught the statute of limitations will run out, he must bear the burden of relying on factors alien to the legality of the act, just like the person who hopes that he will not be punished because all the prisons in the country will burn.

Therefore, I do not believe that the principle prohibiting retroactive criminal legislation is an obstacle to extending or abolishing statutes of limitations for massive human rights abuses. The only issue that may legitimately arise is whether it is just to punish somebody for acts done in the distant past when that person has changed significantly in the interim.

THE SELECTIVITY OF PUNISHMENT

One of the main obstacles to trials for massive human rights violations is the fact that it is politically and practically impossible to prosecute all the persons who bear responsibility. This situation gives rise to a further defense: It is unfair to select, almost randomly, some to be prosecuted. In other words, either everyone must be prosecuted or no one. This feeling clearly explains some of President Vaclav Havel's arguments against trials in the former Czechoslovakia. In Argentina, this feeling was voiced by some defendants in the trials of the commanders. It explained much resistance to the trials and was effective in thwarting the proposed law which would have introduced prosecutorial discretion to deal with the worst cases.

The argument against selective prosecution largely depends on what we understand the requirement of equal treatment to mean, which in turn draws on the familiar distinction between rights and goals. My favorite way to illustrate the difference between rights and collective goals is to focus on some benefit that people may receive. Suppose that the benefit is contraception. This could be conceived as an individual right because it concerns personal autonomy. If the availability of contraceptives is in fact recognized as a right by the state, it cannot be granted to some individuals and denied to others, unless there is a relevant moral difference between one group and the other related to their rights. This means that the recognition of the right for some automatically gives others the right to claim for an extension of the right. Things are quite different if the same benefit is only bestowed as part of a collective goal. Suppose that, as in many Asian countries, the government wants to contain the birth rate and therefore makes contraceptives available only to some people. In this case, the government could circumscribe the class of beneficiaries, although not arbitrarily, by taking into account how particular distributions will help to achieve particular goals. For instance, the government may choose to distribute contraceptives only to couples who are likely to have more children. This decision would not give rise to the claim that others must be treated in a like manner. Therefore, equal treatment accrues to benefits recognized as rights and not necessarily when they are a mere means to achieve collective goals.

When we apply this distinction to the case of punishment, we immediately notice diverse results depending on the theory of punishment we adopt. Under a retributivist view of punishment, society as a whole, and the victims in particular, claim a right to have perpetrators punished in a way commensurate with the crime; the perpetrators also have a right not to be punished to a greater extent than their guilt justifies. Under a retributivist view, therefore, the requirement of equal treatment permeates all aspects of punishment. If only some offenders are prosecuted and the rest are let free, society, the victims, and the offenders can complain in the name of equal treatment.

When punishment instead is viewed in terms of *pure* preventionism, punishment becomes a collective goal rather than a right. Punishment is deemed a means to prevent crimes and is shaped in terms of efficacy in attaining that collective goal. No one has a right to a particular punishment, except for society's amorphous right to have punishment administered in utilitarian terms.

Under my consensual theory, punishment is a mix of goals and rights. Punishment is, on the one hand, a prudential means of social protection and therefore is shaped by its efficacy in attaining that goal. But punishment also requires consent to assume that liability, and, although not discussed herein, there are also some restraints upon the kind of punishment to be imposed.[36] These requirements involve rights, but only rights of the defendants not to be punished when those conditions are not met.

Therefore, under the view of punishment defended here, nobody has a right that certain persons be punished and, consequently, nobody has a right not to be punished because others are not. Punishment does not call for equal treatment because it is not a benefit which is the object of positive rights. Punishment is the object of *positive goals* and only of *negative rights*. Punishment may therefore be selectively relinquished through prosecutorial discretion, amnesties, or pardons without raising claims of equal treatment. This selectivity, of course, should not be arbitrary but rather aimed at efficiently achieving legitimate goals.

A retributivist view of punishment makes selective punishment an almost impenetrable obstacle to prosecutions for human rights violations. Because these crimes are characterized by the "many hands" phenomenon and because political reality and practical difficulties prevent universal prosecutions, one result of retributivism — promoted by defendants, victims, and human rights advocates — is the widespread impunity which I described in the first chapter and which so often is the fate of radical evil. Everyone has to be punished, so no one is.

Conclusion

The Role of International Law

There have been few instances in world history, certainly none in Latin America, of prosecuting those responsible for massive human rights violations. Argentina did just this and, even more remarkably, undertook this endeavor without an invading army or a division of the armed forces backing the trials, relying on nothing more than moral appeal. Given the circumstances, President Alfonsín's investigation and prosecution of human rights abuses held up miraculously well.

The results were the product of the uncoordinated actions of many independent agents and were nearly all that could be morally required under the circumstances — a piece of what Bernard Williams calls "moral luck."[1] The trials contributed to creating a public consciousness about the horrors that can transpire when democracy and the rule of law are forgone. President Alfonsín was able, moreover, to achieve these results without putting democratic institutions under an excessive strain from the reactions of the military. Consequently, the military gradually changed its characteristic mode of discourse, accepting a less holistic view of the nation and a less elitist epistemic view about its needs.

The success of the Alfonsín government, limited though it may be, was the product of a delicate equilibrium between many factors. Some scholars, most notably Diane Orentlicher, argue for an international duty to punish human rights violations of a prior regime.[2] They assume that such a duty could bring the pressure of the international community to bear down on the local situation, so as to strengthen the hand of the new democratic government and further the goals of the prosecution. I am of another mind. I do not think that the equilibrium in Argentina would have been fortified by such an unqualified and unrelenting international duty. In fact, an international duty of that nature would perhaps have even further destabilized the process of promoting the trials. Such a duty would have increased the polarization between human rights groups pressing for maximum prosecutions and the military. Indeed, faced with international economic sanctions for failure to carry out a duty to prosecute, the Alfonsín government might have been forced publicly to admit that it lacked the strength to punish as many as deserved punishment. Such an open confession of weakness would have emasculated the image of the government, with unforeseeable results.

Of course, every punishment may produce valuable consequences. For instance, it can deter similar deeds by demonstrating that no group is above the law and can instill respect for the rule of law. But the value of prosecutions may be limited, and that value must be counterbalanced with the aim of preserving the democratic system. This last caveat becomes all the more cogent once we realize that preserving the democratic system is a prerequisite for carrying out those very prosecutions and the loss of it is a necessary antecedent to massive human rights violations. A duty to prosecute all human rights violations committed under a previous regime is too blunt an instrument to help successor governments which must struggle with the subtle complexities of reestablishing democracy.

In my view, it would be much more helpful for international law to recognize the right of the world community to punish human rights violations in an international forum. The post-Nuremberg spirit of requiring perpetrators of crimes against human rights to answer for their crimes in international courts seems to be quite sensible. Violations of human rights belong with crimes such as terrorism, narcotics trafficking, and destabilizing democratic governments; all involve deeds which may, because of their magnitude, exceed the capacity of national courts to handle internally. Admittedly, it may be too idealistic to hope for the establishment of such courts in the present state of international law; but it is no more idealistic than to hope, as Orentlicher does, that the international community, through external political pressure, will enforce the duty on national governments to prosecute past human rights abuses. In fact, recent experience suggests the opposite. The United Nations War Crimes Tribunal for the former Yugoslavia is an attempt to deal with radical evil through the Nuremberg model. In other situations, it may be impossible to establish international tribunals, but even then intermediate arrangements might be used; the jurisdiction of national courts could be expanded on a global scale, or national courts could stand firm in refusing to recognize amnesties, pardons, or special statutes of limitations for these kinds of crimes.

Beyond this, an international duty could be constructed that is more sensitive to the factual context than that proposed by Orentlicher. The duty should be more forward-looking. Rather than a duty to prosecute, we should think of a duty to safeguard human rights and to prevent future violations by state officers or other parties. There are clear cases, condemned by present international law, in which governments violate human rights in a direct and active way. But there are also cases in which governments fail to preserve human rights in an indirect and passive way, by undermining the institutions, practices, cultural habits, and economic structures which help to safeguard human rights. These actions or omissions are not generally recognized as violations of the general duty to safeguard human rights, although they should be. Sometimes a government's failure to investigate and prosecute violations of human rights committed by a previous regime can justly be categorized as a passive abuse of human rights if it places those rights in future peril.

On occasion, though, what may appear to the international community to be passivity on the part of a government may actually be the active safeguarding against future violations at the cost of forgoing prosecution of past crimes. In other words, the factual context may frustrate a government's effort to promote the prosecution of persons responsible for human rights abuses, except at the risk of provoking further violence and a return to undemocratic rule. In such cases, the international community itself could assume responsibility for upholding the general duty I am proposing. This would be much more useful for the protection of human rights than the imposition of a duty on national governments to punish without regard to the government's particular circumstances and the need to guard against future violations.

With the international mechanism proposed here, foreign states and the international community would not be able to issue simplistic criticisms of a government's omission to prosecute a former regime's violations. Before reacting with criticisms and sanctions, the international community would have to undertake a thorough examination of the factual context and of the complex causal chains leading to the violation of human rights, which might be generated not only by lenience toward past abuses but also by other factors, such as economic or political pressures. Such an examination could reveal that those obstacles originated in agents, such as outside governments, which are usually deemed to be above all suspicion.

In short, what is needed is a system whereby the international community itself must consider the unique problems a particular successor democratic government faces and support the efforts that are needed to secure democracy, and hence human rights, in the future. The required knowledge of the factual circumstances of each case, in order to reach just and prudent solutions, excludes in general the epistemologically elitist attitude of direct intervention by outside powers; at the same time it allows for pressures that tend to provoke the people to discuss and decide for themselves the best way to protect their own rights. By carefully balancing efforts to strengthen democratic institutions and to enunciate and enforce human rights norms, national governments, with the assistance of the international community, can best guarantee the human rights of their citizens in the future.

Notes

Introduction

1. Hannah Arendt, *The Human Condition* (Chicago: University of Chicago Press, 1958), 241.

Chapter 1: Punishment as a Response to Human Rights Violations

1. Telford Taylor, *The Anatomy of the Nuremberg Trials: A Personal Memoir* (New York: Knopf, 1992), 12.

2. Ibid., 29.

3. The London Charter largely reflected the position of the United States, but the charge of conspiracy was restricted to the crime of launching an aggressive war, whereas the U.S. draft had related conspiracy to all of the offenses. With this change, the tribunal could not reach the atrocities against German citizens, mainly Jews, committed before the war, since those atrocities could not be seen as preparation for the war.

4. Taylor, *Nuremberg Trials,* 176.

5. "Charter of the International Military Tribunal," sec. 1, art. 6(a). The charter can be found in U.S. Department of State, *Trial of War Criminals: Documents: 1. Report of Robert H. Jackson to the President: 2. Agreement Establishing an International Military Tribunal: 3. Indictment* (Washington, D.C.: Government Printing Office, 1945), 16.

6. "Charter," sec. 1, art. 6(a), 16.

7. "Charter," sec. 1, art. 6(b), 16.

8. "Charter," sec. 1, art. 6(c), 16–17.

9. Taylor, *Nuremberg Trials,* 168.

10. The decision first dealt with the London Charter, the indictment, the proceedings, and the evidence. It continued with a history of the rise of the Nazi party and an account of the atrocities that pre-war Nazi Germany had committed against different groups, mainly the Jews. Then the decision referred to the crimes the Nazi regime had committed in planning and waging an aggressive war. Finally, the tribunal described the circumstances of the attack and invasion of each country, depicting the atrocities committed in the course of each invasion. Taylor, *Nuremberg Trials,* 574–87.

11. Those organizations considered criminal included the Leadership Corps; the Gestapo; the SD (Sicherheitsdienst) intelligence and clandestine operations agency; and the SS (Schutzstaffel), the Nazi Party's police, intelligence, and security organizatino. The SA (Sturmabteilung, a quasimilitary force commonly referred to as "storm troopers" or "Brownshirts," were, however, not declared to be criminal, nor were the Reich Cabinet, the General Staff, or the High Command.

12. See Jutta-B. Lange-Quassowski, "Coming to Terms with the Nazi Past: Schools, Media, and the Formation of Opinion," in John H. Herz, ed., *From Dictatorship to Democracy: Coping with the Legacies of Authoritarianism and Totalitarianism* (Westport, Conn.: Greenwood, 1982), 97.

13. John H. Herz, "Denazification and Related Policies," *Dictatorship to Democracy,* 20.

14. Ibid., 21.

15. Frederick C. Engelmann, "How Austria has Coped with Two Dictatorial Legacies," *Dictatorship to Democracy,* 144.

16. Giuseppe DiPalma, "Italy: Is There a Legacy and Is It Fascist?" *Dictatorship to Democracy,* 119–20.

17. Ibid., 121.

18. Ibid., 133, n. 50.

19. Roy C. Macridis, "France: From Vichy to the Fourth Republic," *Dictatorship to Democracy,* 169.

20. Ibid., 172. While more than 7,000 death sentences were issued, and approximately 899 people were actually executed, 13,000 people were sentenced to forced labor, 2,750 of them for life.

21. Arthur E. Tiedemann, "Japan Sheds Dictatorship," *Dictatorship to Democracy,* 184.

22. Ibid., 198.

23. Ibid., 199–201. In 1973, this shrine was expanded to memorialize other war criminals.

24. Ibid., 199.

25. The case of John Ivan Demjanjuk, "Ivan the Terrible," the "Butcher of Treblinka," is another example. After he was extradited from the United States, a Jerusalem court in 1988 sentenced Demjanjuk to death for crimes against the Jewish people and for war crimes. The sentence was appealed to the Israeli Supreme Court and was reversed on July 29, 1993, with the court finding reasonable doubt that Demjanjuk had committed the crimes for which he was accused and extradited. See Chris Hedges, "Acquittal in Jerusalem: Israel Court Sets Demjanjuk Free, But He Is Now Without a Country," *New York Times,* 30 July 1993: 1.

26. Eichmann's connection to nazism began in 1932, when he joined the Nazi party and entered the SS. In 1934 he joined the SD, the intelligence arm of the party. In 1938, Eichmann was sent to Vienna to organize the forced emigration of the Jews. In 1939, he similarly organized the expulsion of Jews from Prague and also had the duty of relocating the Jewish people. He concluded that concentration camps were the only feasible alternative. In 1941, Eichmann, in conjunction with Reinhard Heydrich, became conversant with the technology of mass extermination as the only viable means to carry out the Final Solution. Thereafter, Eichmann was the architect of the elaborate transportation system which carried millions of Jews to their deaths. See Hannah Arendt, *Eichmann in Jerusalem: A Report on the Banality of Evil* (New York: Viking, 1963).

27. Quoted by Arendt, *Eichmann*, 225.

28. Ibid., 232–34.

29. The democratization processes in Portugal and Greece were fueled by the failed wars in Angola and Cyprus, respectively. Unlike the case of Germany during World War II, the wars were fought on foreign soil, and consequently there were no foreign invading forces clamoring for democratization.

30. Regional separatists, for example, murdered Adm. Carrero Blanco, the closest of Franco's collaborators, in 1973.

31. Julian Santamaría, "Transición controlada y dificultades de consolidación: El ejemplo español," in Julian Santamaría, ed., *Transición a la democracia en el sur de Europa y America Latina* (Madrid: Centro de Investigaciones Sociologicas, 1982), 387.

32. See Josep M. Colomer, *El arte de la manipulación del poder: Votaciones y teoría de juegos en la política española* (Barcelona: Anagrama, 1990), 63.

33. Harry J. Psomiades, "Greece: From the Colonels' Rule to Democracy," *Dictatorship to Democracy*, 257.

34. Ibid., 263.

35. I follow the account of the trials given by Psomiades, "Greece," 264–65.

36. Ibid., 265.

37. Ibid.

38. See Richard Pipes, *Legalised Lawlessness: Soviet Revolutionary Justice* (London: Institute for European Defence and Strategic Studies, 1986).

39. The repression of the popular uprising in East Berlin in 1953, the Soviet invasion of Hungary in 1956, the similar invasion of Czechoslovakia in 1968 after the "Prague Spring," and martial law in Poland imposed by Gen. Wojciech Jaruselski in 1981 are among the most common examples of particularly repressive moments.

40. The word comes from the Latin *lustratio* and means purification or sacrifice.

41. Vojtech Cepl, a leading Czech law professor and primary force behind the new Czech constitution, has addressed the problem of lustration. See, for example, David Franklin, "Bounced Czechs: Communism's Latest Victims: 'Purging of Secret Police Collaborators in Czechoslovakia," *New Republic*, June 10, 1991: 13. In fact, the lustration procedures have provoked many scandals. For example, Jan Kavan, one of the most prominent leaders of the dissident movement since the 1968 Prague Spring, was accused of being an informer on the basis of information found in one of the StB files. See Lawrence Weschler, "The Velvet Purge: The Trials of Jan Kavan," *New Yorker*, October 19, 1992: 66.

42. See, for example, " 'Lustration Loses in Poland," *New York Times*, 7 June 1992: 18

(editorial), for an account of Polish president Lech Walesa's efforts to restrain the Polish Parliament from making public lists of politicians, judges, and civil servants who were police informers under the communist regime. A20.

43. Victor Yasmann, "Where Has the KGB Gone?" *RFE/RL Research Report* 2, no. 2 (1993): 17.

44. Ibid., 17–20.

45. See Mary Albon, "Project on Justice in Times of Transition: Report of the Project's Inaugural Meeting," unpublished report by the Charter 77 Foundation, New York, summarizing meeting held in Salzburg, Austria, March 7–10, 1992.

46. See a vivid account of the trial in David Remnick's "The Trial of the Old Regime," *New Yorker*, Nov. 30, 1992: 114.

47. Michael Walzer, *Just and Unjust Wars: A Moral Argument with Historical Illustrations* (New York: Basic Books, 1977), 299.

48. See Joseph Goldstein, Burke Marshall, and Jack Schwartz, "The Limits of Law: On Establishing Civilian Responsibility for the Enforcement of Laws Against War Crimes," *The My Lai Massacre and Its Cover-Up: Beyond the Reach of Law? The Peers Commission Report, with a Supplement and Introductory Essay on the Limits of Law* (New York: Free Press, 1976), 7.

49. One soldier shot himself in the foot to avoid participation in the brutalities; another interposed himself between the aggressors and the victims.

50. The report focused on Col. Oran Henderson, commander of the brigade responsible, who was directed by his superior officer to investigate the abuses but failed to make appropriate inquiries.

51. Goldstein et al., "Limits of Law," 3.

52. Ibid., 4.

53. I follow the account given by R. Kirkland Cozine in his paper "International Responses to Bosnia and Cambodia: A Comparison," prepared for my seminar Trials for Human Rights Violations at Yale Law School, spring 1993. Among many sources, he consulted Elizabeth Becker, *When the War Was Over: The Voices of Cambodia's Revolution and Its People* (New York: Simon and Schuster, 1986) and David P. Chandler, *The Tragedy of Cambodian History: Politics, War, and Revolution since 1945* (New Haven: Yale University Press, 1991).

54. John Barron and Anthony Paul, *Murder of a Gentle Land: The Untold Story of a Communist Genocide in Cambodia* (New York: Reader's Digest Press, 1977) and François Ponchaud, *Cambodia: Year Zero* (New York: Holt, Rinehart and Winston, 1978), trans. Nancy Amphoux, cited in Cozine, "International Responses," 11, nn. 31–32.

55. I follow here data provided by Julito Sarmiento in his monograph "Transition to Democracy from Authoritarianism: The Philippines' Past Lessons for the Future," prepared for my seminar Trials for Human Rights Violations at Yale Law School, spring 1993.

56. Ed Garcia, *Dawn over Darkness: Paths to Peace in the Philippines* (Quezon City, Philippines: Claretian, 1988).

57. Jamal Benomar, "Confronting the Past: Justice after Transitions," in Carter Center of Emory University, Conference Report Series, vol. 6, no. 1, *Investigating Abuses and Introducing Safeguards in the Democratization Process* (Atlanta: Carter Center, 1992).

58. See "Trials for Human Rights Violations in Ethiopia," a student paper by Zecharias Hailu, presented in my course Trials for Human Rights Violations at Yale Law School, spring 1993.

59. Guillermo O'Donnell has labeled these regimes "bureaucratic authoritarian." See O'Donnell, *Modernization and Bureaucratic-Authoritarianism: Studies in South American Politics* (Berkeley: Institute of International Studies, University of California, 1973).

60. Lawrence Weschler, *A Miracle, a Universe: Settling Accounts with Torturers* (New York: Pantheon, 1990), 10–76.

61. Ibid., 73, quoting Elio Gaspari.

62. Ibid., 87–88.

63. For instance, in May 1976, two prominent political leaders — Gutierrez Ruiz, the former president of the Chamber of Deputies, and Zelmar Michelini, a well-known senator — were kidnapped and subsequently murdered in Buenos Aires.

64. One hundred and eighty officials were accused of more than four hundred human rights violations. James F. Smith, "Uruguay Vote Strongly Backs Amnesty: Unofficial Results Show Retention of Law That Pardons Officers," *Los Angeles Times,* April 17, 1989: 6.

65. The government tried to obstruct the verification of signatures, launched a counter-campaign for maintaining the amnesty law, and appointed the same Gen. Hugo Medina as defense minister. The Electoral Court announced that 23,000 more signatures were needed for the referendum, sending the organization into a frantic attempt to obtain them. By 1989, the group had gathered the necessary signatures. Weschler, *A Miracle, a Universe,* 175–176.

66. Servicio Paz y Justicia (SERPAJ), *Uruguay: Nunca Más,* trans. Elizabeth Hampsten (Philadelphia: Temple University Press, 1992), discussed in Weschler, *A Miracle, a Universe,* 235.

67. See "Los generales rebeldes: Lacalle negocia con los militares," *Página 12,* June 11, 1993: 18. The particular incident reported has to do with pressures of the chiefs of the armed forces to block investigations and measures being taken against officers who were accused of being involved in the kidnapping and murder of a Chilean intelligence officer. (It is also reported that some deputies received threats for meddling with the military.)

68. It was officially acknowledged that at least 9,000 disappeared or were killed, although human rights groups claim that the number may be as high as 30,000. See, for example, "For the First Time, Argentine Army Admits 'Dirty War' Killings," *New York Times,* April 26, 1995: 13.

69. See Jorge Correa, *Dealing with Past Human Rights Violations: The Chilean Case after Dictatorship,* 67 Notre Dame Law Review 1455, 1455–85 (1992).

70. Ibid., 1462–63.

71. See "Aylwin reprendio a Pinochet," *Página 12,* June 11, 1993: 19.

Chapter 2: Retroactive Justice in Argentina

1. Several constitutional projects resulted in the enactment of two constitutions, one in 1819 and one in 1826. These constitutions, however, failed to gain general acceptance, since they expressed the liberal and centralist ideas of the Buenos Aires intellectual elite,

led by Bernadino Rivadavia, and were thereby rejected by the caudillos of the interior, who were inclined to a more popular and federalist model.

2. See Carlos Santiago Nino, *Un país al margen de la ley* (Buenos Aires: Emece Editores, 1992).

3. This constitution was not ratified by the province of Buenos Aires until 1860.

4. Carlos Santiago Nino, *Fundamentos de derecho constitucional* (Buenos Aires: Astrea, 1992).

5. For instance, confrontations between the conservative president of the first military junta, Cornelio Saavedra, and the young liberal Mariano Moreno, the secretary of the junta, forced Moreno's resignation. Moreno was moved by Rousseau's ideas, as well as those of the French Revolution, and he actively spread such ideas through the first Argentine newspaper, *La Gaceta,* which Moreno himself founded. The traditionalist and populist dictator Rosas and the liberal president Rivadavia (the founder of the National Library and the University of Buenos Aires) were also embroiled in ideological confrontation. Likewise, ideological conflict placed the leading promoter of liberal education, Domingo Faustino Sarmiento, at odds with the caudillo of the province of La Rioja, Juan Facundo Quiroga.

6. See a criticism of Moreno's democratic leanings in Nicolas Shumway, *The Invention of Argentina* (Berkeley and Los Angeles: University of California Press, 1991).

7. See Carlos H. Waisman, *Reversal of Development in Argentina: Postwar Counterrevolutionary Policies and Their Structural Consequences* (Princeton: Princeton University Press, 1987).

8. As we shall see in a later chapter, in political philosophy there has been lately a certain revival of an organic conception of society in the emergence of the movement that has been called "communitarianism." For a description and criticism of this movement, see Carlos Santiago Nino, *The Communitarian Challenge to Liberal Rights,* 8 *Law and Philosophy* 37 (1989).

9. Guillermo O' Donnell, "Corporatism and the Question of the State," in James M. Malloy, ed., *Authoritarianism and Corporatism in Latin America* (Pittsburgh: University of Pittsburgh Press, 1977), 47–87.

10. Latin American corporatism differs from its fascist counterpart in two respects: fascist corporatism was conducted exclusively from within the state and its privileged party; and its degree of control over different social sectors was much more extensive. Latin American corporatism differs also from democratic systems in which interest groups and lobbies attempt to guide official policy. In democracies, spontaneous movements try to influence governmental decisions, while corporatist efforts are highly organized and calculated.

11. O'Donnell, "Corporatism," 67–70.

12. Even during the second period (1853–1930), in which quasidemocratic civilian governments prevailed, many elected presidents were affiliated with the military. For instance, Julio Argentino Roca was the general who conquered much of Patagonia from the Indians.

13. See my discussion of the origin and evolution of anomie in Argentina in *Un país al margen de la ley,* 53–136.

14. See ibid., 53–88.

15. See Juan Bautista Alberdi, *Bases y puntos de partida para la organizacion politica de la Republica Argentina* (Buenos Aires: Centro Editorial de America Latina, 1979), 26–28.

16. See further these specific points and the general formation of hyperpresidentialism in Nino, *Fundamentos*.

17. For a highly detailed account of the origins and evolution of the Montoneros, see Richard Gillespie, *Soldiers of Perón: Argentina's Montoneros* (Oxford: Oxford University Press, 1982).

18. The founders of the Montoneros include Fernando Abal Medina, Norma Arrostito, Carlos Gustavo Ramus, Mario Eduardo Firmenich, Emilio Angel Maza, Carlos Capuano Martínez, and José Sabino Navarro. These founders were highly influenced by nationalist writers and members of the Third World Priests Movement, such as Carlos Mugica and the former seminarian Juan García Elorrio.

19. *Socialismo nacional* in Spanish, as opposed to *nacional socialismo,* which refers to the Nazis' ideology.

20. However, legal technicalities, related to his "leave of absence" from Argentina, prevented Perón from being a candidate in these elections.

21. Gillespie, *Soldiers of Perón,* 123–27.

22. At least twenty-five people were killed in the violence, most of them from the left. Perón, who finally arrived at another airport, justified the repression, claiming that law and order should be reestablished.

23. Gillespie, *Soldiers of Perón,* 155.

24. The Montoneros received $60 million in ransom from the September 1974 kidnapping of Juan and Jorge Born, the leaders of the multinational Bunge y Born Corporation. Ibid., 180–81.

25. Ibid., 215.

26. Ibid., 215, n. 156.

27. By the end of September 1976, workers' real income was less than half of the 1974 level. Ibid., 230.

28. Jacobo Timerman, *Prisoner without a Name, Cell without a Number,* trans. Toby Talbot (New York: Alfred A. Knopf, 1981).

29. See his story in Marguerite Feitlowitz, "Night and Fog in Argentina," *Salmagundi* 94–95 (1992): 40–74.

30. Comisión Nacional Sobre la Desaparición de Personas (CONADEP), *Nunca Más* (Buenos Aires: Editorial Universitaria de Buenos Aires, 1986), 395.

31. Ibid., 64–65.

32. Ibid., 75.

33. Ibid., 252–53.

34. *Clarín,* May 30, 1980, cited in Emilio F. Mignone, *Derechos humanos y sociedad: El caso argentino* (Buenos Aires: Centro de Estudios Legales y Sociales, 1991), 69.

35. Ibid.

36. Ibid.

37. Ibid.

38. See the statement of General Roualdes in a private conversation with Mignone, in *Derechos humanos,* 67.

39. Included among such lower-level officers were the commanders of the First and Third Army Corps, Gens. Carlos Suarez Mason and Benjamin Menendez; the chief of police in the province of Buenos Aires, Gen. Ramón J. Camps; and the commander of the ESMA, Adm. Ruben J. Chamorro.

40. Tina Rosenberg, "The Good Sailor," in *Children of Cain: Violence and the Violent in Latin America* (New York: Morrow, 1991).

41. *Nunca Más,* 329.

42. Gillespie, *Soldiers of Perón,* 231.

43. Ibid., 238.

44. Sometimes strange relationships developed between the "disappeared" and their custodians. The most bizarre was the marriage of a Montonero woman to the head of the ESMA, Admiral Chamorro.

45. Mignone, *Derechos humanos,* 91.

46. John Simpson and Jana Bennett, *The Disappeared and the Mothers of the Plaza: The Story of the Eleven Thousand Argentinians Who Vanished* (New York: St. Martin's, 1985).

47. Inter-American Commission on Human Rights, *Report on the Situation of Human Rights in Argentina* (Washington, D.C.: General Secretariat, Organization of American States, 1980).

48. Carlos Santiago Nino and Jaime Malamud Goti, memorandum, "La responsabilidad jurídica en la represión del terorismo," in Horacio Verbitsky, *Civiles y militares: Memoria secreta de la transición,* (Buenos Aires: Contrapunto, 1987), 389–91.

49. See my expansion of this idea in Chap. 5 below, where I deal with the issue of the statute of limitations.

50. Verbitsky, *Civiles y militares,* 38.

51. *La Ley* 1983-D, 935.

52. In response, the leader of the metallurgic trade union, Lorenzo Miguel, charged Alfonsín with criminal libel. Alfonsín was to be defended by Genaro Carrió, but the case never advanced.

53. Decree 157 called for the prosecution of the following suspected leaders of guerrilla movements: Firmenich, Vaca Narvaja, Obregon Cano, Galimberti, Perdia, Pardo and Gorriaran Merlo. Decree 158 called for the prosecution of the following junta members: Videla, Viola, and Galtieri of the army; Massera, Lambruschini, and Anaya, of the navy; and Agosti, Graffigna, and Lami Dozo of the air force.

54. This is also the procedure for other administrative trials, such as those entailing tax issues.

55. See Andrés Fontana, "La política militar en un contexto de transición. Argentina 1983–1989," paper presented at the Symposium on Transition to Democracy organized by the Schell Center for Human Rights at Yale University and the Center of Institutional Studies of Buenos Aires, New Haven, Connecticut, March 1990.

56. In the end, only three national deputies, all Radicals, became members of CONADEP: Santiago Lopez, Hugo Piucill, and Horacio Huarte.

57. Other members of the Supreme Council included Adms. León Mario Scasso and Juan Carlos Fourcade, Brig. Jorge Alberto Filipini, and Gen. Tomás Sanchez de Bustamente. See Jorge Camarasa, Ruben Felice, and Daniel González, *El juicio: Proceso al horror* (Buenos Aires: Sudamericana/Planeta, 1985), 36.

58. The Federal Court of Appeals later convicted Galtieri, Admiral Anaya, and Brig. Lami Dozo for these crimes.

59. Admiral Massera was already detained by judicial order for orchestrating the abduction of a businessman to safeguard his intimate relationship with the businessman's wife.

60. Camarasa et al., *Juicio,* 62.

61. For details, see ibid., 63.

62. Mansur was an old friend and former partner of mine, whom I always admired for his decency and work ethic, despite the fact that I dissented from his Peronist sympathies. Everyone agrees that his work in CONADEP was pivotal to its success, forging an equilibrium between the pressures of the human rights groups, represented by Graciela Fernandez Meijide, and the government's aspirations, as well as drafting, with Rabossi, much of *Nunca Más.*

63. Of course, this provoked several custody battles in the courts between the families in possession of the children and the relatives of their natural parents.

64. *Nunca Más,* 77.

65. Ibid., 137.

66. Ibid., 143.

67. Ibid., 27, 61, 64.

68. Ibid., 50–51.

69. Ibid., 48.

70. Ibid., 18.

71. Ibid., 286.

72. Ibid., 303.

73. Ibid., 330.

74. CONADEP presented these cases to civilian judges, to avoid upsetting the victims of the abuses and the human rights groups. These judges would decide these cases, taking into account the existing legislation.

75. Jaime Malamud and I had many discussions about this project with our colleagues Gabriel Bouzat, Hernán Gullco, Carlos Rosenkrantz, and Agustín Zbar.

76. See Nino and Malamud memorandum in Verbitsky, *Civiles y militares,* 389–91.

77. See details of these events in Camarasa et al., *Juicio.*

78. For example, there was no documentation of the different operations, prisoners, and casualties.

79. A public meeting would of course have been scandalous because the tribunal was preparing the decision and the government would have been accused of orchestrating the trial.

80. See an account of this meeting, with some departures from the facts, in Verbitsky, *Civiles y militares,* 156–57.

81. Federal Criminal and Correctional Court of Appeals for the Federal District of Buenos Aires, judgment in Case no. 13 (Dec. 9, 1985), trans. Alejandro M. Garro and Henry Dahl, 8 *Human Rights Law Journal* 368, 373.

82. Ibid., 415–17.

83. This point was considered an interpretation of the due obedience provision and thus a gesture toward the government's concerns.

84. In fact, the government ordered that all the television coverage be silent to mitigate the military's irritation.

85. Verbitsky, *Civiles y militares,* 157.

86. Ibid., 167.

87. In fact, Joaquín Morales Solá, in an editorial in *Clarín,* accused me of being an obstacle to that solution. See Sola, "El punto final," *Clarín,* May 4, 1986: 14.

88. Verbitsky, *Civiles y militares,* 198.

89. On Dec. 19 there was a public demonstration against the law.

90. Verbitsky, *Civiles y militares,* 319.

91. Bacqué was my professor of legal philosophy at the Law School of the University of Buenos Aires. Afterwards, I worked with him there as an assistant. Malamud and I suggested his nomination for the Supreme Court after Carrió resigned due to poor health. Some government officials, but not President Alfonsín, would not let us forget this nomination when Bacqué took quite independent stands on issues deemed crucial for the government's strategy.

92. *New York Times,* March 2, 1982: 30.

93. One day, after lunch with Minister Troccoli, he suggested that I speak with Justice Bacqué about the due obedience issue. I did not believe that the Supreme Court would take such a political step. Troccoli, rather upset, told me that the country would suffer if the issue was not resolved.

94. See details in "Día de vigilia en la Casa Rosada: el presidente Alfonsín ratificó al general Ríos Ereñu," *La Rázon,* April 18, 1987: 11.

95. See Horacio Verbitsky, *Medio siglo de proclamas militaras* (Buenos Aires: Per Abbat, 1987), 162–66.

96. Verbitsky, *Civiles y militares,* 362.

97. See "Solución política para la crisis" and "Los dos temas en discusión," *Rázon,* April 22, 1987: 3.

98. Verbitsky, *Civiles y militares,* 364–65.

99. Gen. Fausto Lopez, who openly praised the mobilization of the population in defense of democracy, was appointed deputy chief.

100. See this version by a journalist who always pressed for leniency toward the military: Joaquín Morales Sola, *Asalto a la ilusión* (Buenos Aires: Planeta, 1990), 158–62.

101. See, for instance, Rama Argentina de la Asociación de Juristas, *Argentina: Juicio a los militares: Documentos secretos decretos-leyes jurisprudencia* (Buenos Aires: Rama Argentina de la Asociación Americana de Juristas, 1988).

102. On Dec. 3, 1990, Colonel Seineldín rebelled again, killing innocent civilians. The armed forces reacted swiftly, and Seineldín and his fellows were put to trial and harshly sentenced.

Chapter 3: Political Problems of Trials for Human Rights Violations

1. This analysis parallels that undertaken by Mark Osiel, "The Making of Human Rights Policy in Argentina: The Impact of Ideas and Interests on a Legal Conflict," *Journal of Latin American Studies* 18 (1986): 135–80.

2. Juan J. Linz, "Crisis, Breakdown, and Reequilibration," in Juan J. Linz and Alfred

Stepan, eds., *The Breakdown of Democratic Regimes* (Baltimore: John Hopkins University Press, 1978), 71–74.

3. This also shows the deficiency of a presidential system of government, where the president becomes the ultimate object of corporatist pressures. A diffusion of decision-makiR centers would dilute the possibility of these pressures becoming successful. See Carlos Santiago Nino, *Fundamentos de derecho constitucional* (Buenos Aires: Astrea, 1992), chap. 3.

4. Adam Przeworski believes democracy will be self-sustaining only if all relevant actors view democracy as an equilibrium in which they are better off than in any alternative institutional arrangement. I believe this view is too unrealistic because democracy, almost necessarily, must have losers who would benefit from an authoritarian regime. But it is obvious that, in order to stabilize democracy, a balance of power must be struck by the prevalence of groups that are not irreversible losers in a democracy. The law of due obedience attempted to achieve such a balance, as shown by the reaction of the bulk of the military to the unity at Campo de Mayo and elsewhere. Przeworski, *Democracy and the Market: Political and Economic Reforms in Eastern Europe and Latin America* (Cambridge: Cambridge University Press, 1991).

5. Carlos H. Acuña and Catalina Smulovitz, "¿Ni olvido ni perdón? Derechos humanos y tensiones cívico-militares en la transición argentina," paper presented at the annual International Congress of the Latin American Studies Association, Washington, D.C., April 4–6, 1991, 47 (trans. by the author).

6. Samuel P. Huntington, *The Third Wave: Democratization in the Late Twentieth Century* (Norman: University of Oklahoma Press, 1991), 221.

7. Josep M. Colomer, *El arte de la manipulación política: Votaciones y teoría de juegos en la política española* (Barcelona: Anagrama, 1990), 20–34.

8. David Pion-Berlin, "To Prosecute or to Pardon? Human Rights Decisions in the Latin American Southern Cone," *Human Rights Quarterly* 16 (February 1994): 105–30.

9. Ibid.

10. See references to the racial factor in Joseph Goldstein, Burke Marshall, and Jack Schwartz, "The Limits of Law: On Establishing Civilian Responsibility for the Enforcement of Laws against War Crimes," *The My Lai Massacre and Its Cover-Up: Beyond the Reach of Law? The Peers Commission Report, with a Supplement and Introductory Essay on the Limits of Law,* prepared at the request of the United States Department of the Army (New York: Free Press, 1976), 7.

11. See, for example, Ken Adelman, "The Drama of Rectifying History," *San Diego Tribune,* April 6, 1994: B6. The article quotes Havel as explaining his opposition to holding trials for past human rights abuses: "All of us are responsible, each to a different degree, for keeping the totalitarian machine running. None of us is merely a victim of it, because all of us helped to create it together."

12. Huntington, *Third Wave,* 220–21.

13. Ibid., 221.

14. Ibid., 215.

15. Ibid., 231.

16. Bruce Ackerman, *The Future of Liberal Revolution* (New Haven: Yale University Press, 1992), 72–73.

17. Ibid., 80.

18. Linz, "Crisis, Breakdown, and Reequilibration," 42, 45–46.

19. Bruce Ackerman, *We the People* (Cambridge: Harvard University Press, 1991).

20. See, for example, John J. Bailey, "Pluralist and Corporatist Dimensions of Interest Representation in Colombia," in James M. Malloy, ed., *Authoritarianism and Corporatism in Latin America* (Pittsburgh: University of Pittsburgh Press, 1977), 259–302.

21. Carlos Santiago Nino, *Un país al margen de la ley* (Buenos Aires: Emecé, 1992).

22. See Carlos Santiago Nino, *The Constitution of Deliberative Democracy* (New Haven: Yale University Press, 1996).

23. Ronald Dworkin, *Law's Empire* (Cambridge: Harvard University Press, 1986), 208–24.

Chapter 4: The Morality of Punishing and Investigating Human Rights Violations

1. Hannah Arendt, *The Human Condition* (Chicago: University of Chicago Press, 1958), 241.

2. Donald Davidson, "Agency," repr. in *Essays on Actions and Events* (London: Oxford University Press, 1980), 59.

3. See a discussion of this in Carlos Santiago Nino, *Introducción a la filosofía de la acción humana* (Buenos Aires: EUDEBA, 1987).

4. Carlos Santiago Nino, "A Consensual Theory of Punishment," 12 *Philosophy and Public Affairs* 289 (1983).

5. P. F. Strawson, "Freedom and Resentment," in *Freedom and Resentment and Other Essays* (London: Methuen, 1974).

6. See, for instance, R. A. Duff, *Trials and Punishments* (Cambridge: Cambridge University Press, 1986), 47–54.

7. Robert Audi, "Responsible Action and Virtuous Character," *Ethics* 101, no.2 (1991): 314.

8. Jonathan Glover, *Responsibility* (London: Routledge and Kegan Paul, 1970).

9. See some answers to critics of the character theory of blame in Peter Arenella, "Character, Choice, and Moral Agency: The Relevance of Character to Our Moral Culpability Judgments," in Ellen Frankel Paul, Fred D. Miller, Jr., and Jeffery Paul, eds., *Crime, Culpability, and Remedy* (Cambridge, Mass.: Blackwell, 1990), 59–83.

10. Michael S. Moore, "Choice, Character, and Excuse," ibid., 29–58.

11. See Carlos Santiago Nino, "Towards a General Strategy for Criminal Law Adjudication" (doctoral diss., Oxford University, 1976) and Carlos Santiago Nino, *Los límites de la responsabilidad penal: Una teoría liberal del delito* (Buenos Aires: Astrea, 1980).

12. George P. Fletcher, *Rethinking Criminal Law* (Boston: Little, Brown, 1978), 800.

13. See Strawson, "Freedom and Resentment."

14. See Marguerite Feitlowitz, "Night and Fog in Argentina," *Salmagundi* 94–95 (1992): 40–74.

15. Alfonsín espoused a preventionist theory of punishment in his Dec. 13, 1983 speech mentioned in Chap. 2.

16. See Nino, "Consensual Theory of Punishment."

17. Duff follows Hegel in thinking that the threat of punishment involved in the existence of a criminal law is justified because the subject of that threat is not entitled to the respect due to a free man. Duff argues that my consensual theory of punishment is flawed for not providing that justification. This is a mistake and derives from the fact that the distinction between threats and other alternatives, like offers, depends on value judgments. If the criminal law is just—as it is assumed to be here—it does not involve any threat, and it is not perceived in that way by the people who acknowledge its justice. The same occurs in the case of a just civil law. I can only get something that I want if I pay the owner what he wants (of course, the civil law could be very threatening if it were unjust— if, for instance, it obliged me to pay people for not harming me with deafening noises). Therefore, when we speak of the "threats" of the criminal law, we should put the word in quotation marks, as though it were being uttered by someone presuming the criminal law is not just. See Duff, *Trials and Punishments*, 180.

18. Negligent crimes present problems, since these conditions are not met. However, I have defended a view under which their unlawfulness—what the law should seek to prevent—stems not from the harm they produce but from the danger that the agent knows he is producing. The risk of punishment is attached to that danger and not to the harm, which justifies a lesser penalty than the corresponding intentional offense. The requirement of actual harm is an objective condition not for the punishability of the offense but for enforcing that punishment, since it provides hard evidence that the danger was real and high. Unconscious negligence should not be punished.

19. See Jaime Malamud Goti, "Punishment and a Rights-Based Democracy," *Criminal Justice Ethics* 10, no. 2 (1991): 3–13, 7.

20. In Haiti, for example, Cedras and his military comrades were unwilling to transfer power to President Aristide because they feared some type of trials.

21. Judith N. Shklar, *Legalism: Law, Morals, and Political Trials* (Cambridge: Harvard University Press, 1986).

22. A reference to Nagel's contribution to a meeting of the Aspen Institute appears in Lawrence Weschler, *A Miracle, a Universe: Settling Accounts with Torturers* (New York: Pantheon, 1990), 4.

Chapter 5: Legal Problems of Trials for Human Rights Violations

1. This is an adaptation of a fictional judicial debate I used in my book *Introducción al analisis del derecho* (Buenos Aires: Astrea, 1980), 18–30.

2. Saul A. Kripke, *Naming and Necessity* (Cambridge: Harvard University Press, 1980) and Hilary Putnam, *Mind, Language, and Reality* (Cambridge: Cambridge University Press, 1975), 215–271.

3. There may be also *mixed* concepts of law, like those advocated by Ronald Dworkin, that refer to the standards actually recognized by judges as well as to those they ought to recognize. See Dworkin, *Taking Rights Seriously* (Cambridge: Harvard University Press, 1977) and Carlos Santiago Nino, "Dworkin and Legal Positivism," 89 *Mind* (1980): 519–543.

4. My thesis about the plurality of concepts of law appears similar to the distinction

between the internal and the external points of view as proposed by H. L. A. Hart in *The Concept of Law* (Oxford: Oxford University Press, 1961). However, my claim transcends Hart's distinction, since the latter presupposes a descriptive concept of law which Hart defends as the exclusive one. If we start, instead, from an emphasis on the plurality of concepts of law, the internal and the external points of view acquire different forms. While a descriptive concept of law engenders descriptive discourse within which the discourse of the participants can be taken into account, a normative concept of law gives pride of place to the committed discourse of participants. From within, the observer's discourse cannot be detected but her possible actions may be taken into account in a parametric way. In this way, the distinction between different concepts of law transcends the distinction between different points of view toward law.

5. Carlos Santiago Nino, *La validez del derecho* (Buenos Aires: Astrea, 1985). For a more succinct account, see Nino, *Ethics of Human Rights* (Oxford: Oxford University Press, 1991), chaps. 2–3.

6. I think that this is not a genuine fallacy but just the mistake of associating moral predicates with certain factual properties that are not conceptually tied to them. See William K. Frankena, "The Naturalistic Fallacy," 48 *Mind* (1939): 464–77.

7. See discussion of these cases in Carlos Santiago Nino, *Fundamentos de derecho constitucional* (Buenos Aires: Astrea, 1992).

8. Genaro Carrió, *Análisis filosófico, jurídico y politológico de la práctica constitucional* (Buenos Aires: Astrea, 1992).

9. To reject the ideological positivism expressed in Caius's opinion implies that legal discourse is not an autonomous species but that it is a special modality of moral discourse — what Robert Alexy calls the *Sonderfall* thesis in *A Theory of Legal Argumentation: The Theory of Rational Discourse as Theory of Legal Justification* (Oxford: Oxford University Press, 1989), trans. Ruth Adler and Neil MacCormick. Legal discourse is not insular but is part of a broader justificatory discourse that aims at establishing morality. (The integration of all justificatory discourses into one which ultimately seeks to establish reasons that have the distinctive features of morals — autonomy, universality, generality, etc. — is the hallmark of modernity.) Much confusion in legal philosophy results from attempts to isolate legal discourse from the wider justificatory moral discourse, for instance by proposing a purely descriptive notion of legal validity. The substitution of a descriptive notion of validity for the normative concept current among lawyers generates a host of problems, like those related to the conflict between higher and lower norms and those of the reform of the highest norms of the system, which do not appear under the latter concept. A good deal of the work of analytical jurisprudence consists of solving these problems that it itself had created.

10. Nino, *Ethics of Human Rights;* Nino, *The Constitution of Deliberative Democracy* (New Haven: Yale University Press, 1996).

11. Philosophical anarchism — the belief that no government or other source of heteronomous reasons is justified — has been defended by authors such as Robert Paul Wolff. On similar reasoning — namely, the autonomy of justificatory reasons — see Wolff, *In Defense of Anarchism* (New York: Harper Torchbooks, 1970).

12. Telford Taylor, *The Anatomy of the Nuremberg Trials: A Personal Memoir* (New York: Knopf, 1992), 635.

13. Judith N. Shklar, *Legalism: Law, Morals, and Political Trials* (Cambridge: Harvard University Press, 1986), 162–65.

14. See Carlos Santiago Nino, *Los límites de la responsabilidad penal: Una teoría liberal del delito* (Buenos Aires: Astrea, 1980), 470–475.

15. See Nino, *Ethics of Human Rights,* chap. 7.

16. See Robert Nozick, *Anarchy, State, and Utopia* (New York: Basic Books, 1974), 130.

17. H. L. A. Hart and A. M. Honoré, *Causation in the Law* (Oxford: Oxford University Press, 1985), 2d ed., 217.

18. See these characterizations in Carlos Santiago Nino, *Introducción a la filosofía de la acción humana* (Buenos Aires: Eudeba, 1987), 96.

19. Federal Criminal and Correctional Court of Appeals for the Federal District of Buenos Aires, judgment in Case No. 13 (Dec. 9, 1985), trans. Alejandro M. Garro and Henry Dahl, 8 *Human Rights Law Journal* 368, 373.

20. Michael Walzer, *Just and Unjust Wars: A Moral Argument with Historical Illustrations* (New York: Basic Books, 1977), 323.

21. Thomas Nagel, *Mortal Questions* (Cambridge: Cambridge University Press, 1979), 53–74.

22. Ibid., 68.

23. Bernard Williams, "A Critique of Utilitarianism," in J. J. C. Smart and Bernard Williams, *Utilitarianism: For and Against* (Cambridge: Cambridge University Press, 1973), 98–99, 108–110.

24. See Garro and Dahl translation, 404.

25. See a fuller treatment of this subject in Carlos Santiago Nino, *La legítima defensa: Fundamentación y régimen jurídico* (Buenos Aires: Astrea, 1985).

26. Johannes Wessel, *Derecho penal: Parte general,* trans. Conrado Finzi (Buenos Aires: Depalma, 1980), 95 (English trans. by author).

27. Jean-Jacques Rousseau, "The Social Contract," in Sir Ernest Baker, ed., *Social Contract: Essays by Locke, Hume, Rousseau* (Oxford: Oxford University Press, 1971), 200.

28. Thomas Nagel, *The View from Nowhere* (Oxford: Oxford University Press, 1986), 184–185.

29. See Garro and Dahl translation of judgment in Case No. 13, 404.

30. Carlos E. Alchourrón and Eugenio Bulygin, *Normative Systems* (New York: Springer, 1971).

31. Walzer, *Just and Unjust Wars,* 41–46.

32. See, for instance, Herbert C. Kelman and V. Lee Hamilton, *Crimes of Obedience* (New Haven: Yale University Press, 1989), 136–66.

33. Walzer, *Just and Unjust Wars,* 314.

34. Mark Osiel, "The Making of Human Rights Policy in Argentina: The Impact of Ideas and Interests on a Legal Conflict," *Journal of Latin American Studies* 18 (1986): 153.

35. Derek Parfit, *Reasons and Persons* (Oxford: Oxford University Press, 1984), 326.

36. See Nino, *Fundamentos de derecho constitucional,* chap. 1.

Conclusion

1. Bernard Williams, *Moral Luck: Philosophical Papers, 1973–1980* (Cambridge: Cambridge University Press, 1981).

2. See Diane F. Orentlicher, *Settling Accounts: The Duty to Prosecute Human Rights Violations of a Prior Regime,* 100 *Yale Law Journal* 2537 (1991).

Editor's Note

Carlos Santiago Nino was born in Buenos Aires in 1943. He received his first law degree from the University of Buenos Aires and his doctorate in jurisprudence from Oxford. He became involved in politics in the early 1980s in an effort to restore democracy in Argentina and later served as an advisor to President Raúl Alfonsín on human rights and constitutional reform. He held a chair in philosophy of law at the University of Buenos Aires and, starting in 1986, was a regular visiting professor at the Yale Law School.

Professor Nino died suddenly on August 29, 1993 while on a trip to La Paz to work on the reform of the Bolivian constitution. Immediately before his death, Owen Fiss of the Yale Law School had visited Professor Nino in Buenos Aires and received the manuscripts of two books, *The Constitution of Deliberative Democracy* and *Radical Evil on Trial,* both written in English. The two men discussed the manuscripts and a number of revisions that Professor Nino was contemplating.

Upon Professor Nino's death, Professor Fiss assumed the responsibility of readying the two manuscripts for publication by Yale University Press. On *Radical Evil on Trial* he was principally assisted by Janet Koven Levit, a student close to Professor Nino at Yale. Sunny Chu, Leah Cover, Gadi Dechter, Zecharias Hailu, Elisabeth Layton, Noah B. Novogrodsky, and Gregory H. Woods III also helped in bringing this project to completion. A copy of the manuscript for *Radical Evil on Trial* as it existed upon Professor Nino's death is at the library of the Yale Law School.

Index